# ODD COUPLES

# ODD
# COUPLES

Friendships at the

Intersection of Gender

and Sexual Orientation

## ANNA MURACO

*Duke University Press*
*Durham & London 2012*

© 2012 Duke University Press

All rights reserved

Printed in the United States of America on

acid-free paper ∞

Designed by Nicole Hayward

Typeset in Quadraat by Keystone

Typesetting, Inc.

Library of Congress Cataloging-in-

Publication Data appear on the last

printed page of this book.

In memory of my dad, Natali Anthony Muraco

# CONTENTS

# ACKNOWLEDGMENTS

THE EFFORTS AND GENEROSITY of many people have made the completion of this work possible. I want to start by thanking my committee members at the University of California (UC), Davis, for their academic and personal contributions to this project: Diane Femlee, Lyn Lofland, Stephen T. Russell, and Laura Grindstaff. Diane Felmlee, provided support, encouragement, and mentorship, as well as time and effort, to my development as an academic. Lyn Lofland provided much guidance throughout the early versions of the manuscript; her apparent confidence in me and my work helped to bolster not only my own perception of the project, but also my abilities as an academic. Stephen T. Russell challenged my assumptions about family, friendship, and sexuality, which improved the quality of my thinking. He not only helped me with this work but also provided generous assistance with other projects and gave me steady employment while I attended graduate school. Laura Grindstaff and the other faculty members in women's and gender studies at UC Davis, especially those who taught in the Designated Emphasis in Feminist Theory and Research, helped me to nuance the feminist perspective that underlies the analyses in this book. The Consortium for Women and Research and the Sociology Department at UC Davis provided varied forms of funding while I was in graduate school.

I thank the editorial staff I worked with at Duke University Press: Courtney Berger, Christine Choi, Reynolds Smith, and Sharon Torian, as well as the three anonymous reviewers whose comments wholly improved the manuscript.

Many thanks to the administrators of and participants in the University of Michigan Applied Issues in Aging Postdoctoral Fellowship Program (and NIA Grant AG000117) for providing financial and academic support. In particular, Ruth Dunkle, Berit Ingersoll-Dayton, Karin Martin, and the pre- and postdoctoral fellowship participants contributed to this work and other projects in their various stages of development.

Many thanks also to those who have provided me with meaningful professional experiences. Karen Fredriksen-Goldsen has been a wonderful mentor and gracious collaborator. My development as an academic blossomed during my postdoctoral work with her and continues to grow through our work together. Allen LeBlanc also has been an unwavering advocate and mentor.

Many people at Loyola Marymount University (LMU) in Los Angeles have nurtured my work. The Bellarmine College of Liberal Arts (BCLA), including Dean Mike Engh and Dean Paul Zeleza, funded my work through the BCLA College Fellowship and BCLA Summer Research Fellowships and provided informal forms of support. The faculty members of the Sociology Department at LMU—especially my dear friends Nadia Kim, Rebecca Sager, Rachel Washburn, and Stephanie Limoncelli—have been an excellent cheering section, indignant on my behalf when needed, and a vast source of humor. Carla Bittel, Adam Fingerhut, Diane Meyer, and Kirstin Noreen have been my sources of fun and stability in Los Angeles. Big thanks to all of my research assistants at LMU— Kiana Dyen, Ashley Narramore, Marisa Parker, Caitlin Pickering, and especially Nerissa Irizarry—for all of their hard work.

Jeff Sweat and Clare Stacey, my UC Davis writing group, provided friendship, moral support, and careful feedback while this book was still a dissertation. Over the years that it took me to complete this manuscript, many people provided places to stay (for nights, weeks, and sometimes months), kept me company, recruited potential study participants, helped me move, cheered me on, and cared for me when I was very ill: Clare Stacey and Zach Schiller, Michael Flota, Joanna Conley-Flota, Jonathan Isler, Jennifer Gregson, Jennifer Hoofard, Magdi Vanya, Joan Meyers, Stephanie Wells and Scott Godfrey, Gordon Edgar, Brian Chao, David Hutson, Heather Worthley, Nate Fox, Heather Smith, Shira Richman, Tracy Goodsmith, Liz Jones, Susannah Kirby, and Erin MacDougall. Special thanks to Thomas Burr for his willingness to read a copy of this manuscript and provide comments when I most needed them.

My thanks to all of my family: my parents, Nat Muraco and Kathy Muraco, as well as Pete Muraco, Marlene Muraco, Katie Muraco, Ashley Muraco, and Lexi Muraco, for feeding me, giving me hugs and kisses, providing a place to stay, and handing down frequent-flier miles and for all of your love and support. Thanks to Vicki, Ron, Aaron, and Dan Kleinman and to Charlene Biagi for continuously being interested in what I am doing and asking about my work at family gatherings. Many thanks also to my sister, Christina Muraco, and Ben Durbin for keeping me company across hundreds of miles, spending hours on the phone and Skype with me, visiting me in all of the places I have lived, driving me up and down the West Coast, and bringing the delightful Vivian Calliope Muraco Durbin into this world. Christopher Duke, Elizabeth Coleman, Laurie Jones-Neighbors, and my roommate, friend, and colleague, Andreana Clay, cheered me on in my successes and supported me in harder moments. Buddy, the Angel Dog, as well as Jesse and Dessa also kept me great company over the years.

A special thank you goes to my dad, Natali Anthony Muraco, who was always my biggest fan. Unfortunately, he did not live to see the publication of this book, but I know that he is very proud of this and all of my accomplishments.

Two other people have been central to the completion of this project. Jennifer Reich has been a supportive friend, mentor, and colleague. She has read nearly every word of this manuscript and has helped me to clarify and organize my thoughts many times over. I could never have thought to ask for the kind of personal and academic support she has given me. My successes are her successes.

Michael Borgstrom inspired this work. Not only is Mike my best friend; he is also a superstar academic who challenges me to think beyond my assumptions, refuses to let me doubt my abilities, and makes me laugh almost every day. While I certainly value his intellectual attributes, I cherish Mike most for the everyday happiness and stability he brings to my life.

Finally, I must thank all of the individuals who participated in this study for the candor and depth of what they were willing to share and for taking time out of their lives to talk to me. Their accounts convinced me that this work was not only worth undertaking, but also that their stories of friendship and love deserve concerted attention.

# INTRODUCTION

IN THE LATE 1990S, *Will and Grace*, a television sitcom about a gay man and a straight woman who were best friends, was one of the most watched and awarded shows. I watched the show and compared it to my own twenty-plus-year friendship with Mike, a gay man (I am a straight woman) who is my best friend. I related to how Will and Grace made each other laugh and finished each other's sentences. And whenever I was introduced to the few of Mike's friends I had not met previously, they nearly always characterized me as his "Grace."

Through my casual conversations with friends and acquaintances, it seemed that "Wills" and "Graces" were everywhere. As both a scholar who studies relationships and interaction and someone with this kind of friendship, which I refer to as "intersectional,"[1] I paid close attention to television and cinematic representations of relationships that looked similar to my friendship, at least on the surface. These friendships also were portrayed in such feature films as *My Best Friend's Wedding* (1997), *The Object of My Affection* (1998), and *The Next Best Thing* (2000), just to name a few. Yet television and other media portrayals of these friendships were distorted and exaggerated in ways that seemed to mock the significance of these ties. They also focused on gay men and heterosexual women; there was a conspicuous absence of portrayals of friendships between lesbians and straight men. I knew that these relationships existed. At the time, my roommate was a lesbian with a best friend who was a straight man. Her girlfriend at the time also had a straight male friend whom she talked about incessantly. Yet none of us could recall a single depiction of the lesbian–straight man friendship on television. The more I thought about these differences, the more interesting the topic became. Why were friendships between gay men and straight women portrayed as "natural," while a similar expectation was lacking for lesbians and straight men? Over time, my initial curiosity grew into a full-fledged sociological examination of these friendships.

*Odd Couples* examines intersectional friendships between gay men and straight women and between lesbians and straight men to show how these friendships serve as a barometer for shifting social norms, particularly with respect to gender and sexual orientation.[2] More than simply an examination of changing social norms, *Odd Couples* explores intersectional friendships as they challenge the idea that gender differences are indelible and can never be fully bridged. What I mean is that we, as a society, have a set of social norms that guide our behaviors and social relationships. Inter- and intra-personally, with rare exceptions, men and women are expected to have different emotional lives, interests, goals, and expectations. Relationally, men and women are expected to interact in known ways: they are romantic or sexual partners, co-workers, or relatives, and rarely do these roles intersect. These social norms are based on an assumption of heterosexuality. The question that has continually interested me was how differences in sexual orientation may alter these expectations, both behaviorally and in relationships. From media images and from my own life, I know that bonds between a gay man and a straight woman break some social norms but also bring new expectations. This is the dynamic that I explore throughout *Odd Couples*.

Intersectional friendships, most profoundly, challenge two widespread assumptions about friendships between men and women. First, these relationships challenge the idea that men and women are fundamentally different from one another; and second, they challenge the widespread understanding that men and women who are not related by biology or law can forge significant bonds only within romantic relationships. Intersectional friendships also challenge us to think through a spectrum of other ways that social norms are taken for granted or are challenged in our everyday interactions.

In *Odd Couples*, I argue that intersectional friendships represent a resistance against social norms that define and regulate gender, sexuality, and social institutions. Intersectional friendships often are strong bonds that provide support and companionship, like many other types of friendship. What distinguishes them from other relationships is the way that intersectional friends allow each other to embody identities that feel more genuine than those allowed by social norms, particularly those norms related to gender and sexual orientation. These friendships highlight what is unsatisfying about the limited roles that men and women are expected to play in one another's lives, as they offer an alternative. Throughout this book, I propose that individuals who are dissatisfied with the limited expressions of gender and sexual orientation dictated by social norms hold dear their intersectional friendships when they allow flexibility in gendered behavior. I acknowledge, however, that social norms, particularly those related to gender and sexual orientation, are difficult to resist because they are built into nearly every aspect of our lives through the processes of socialization and interaction. As a result, people's behavior is often conflicting with respect to being able to wholly resist or embody norms. In rewriting possibilities for gender and sexuality, individuals behave inconsistently. The friendships I highlight thus are neither entirely revolutionary nor entirely normative. They are both.

## THE SIGNIFICANCE OF INTERSECTIONAL FRIENDSHIP

Studying intersectional friendships between gay men and straight women and between lesbians and straight men can help us to better understand how our expectations about gender and sexual orientation shape the assumption that gay men and straight women make the best of friends. The same expectation fuels the belief that friendship between a lesbian woman and a straight man is a rare occurrence. Both assumptions are mired in conventional norms about gender and sexual orientation. A friendship pairing between a lesbian and a straight man rarely enters the public consciousness as a feasible bond because these groups are not perceived as having anything in common (aside from an attraction to women). Also, people may perceive straight men as having romantic or sexual feelings about the lesbian friend (i.e., the film *Chasing Amy*), which motivates his pursuit of a friendship. On the other end of the spectrum, gay men are expected to be feminine or female-like and to embody a conventional version of femininity; as seen in their images on television and in film, they enjoy shopping and gossiping and are focused on appearance and making everything fabulous. The friendships gay men share with straight women are perceived of as ideal because they are expected to provide a context in which men and women can interact as equals, without sexual tension. Throughout the book, I explore the varied embodiments and expectations of gender; ultimately, intersectional friendships allow us to see the nuances in gendered behaviors and identities.

Intersectional friendships challenge gender and sexual orientation norms by virtue of their existence. Nardi (1999) found that gay men's friendships challenge the heterosexual norms implicit in the dominant culture, a dynamic that Warner (1991) defines as heteronormativity. He explains heteronormativity as "the institutions, structures of understanding, and practical orientations that make heterosexuality seem not only coherent—that is, organized as a sexuality —but also privileged" (Warner 1991: 3–17).[3] Extending this principle to intersectional friendships, we see how these bonds give friends the opportunity to construct identities and a sense of belonging that runs counter to heteronormativity. In particular, intersectional friendships defy expectations of what men and women can be to each other. Intersectional friendship provides a space where not only gay men but also straight women, straight men, and lesbians may reject social norms of gender and sexual orientation, not only in their own identities, but also in their ways of relating to each other, without losing support.

MORE THAN "JUST FRIENDS"

In this work, I also tackle how social interaction is imbued with assumptions about compulsory heterosexuality, which Rich (1980) describes as the dominant cultural expectation that women will be innately sexually attracted to men and men, to women. The norm of compulsory heterosexuality structures our social perceptions of all social relationships, including friendships. As Shepperd, Coyle, and Hegarty (2010: 208) explain, "Not only are men and women expected to be sexually involved with one another, but non-sexual relationships often have difficulty justifying themselves as psychologically important. . . . Friendships are treated less seriously than romantic relationships by the general public, by social scientists, and by society." Gender and compulsory heterosexuality thus shape not only our social expectations of interactions and relationships, but also our relegation of friendship itself to less importance than romantic interactions and, by extension, biological family relations. By making friendship between men and women, gay, lesbian, and straight, the focus of study, this work challenges the assumptions of compulsory heterosexuality.

In addition to showing how gender shapes and is challenged by intersectional friendships, I incorporate the goal proposed by the queer theorist Steven Maddison (2000: 71), which is to better understand the "structural nature of affiliations between women and gay men so as to foreclose purely frivolous understandings of their relations and to validate the institutional difficulties that such bonds endure, as well as the dissent potential they hold." Accordingly, I highlight the potential that these friendships have to challenge and change the way we understand gender, sex, sexual orientation, and friendship. (In chapter

3, I address how our cultural understanding of family represents what Maddison identifies as an "institutional difficulty" that intersectional friendships face, as family life is given primacy over friendships, both structurally and interpersonally. I explore how, in some cases, the friendships provide alternative ways to view and experience family life.)

In making intersectional friendship the focus of the study, my intent is to raise awareness of friendship in analytical discussions. A gap exists in social science research: the friend relationship has been largely ignored as an important influence on the social behavior of adults and the organization of social life because it does not fit with the norms that place family at the center of adult life. Prior research has focused on the role of adolescent and young adult friends as a socialization influence (Eder, Evans, and Parker 1995) and in adulthood, on the principle of substitution, which is the idea that when people lack conventional family relationships, they often turn to friends as a form of chosen kin (Stack 1974; Townsend 1957). Yet rarely is friendship considered as a way to organize adult lives. This work serves as a case study about how gender and sexual orientation operate within a specific context (intersectional friendship), elucidating the potential of friendships to challenge social norms and create alliances.

I also aim to highlight the significance of friendship as a central means of understanding personal connection in light of the ways that family life continues to evolve in the twenty-first century. Contemporary heterosexual family life is in flux, with lower rates of marriage, higher rates of cohabitation, and greater acceptance of divorce (Musick 2007; Stacey 1998a); these demographic shifts suggest that normative family life is not necessarily a stable means for organizing adults' lives, yet it remains the focus for policymakers, extended family members, and even much of social science analysis. *Odd Couples* offers a lens to examine all friendship as intersectional by focusing on the hierarchy of different relationship forms and the different structural position of those within them.

This work also connects the realms of the personal and the political by exploring how power and representation play out in close interpersonal relationships. Prior research supports the idea that power differences are reinforced in social relationships (Cancian 1987; Cohen 1992; O'Connor 1992). Specifically, styles of relating in which women do the often invisible relationship work of maintaining emotional intimacy disproportionately benefit heterosexual men and reinforce their position at the top of the societal hierarchy

(Cancian 1987; Strazdins and Broom 2004). In addition to interaction dynamics, structural inequalities that place women below men in terms of employment hierarchies (Acker 1988) still affect women's earnings and economic independence; as of September 2010, the wage gap showed women earning 77 percent of every dollar earned by men (Institute for Women's Policy Research [IWPR] 2010). These structural inequalities color the romantic relationships and marriages between straight men and women such that men typically have greater earning power and women provide greater unpaid and, often, unacknowledged emotional and domestic labor (Hartmann 1981; Hochschild and Machung 1989).

Through this research I sought to understand whether inequality between men and women in close relationships was mitigated by sexual orientation. Prior scholarship about friendships answered parts of this question. Werking (1997), for example, addressed how cross-sex friendships between straight men and women navigated sexual tension and to some extent defied traditional gender norms. Tillmann-Healy (2001) discussed the various ways that she, as a straight woman, developed and maintained intimate friendships with a group of gay men. Yet these previous studies did not answer the question that most interested me: in the absence of socially sanctioned sexual tension and expectations of a romantic relationship, can men and women maintain egalitarian relationships? Furthermore, I wanted to know how gender norms would operate in contexts in which sexual orientation seemingly ruled out or prohibited sexual relationships.

## INTERSECTIONAL FRIENDSHIPS
## AND TERMINOLOGY

For the sake of clarity, it is important to explain some terminology used throughout the book. I refer to the friendships between people of different sexes and sexual orientations—in particular, the bonds between gay men and straight women and the bonds between lesbians and straight men—as "intersectional" because they create contexts in which multiple identities converge, the most salient in my study being gay and straight, male and female. There also are dialectical tensions that influence these relationships: the pairings of friendship and family, feminine and masculine, sexual and platonic.

Intersectionality is a concept that calls for an integrated approach to examining interlocking systems of oppression (i.e., race, class, sex, and gender oppression, among other social categories) as they influence everyday life (Collins 1991, 1998; Dillaway and Broman 2001). An intersectional approach considers inequalities to be components of social structure and interaction (Zinn and Dill 2000) and examines how sexuality and sexual orientation are intertwined with the cultural creation of other categories of inequality (Gamson and Moon 2004). The specific focus of this book is intersections of sex and sexual orientation, but throughout I consider gender, race, and class, because they are significant components of one's identity and experiences, as well.

Terminology, with respect to identity and social location, can be tricky because naming is imbued with political meaning. In this study, I use the term "sex" purposefully, to indicate that the friendships are between women and men. I discuss the norms of behavior in terms of "gender." Sex and gender are not synonymous categories; sex is a biological category, while gender is a socially determined and reinforced category that is produced and reproduced through interactions with others (West and Zimmerman 1987), and I treat these terms accordingly. In general, I also address whether or not someone is straight, gay, or lesbian as one's "sexual orientation."[4] While "sexual orientation" is a sufficiently common term, for the sake of clarity, I use the definition offered by the American Psychological Association (2008: 1): "An enduring emotional, romantic, sexual, or affectional attraction toward others. It is easily distinguished from other components of sexuality including biological sex, gender identity (the psychological sense of being male or female), and the social gender role (adherence to cultural norms for feminine and masculine behavior)." Thus, straight people; gay men; lesbian women; and bisexual, transgender, and intersexed individuals all have sexual orientations. Sexual orientation is not equal to sexual behavior. Sometimes a lesbian may have sex with a man and still consider herself a lesbian; in other cases, a man identifies as straight even if he has had sexual contact with other men. These identities can fluctuate over time and in varying contexts.

"Queer" is another term that the participants in this project and scholars use to describe identities, theories, and analytical frameworks. Jagose (1996: 3) provides a useful definition of the term:

> Broadly speaking, queer describes those gestures or analytical models which dramatise incoherencies in the allegedly stable relations between chromosomal sex, gender and sexual desire. Resisting that model of stability—which claims heterosexuality as its origin, when it is more properly its effect—queer focuses on mismatches between sex, gender and desire. Institutionally,

queer has been associated most prominently with lesbian and gay subjects, but its analytic framework also includes such topics as cross-dressing, hermaphroditism, gender ambiguity and gender-corrective surgery. Whether as transvestite performance or academic deconstruction, queer locates and exploits the incoherencies in those three terms which stabilise heterosexuality. Demonstrating the impossibility of any "natural" sexuality, it calls into question even such apparently unproblematic terms as "man" and "woman."

When individuals use the term "queer" to describe their identities, they may be identifying themselves as gay, lesbian, bisexual, transgender, straight but gender-ambiguous, the partner of someone who has undergone sexual reassignment, or countless other possibilities. "Queer" is a term used purposely to identify oneself as not aligning with norms of gender, sex, or sexual orientation. Queer theoretical positions or frameworks are used to make problematic the assumptions that heterosexuality is the central defining feature of everyday life. In other words, people or groups who identify themselves as queer do so as a means to show that they reject the social norms that define them as marginal.

THE STUDY

*Odd Couples* is based on interviews with individuals engaged in close intersectional friendships, which I conceived of as affectionate and ongoing relationships between individuals that are not of a biological, legal, or romantic nature. I relied on the participants' self-identification of being in a close intersectional friendship as sufficient to include them in the study and during our interviews, I asked them to characterize what "close" friend meant to them. The closeness of friendship bonds is an important element in this study for two reasons. First, it is unlikely that the interactions in casual friendships will have the same degree of impact on an individual's everyday life as more significant ones. Second, previous research has shown that mere casual contact between individuals from different sexual orientations does not necessarily bring the same sense of understanding and affiliation as close bonds (Fee 1996; Price 1999). Consequently, I focus on close friendship bonds because my interest centers on the relations between those individuals whose friendship has an impact on the ideology and identity of their members.

My interest in researching intersectional friendships originated from my own personal biography. I am a straight woman who has a very close friendship with a gay man, and I consider this relationship central to my life. Thus, I approached this research as an exercise in "starting from where you are"—in other words, subjecting matters that are relevant in the life of the researcher to sociological analysis (Lofland and Lofland 1995). O'Connor (1992) critiques that, while discounted by some as a frivolous or an insignificant topic of scientific inquiry, the study of friendship is a means of examining the everyday experiences and interactions that make people's lives meaningful. In fact, as more and more individuals create adult lives outside traditional family norms (Cagen 2004; Watters 2003; Weston 1991), friends increasingly serve the roles of surrogate parent or sibling and fulfill the many domestic functions necessary in contemporary life: daycare provider, handyman, taxi service, career counselor, and therapist. Studying intersectional friendships, then, not only contributes to our greater understanding of friendships across categories of difference, it also adds to sociological knowledge about the relationships people rely on to build and support their lives.

The people at the center of this book are those engaged in intersectional friendships. In 2002 and 2003, I interviewed fifty-three people involved in twenty-six close friendship dyads and one triad primarily in the San Francisco Bay Area and surrounding counties. My interviews with the intersectional friends provide the foundational data for the research; thus, it is important to provide a brief explanation of how I went about studying them here. A more detailed discussion of my research methods is in appendix 1. Using a convenience and purposive snowball sampling method, I recruited the study participants beginning with my contacts in the lesbian, gay, bisexual, and transgender (LGBT) communities of the San Francisco Bay Area and expanding through participants' social networks. I also targeted LGBT community organizations in the Bay Area for recruitment by distributing electronic and paper fliers describing the study and ran free advertisements on electronic community bulletin boards.

From my recruitment, I found the fifty-three participants. Of the people included in the study, twenty-eight were women (thirteen lesbian, fourteen straight, one queer) and twenty-five were men (thirteen gay, twelve straight). There are more women than men in the study because I was unable to interview the male halves of the friendship pairs in two cases; also, the triad included in the study was composed of two women and one man. The age range of study participants is twenty-one to sixty-four, with a median of thirty-two. The racial composition is 59 percent white, 17 percent Latino, 19 percent Asian, and 4 percent black. Appendix 2 contains a more detailed list of participants with corresponding demographic information and identifies their intersectional friend.

The interviews took place as structured conversations guided by my questions; typically, the discussions lasted forty-five minutes to two hours and were held in a location chosen by the participant. The vast majority of participants were interviewed separately, though in one case I interviewed both members of the friendship dyad together at their request, and in another case, both members of a lesbian couple were present to discuss their straight male friend. My questions covered a range of topics, from how the friends met to how often they communicate, the types of activities they enjoy together, and the significance of the relationship in their lives. To make analytical sense of their accounts, I transcribed the interviews and qualitatively analyzed the data transcripts to look for prevalent themes under the principles of grounded theory, which uses a systematic set of procedures to develop and inductively derive theory about a phenomenon (Glaser and Strauss 1967; Strauss and Corbin 1990). In other words, I used the words of the people I interviewed to create a more in-depth understanding of the dynamics of intersectional friendships.

I sought to examine the issues that interested me in two distinct ways: by constructing the interview questions and by coding the interview transcripts. First, I created interview questions that addressed some of the aspects of these friendships that interested me most and then scrutinized the interviewees' responses to those questions. The particular areas that I wanted to explore were the processes of the friendship (what the friends do, how often they talk and see each other, how they met), the meanings of the friendship (the salience of the friendship in each individual's life, how the individuals describe and characterize the friendship), and what the friendships provide that other relationships do not (targeting issues of gender and sexual orientation). I include a list of the questions that guided the research in appendix 3.

I identified themes in the process of coding the interview transcripts in several ways. First, I kept a journal that noted interesting observations I had throughout the process of conducting face-to-face interviews and transcribing the recorded interviews. Second, once I completed the interview transcription, I reviewed the transcripts repeatedly, looking for repetition of phrasing. Some of the themes that emerged from this process were "a gay man trapped in a straight woman's body" and "chosen family is better than biological family," whose meanings I explored more fully. I conducted a third type of coding by identifying several concepts that I saw as central to the discussion of intersectional friendship: gender, family, identity. I thought about the data in terms of what they could tell us about these concepts by looking at them holistically— that is, rather than examining specific phrasing, I sought to glean the interviewees' perceptions and experiences of these areas by examining the entirety of the interview transcript.

As a whole, the work provides a glimpse into the lives of a particular sampling of intersectional friends, as well as a framework for thinking about friendships more broadly. Thus, the study is not intended to be representative of all intersectional friendships. Rather, it provides insight into the bonds that I studied, which also may be applicable to many types of social relationships.

THE ORGANIZATION OF ODD COUPLES

The chapters of this book explore the issues that arise in these friendships in more detail, drawing on the voices of those interviewed. Each chapter but the last begins with a brief vignette of one of the friendships in the study in order to help the reader get to know a bit more about the intersectional friends included in the book.

Any good study of a sociological phenomenon rests on the work that came before it. Chapter 1 discusses the theoretical foundation and prior literature on which this work is built. In this chapter, I outline the various theoretical perspectives that create the backbone of research on intersectional friendships. The chapter outlines the general findings about friendship as a social relationship and addresses the unique dimensions of "bridging" friendships (de Souza Briggs 2007), or those that cross various categories of difference. By outlining what we already know, I situate this study at the intersection of several literatures on inequality, friendship, sexual communities, and gender.

Chapter 2 introduces the reader to three pairs of intersectional friends. I use these friends to highlight some of the common themes present in many of the pairs in the study.

In chapter 3, I explore the notion of the intersectional friendship as a chosen family connection. Challenging the notion that friends are less important than family, I demonstrate how friends often act as families. In chapter 4, I specifically analyze the gender dynamics in these friendships. I look at how power and privilege operate in these friendships around meanings and experiences of gender and how friends understand each other's identity. I also highlight the tensions between these friends that reinforce and resist traditional gender norms. In chapter 5, I examine the role of sexuality and sexual orientation in shaping intersectional friendship processes. Again, we see how friends under-stand each other's identity but also challenge the notion that friendships that cross sexual orientation would be free of all sexual tension. In each of these chapters, I not only analyze the respective topics but also address the tensions present between the friendships' tendency to both subvert and reinforce tradi-tional expectations of gender, family, and sexuality.

This study also explores various political dimensions of befriending some-one from a different social location. Chapter 6 analyzes the extent to which intersectional friendships constitute political bonds. I analyze the liberatory potential of these friendships, a possibility that is inherent in the ways they challenge categories of privilege and oppression. I highlight the promise in intersectional friendships' ability to transform social life and promote equality and analyze the ways in which dyads can fall short of this possibility.

Finally, *Odd Couples* concludes with chapter 7, which connects each of these empirical discussions to identify the implications of these friendships for those in the relationships, as well as for those around them, and considers the future of intersectional friendships.

# YOU'VE GOT
# TO HAVE FRIENDS

[Gay/straight friendship] makes the straight person, I think, more of a whole person. Straight people can so easily, because they comprise 80–90 percent of the population, just erase the gay and lesbian, bisexual, transgender people out of their lives, it's not easy, but they could do it—I'm not breaking my own arm patting myself on the back, it's just that for a straight person to accept, it forces you to become more open and if you become more open, you become, to me, a more human person.

—Bob, a sixty-four-year-old straight white man

## FRANK AND REBECCA

Frank and Rebecca's friendship began inauspiciously when they were quite young. Frank explained:

> When we were four years old, my sister was taking piano lessons [in the home of] one of our neighbors. We lived in a town of probably 300 people . . . at the time. So we were all neighbors, but it was the other side of town, and we'd gone over there for my sister's piano lessons. I, of course, got bored and went outside to play. It was wintertime; there were mud puddles, so I was out playing in mud puddles, and I suddenly got a swift kick in the ass and went head first into the mud puddle. When I turned around, that's when I met her. I said, "You got me all wet," and she said, "Uh-huh. Wanna come over and play on my slide?" And I said, "Uh-huh."

Since they lived in a small town, Frank and Rebecca were in all of the same classes in elementary school and spent afternoons and summer days together catching lizards and playing in creek beds. Rebecca seemed to need an alliance with Frank. She was the only child who was not white in her small town (she is half-Japanese) and endured a difficult home life. Time spent with Frank was an escape. While the children built a strong friendship, it also was a bond of intense competition. Frank and Rebecca tried to outdo each other in earning grades and academic accomplishments as children. Teachers separated them in junior high because they were so competitive with each other.

In high school, the friends ran in different social circles. Rebecca partly attributes their relative distance in high school to the fact that Frank disliked her boyfriend. Rebecca and Frank remember the details of his coming out as gay to her very differently. Rebecca noted that she was not surprised to learn the news, but Frank has an entirely different memory of the conversation. Frank remembers that Rebecca was very angry with him when she found out he was gay and that she was not the first person he had told. Rebecca noted that she and Frank often remember details from their past differently. Both recalled a night when they discussed whether or not they should have sex and try to be in a relationship together—this was before Frank had come out as gay. As children, they had pretended to have weddings, and many of the adults in their small town had assumed they would marry at some point because of their strong bond. They decided that having sex would be too weird to deal with afterward and decided against it. Frank acknowledges that his friendship with Rebecca confirmed for him that he is gay:

> My friendship with Rebecca has pretty much convinced me of my sexual orientation because of the fact that, you know, by typical standards, she's a freakin' babe, she's so hot, and I've never had the hots for her, and that more than anything has helped to convince me that, oh, yeah, I really am gay.

Frank and Rebecca are now in their mid-thirties and live several hundred miles away from each other but talk on the phone once a week. Rebecca is married, and her husband and Frank get along very well; this encouraged the longtime friends to commit to seeing each other more regularly. Recently, Frank traveled with Rebecca and her husband on a ski trip to Tahoe, and they were planning a mountain biking trip in the winter. Rebecca and Frank still talk to each other when they are making big life decisions; Frank stated that he would not have bought his house without Rebecca's encouragement, and Rebecca said that when she needs to talk to someone about important issues, Frank is the person she calls.

FRIENDSHIP FULFILLS many roles in our lives. Friendship satisfies a desire for affiliation with those who are like us in some ways but unlike us in others. Not only do friends provide feelings of belonging; they also enhance our sense of self. A friendship bond brings meaning to an individual's life and increases feelings of happiness (Bersheid et al. 1989; Fehr 1996; Larson and Bradney 1988), but often its significance is overshadowed by the intensity of familial or romantic relationships, which come with higher cultural expectations and obligations (Felmlee and Sprecher 2000; Rubin 1985). Friendship provides emotional benefits but can also lead to emotional pain, rejection, and annoyance (Duck and Wood 1995). Cited as bringing both joy and conflict to our lives (Argyle 1987; Duck and Wright 1993; Rose and Serafica 1986), friendship is one of the most significant, yet socially ignored, relationships.

Intersectional friendships face novel challenges compared with traditional within-group bonds. These dyadic friendships resist homosexual ghettoization, in which gay men and lesbians become socially segregated in their own communities in reaction to societal heterosexism and homophobia. Friendships between gay men and straight women and between lesbians and straight men enter uncharted relational territory by successfully (and voluntarily) uniting in the face of both homosexual segregation and the belief that friendships between men and women will always result in romance.[1] Thus, intersectional friendships can provide an alternative model for male–female interaction. In so doing, the intersectional dyads create a unique friendship form that may allow expressions of atypical gender behavior and yet also abide by traditional gendered norms in terms of the activities performed in the dyads. In this chapter, I provide a foundation for the rest of the book by examining the prior research, both empirical and theoretical, that helps us to better understand intersectional friendships. The chapter provides an overview of the roles that friendships play in our everyday lives, starting with how we build friendships and common characteristics of friendships, according to the existing body of research. I also address the qualities of various friendship compositions. I start by discussing what we currently know about intersectional friendships between gay men and straight women and between lesbians and straight men, then move on to address friendships between and among gay men and straight women, as well as same- and cross-sex friendships for gay men, lesbians, and heterosexuals. The chapter concludes by highlighting the various theoretical perspectives that inform this study.

## THE ROLES OF FRIENDSHIP IN OUR LIVES

People desire connection to others. According to Baumeister's and Leary's (1995) discussion of the belongingness hypothesis, humans have a desire to form and maintain a minimum quantity of positive, significant relationships. The desire to belong consists of frequent and emotionally pleasant interactions, combined with the stability of such relationships over time (Baumeister and Leary 1995). Friendships are significant bonds that provide many benefits. Friends meet material, cognitive, and social-emotional needs, such as providing love and esteem (Solano 1986), and create a bond where individuals may self-disclose and share activities (Adams, Blieszner, and de Vries 2000). Another benefit of friendship is the pleasure of companionship: people say they are happier when they are with friends than when they are alone or with family members (Larson and Bradney 1988). Friendship ties may benefit individuals' overall health (Baumeister and Leary 1995; Myers 2000). Positive friendship ties are associated with lower mortality rates and a relatively long life (Rasulo, Christensen, and Tomassini 2005; Sabin 1993), as well as higher self-esteem and better overall mental health (Ueno 2005; Wright 1999).

Friendships are formed in a variety of manners and contexts. One element that influences friendship formation is similarity. We tend to form friendships with people who are similar to us with regard to demographic characteristics, social status, attitudes, and other factors, such as common interests and common educational levels (Brehm 1985; Verbrugge 1977; Weinstock 2000). In long-term friendships, a sense of shared history provides similarity, connection, and love (Shea, Thompson, and Blieszner 1988). Similarity alone is insufficient for the development of a significant friendship; another factor that promotes friendship formation is physical and geographical proximity, where people have regular exposure to each other (Fehr 2000; Hendrick 2003) as well as positive contact; the more positive interactions people have, the more they will like each other (Homans 1961). The principle of proximity explains how we form close bonds with those individuals who are roommates and neighbors. With changing technology, however, the issue of proximity has shifted so that people are now able to be in nearly constant communication with others, even when they are not in the same geographical location (McKenna, Green, and Gleason 2002; Morahan-Martin and Schumacher 2003). People stay in touch via email, text messaging, cell phones, and online videoconferencing and are likely to continue to do so as technology develops. As such, we expect that intimate friendships can thrive by putting effort into maintaining closeness and sense of involvement (Rubin 1985), despite a lack of physical or even geographical proximity.

Workplaces blend two of the necessary ingredients for friendship formation: proximity and similarity. Thus, it is not surprising that many friendships are formed on the job. According to Fine (1986: 190), in professional occupational settings, "the content of work affects friendships that are likely to develop, in part because of the people that an occupation attracts, and in part because of the nature of the work."[2] Workplace friendships typically reinforce class similarity, as individuals are more likely to interact with those who share a workplace status than with those at different levels of professional achievement (Cohen 1992), although one study found that cross-orientation friendships commonly occurred in the workplace (Rumens 2008). Whether friendships are formed in the workplace or in childhood, they mold and reflect aspects of individuals' identities in relation to each other.

### Bridging Friendships

While the tendency is toward friendship formation on the basis of similarity—also known as homophily (McPherson, Smith-Lovin, and Cook 2001)—a number of recent studies have focused on friendship between people across different racial, ethnic, and socioeconomic categories. One study showed that between 1985 and 2004, those reporting someone of another race being a "confidant" rose from 9 percent to 15 percent (McPherson, Brashears, and Smith-Lovin 2006). Yet others found that interracial friendships remained the exception rather than the norm (Kao and Joyner 2004). Best friendships most frequently occur between people from the same racial and ethnic group; these individuals are more likely to participate in shared activities, which lead to greater emotional intimacy (Kao and Joyner 2004). Moreover, interracial friendships are less likely to be reciprocal than intra-racial friendships, meaning that they are less likely to be emotionally intimate (Vaquera and Kao 2008). Studies point to miscommunications, a perceived lack of self-disclosure, and a perceived lack of responsiveness across racial or ethnic group to negatively affect the development of intimacy in friendships (Shelton, Trail, West, and Bergsieker 2010; Trail, Shelton, and West 2009).

Some studies have theorized that adolescents' misconceptions about other races partly explain why interracial friendships are less common than same-race friendships (Fujino 1997; Kao and Joyner 2004). Even when racial barriers were broken in friendships, research showed they faced greater challenges than same-race friendships (Kao and Joyner 2004). Despite the challenges, interracial friendships provide valuable connections and have a strong effect on positive attitudes toward interracial marriage, an indicator that interracial friendship promotes greater racial equality (Johnson and Jacobson 2005) and may help lessen anxiety about intergroup interactions (Page-Gould, Mendoza-Denton, and Tropp 2008). A traditionally marginalized social status may affect the patterns of friendship formation. For instance, the social networks of sexual-minority adults reflect larger societal patterns of friendship in terms of race.

One study found that white lesbians and gay men report having more same-race friends than other-race friends, with lesbians of color reporting more cross-race friends than any other group (Galupo 2007b).

Friendships that bridge socioeconomic status also can have a positive social influence. Ties that cross social boundaries can reduce inequality by providing access to information, mentoring, and other forms of social capital, according to one study (de Souza Briggs 2007). Yet researchers also find that class status may be reproduced throughout the life cycle. Vaquera's and Kao's (2008) study of reciprocity in adolescent friendships found that children from more advantaged socioeconomic levels make friends more easily because they are perceived as being more socially desirable, a pattern that likely continues throughout the life course. Moreover, according to these findings, children with greater socioeconomic class advantage were more likely to have reciprocal, emotionally intimate friendships (Vaquera and Kao 2008). More generally, individuals are most likely to form friendships with people who share a common socioeconomic status because they value similar social exchanges and are more likely to interact with each other as peers (Jackson 1977).

When taken together, socioeconomic status and race affect rates of friendship across categories such that bridging friendships are more likely to occur when neighborhoods are integrated, when one's neighborhood of residence is in an urban area with a high degree of racial heterogeneity, and when one engages in a high frequency of socializing with co-workers (de Souza Briggs 2007). Studies of bridging friendships have provided evidence that affectionate ties across categories of difference, while less common than friendships between those from similar backgrounds, were beneficial in facilitating greater understanding across the racial (Johnson and Jacobson 2005), class (de Souza Briggs 2007), sex (Werking 1997), and sexual orientation categories (Tillmann-Healy 2001).

## THE FRIEND RELATIONSHIP BY SEX AND SEXUAL ORIENTATION

When people think of friendships, they generally envision male buddies or best female friends—in other words, a same-sex pairing that fits our dominant cultural image (Rubin 1985; Werking 1997). This normative assumption stems, at least in part, from patterns of gender socialization and norms of compulsory heterosexuality, which Rich (1980) describes as the dominant cultural expectation that women will be innately sexually attracted to men and that men will be attracted to women. From early childhood, people are sex-segregated in play and activities, a practice that influences the friendship bonds they form with other children (Myers and Raymond 2010; Thorne 1986). Throughout the life cycle, men and women primarily maintain friendships with members of their own sex, even as boundaries between sexes have relaxed (Werking 1997). Other research shows that the majority of friendships are between people of similar sexual orientation (Galupo 2007b; Nardi 1999).

## Same-Sex, Same-Orientation Friendships of Gay Men and Lesbians

Some argue that friendships generally play a more important role for gay men and lesbians than they do for straight people, especially those friendships between gay men and between lesbian women. Friendships may be especially important at midlife and beyond for lesbians and gay men (Grossman, D'Augelli, and Hershberger 2000; Quam and Whitford 1992); typically, friends provide more support for gay and lesbian individuals in need of caregiving compared with straight individuals (Dorfman, Walters, Burke, Hardin, Karanik, Raphael, and Silverstein 1995). Moreover, prior research finds that friendships are often the main source of support, affirmation, and love in the lives of gay men and lesbians (Stanley 1996), while straight individuals are assumed to have greater access to social support through normative family life (Nardi 1992).

A common theme in the literature about gay male and lesbian friendships is the chosen family connections that they embody (Nardi 1992; Weinstock 2000; Weston 1991); this may be particularly true for current cohorts of midlife and older lesbians and gay men who came of age in a more repressive social context (Weinstock 2000). The greater importance of friendship for gay men and lesbians in the current generation of older gay and lesbian adults, as compared with straight people, emerged from a greater need to form a supportive community of individuals to provide support and care in the wake of the heterosexism of larger society (Nardi 1999; Weston 1991).

The majority of gay men and lesbians form friendships based on similarity of sex, sexual orientation, and other demographic dimensions such as race, age, and socioeconomic status (Weinstock 2000). Similarities also exist between gay men's and lesbian women's friendship experiences and networks. Nardi and Sherrod (1994) compared gay men's same-sex friendships with lesbians' same-sex friendships and found many similarities in terms of satisfaction with the relationships and the high value placed on them. In their same-sex friendships, gay men and lesbians were more likely than straight men and women to express gender-atypical behavior in terms of emotional and instrumental behavior (Nardi and Sherrod 1994). Thus, to some extent, some gender norms may be relaxed in same-sex gay men's and lesbians' friendships.

Same-sex, same-orientation friendships for gay men and lesbians not only provide a buffer against heterosexism (Kocet 2001); they also provide a link to gay and lesbian communities. In fact, some gay men identify their particular "gay" community as defined by their friendships (Woolwine 2000). Friendship, according to Nardi (1999: 13), represents "the central organizing element of gay men's lives—the mechanism through which gay neighborhoods get transformed, maintained, and reproduced." Social support is present in gay men's friendships, where friends assist with the coming-out process by providing a feeling of acceptance (Kocet 2001). The importance of friendship becomes especially tangible in later life, as older gay men and lesbians characterize themselves as encircled by friends and describe their friendship bonds in affective ways (e.g., "They are part of my inner landscape") (de Vries and Megathin 2009: 90). Gay men's and lesbian women's friendships are often described as a site of refuge and power building that also serves as a source of affiliation and a context for the reaffirmation of identity (Nardi 1999; Stanley 1996). Lesbian friends may serve as each other's role models in learning how to thrive as lesbians in a heterosexist and sexist society; through friendship, the traditions and norms of lesbian identity are learned and reproduced (Stanley 1996). Especially for lesbians, former partners play a complex yet central role, not only as friends, but also as extended family members and connections to the lesbian community (Weinstock 2004).

The same-sex friendships of gay men and lesbians encounter many benefits and challenges, according to prior research. Same-sex friendships of gay men and lesbians introduce a potential sexual tension that generally is not expected to be present in friendships between straight women or straight men or in gay and lesbian cross-sex friendships (Nardi 1999; Weinstock 2000). Prior research shows that, unlike other types of friendships, gay men's friendships may include a sexual component that serves as a way for both casual and close friendships to be formed (Nardi 1999). Rather than redefining these friendships as a different relational form, sexual friendships between gay men seem to be common, according to prior research (Nardi 1999). Young sexual-minority women may also have "passionate friendships," which include intense emotional, sometimes romantic interactions that may or may not have a sexual component (Diamond 2002).

### Intersectional Friendships

We know little about intersectional friendships—the friendships between gay men and straight women and between lesbians and straight men. The majority of existing scholarship about intersectional friendships—those that cross sex and sexual orientation categories—consists of personal accounts and theoretical analyses (e.g., de la Cruz and Dolby 2007; Hopke and Rafaty 1999; Maddison 2000; Moon 1995; Nestle and Preston 1995; Rafaty and Hopke 2001; Thompson 2004). One possible explanation for the lack of empirical work on this topic is that, despite the attention the media pays to friendships between gay men and straight women—such as *Will and Grace*, *My Best Friend's Wedding*, or even use of the term "fag hag"—scholars perceive these friendships to be uncommon. Although some studies claim that 50 percent of gay men reported having at least one close straight female friend (Rubin 1985), most research finds that gay men's and lesbians' closest social networks are composed of other gay men and lesbian women (Nardi 1999; Weinstock 1998). For example, Nardi (1999) discussed relationships between gay men and straight women in a larger examination of gay men's friendships and concluded that, although some very significant friendships exist between these individuals, the perceived commonality of gay man–straight woman reflects stereotype rather than reality.

It is interesting to imagine these friendships as uncommon, considering that most gay men and lesbian women have little choice but to interact with straight people because heterosexuality is the social norm and statistically, heterosexual people make up the majority of the population. In reality, their extensive, unavoidable interactions with straight co-workers, family members, classmates, neighbors, and community members lead gay men and lesbian women sometimes to forge significant, mutual bonds with straight individuals (Muraco 2006; Rumens 2008). Out of these connections intersectional friendships are born.

Given their connections to broader (heterosexual) society and greater social power, we may wonder what motivates straight people to form close relationships with gay men and lesbians. One motivation may be the benefits provided by intersectional friendships. For example, in one study straight women expressed feelings of enhanced attractiveness and self-esteem as a result of attention from their gay male friends (Bartlett, Patterson, VanderLaan, and Vasey 2009). Other possible motivations exist for straight individuals to form close friendships with gay men or lesbians, including the relaxing of gender norms and sexual expectations. Moreover, some research has concluded that straight women seek out the friendship of gay men to gain positive, validating male attention (Bartlett et al. 2009) that is free from sexual overtones (Grigoriou 2004). Others noted that friendships between gay men and straight women allow both parties to reject gender and sexuality norms if they choose to (Maddison 2000; Shepperd, Coyle, and Hegarty 2010), thus allowing individuals to express less traditional gendered behavior and identities. Tillmann-Healy (2001) provides an ethnographic study of the friendship connection between gay men and straight women and discusses how challenging her own heterosexist attitudes and immersing herself in a gay male context queered her perspective and thus allowed her greater freedom to enact more fluid identities.

Grigoriou (2004) reported that intersectional friendships help gay men to feel more "normal," given the privilege and normative social context of heterosexuality. Accordingly, some gay men view straight women as serving as bridges between the gay and straight worlds (Grigoriou 2004). Gay men also stressed that their friendships with straight women provide a level of trust that they do not have in friendships with other gay men, due to the lack of competition and possibility for sexual contact in their relationships with straight female friends (Grigoriou 2004). Research also shows that intersectional friendships between gay men and straight women have political implications, where the friendships give gay men and straight women a space in which they can resist heterosexist and patriarchal power structures by rejecting gender and sexuality norms (Shepperd et al. 2010), even as they may not directly identify their friendships as political acts (Maddison 2000; Rumens 2008; Thompson 2004; Ward 2000).

An examination of workplace friendships between gay men and straight women by Rumens (2008) found that, in gendered work hierarchies, gay men are more comfortable confiding in straight women than in other men, which often leads to the development of close friendships. Both gay men and straight women in the study identified trust and closeness as being a specific quality they experience in their intersectional friendship (Rumens 2008). This is not to suggest that all intersectional interaction is supportive. Some gay men noted that within the workplace, they experienced homophobic comments from straight women, while some straight women took issue with sexist attitudes of gay men (Rumens 2008). Moreover, Shepperd, Coyle, and Hegarty (2010) found that intersectional friends managed heterosexist norms in providing accounts of the friendships so that great emphasis was placed on constructing the friendship as non-sexual.

Friendships between lesbians and straight men may be the bond that has been most neglected in social research. I found only one case study that addressed a friendship between a lesbian woman and straight man as its focus. In part, the lack of research on the topic may stem from lesbian culture's focus on the romantic, committed partnership as the common organizing structure of relational life, particularly during midlife (Weinstock 2000). Another possibility is that lesbian women choose not to engage in bonds with people who represent heterosexist and sexist normative society, which is aligned with some forms of lesbian separatism that was most prominent in second-wave feminist thought (e.g., Frye 1983). Consistent with Weinstock's (2000) review of literature, the majority of research that examines lesbian friendship focuses on the roles of lesbian and straight women friends in supporting lesbians' psychosocial adjustment and well-being.

The single study about lesbian and straight male friends was an autobiographical account of this pair's friendship. The authors characterized their bond as "cerebral," with issues such as differing sexual orientations, politics, and the potential for sexual attraction having arisen as challenges to the friendship (Conner and Cohan 1996). Another study of lesbian family life by Goldberg and Allen (2007) hinted at the presence of male friends, particularly when discussing rearing male children. Of those lesbian women who identified male friends who they hoped would play a significant role in their children's lives, the most commonly named men were gay, husbands of straight female friends, or the sperm donors (Goldberg and Allen 2007). One additional study, Levitt's and Hiestand's (2004) article about lesbian gender identities, included a paragraph about friendships between lesbian women and straight men and characterized them as full of camaraderie and respect. The article also addressed how straight men sometimes talked about sexual topics with a lesbian friend, who became uncomfortable when she perceived the male friend as objectifying women and therefore forgetting she was a woman (Levitt and Hiestand 2004: 616). So little research exists on straight man–lesbian woman friendships that any suggestion of motivations are speculative, but straight men may seek out such friendships to have close interactions in which they do not feel normative gender pressure to enact masculinity.

## Lesbian Woman–Gay Man Friendships

While lesbian women and gay men have in common a sexual-minority status and the oppression that comes with it, empirical studies of friendships between individuals from these groups are scarce. More common are reports that address one particular friendship dyad. Anderson (1998) provides a theological reflection on a friendship between a black gay man and a black lesbian, focusing on how their similar races and different religious orientations and sexes influenced their spiritual practices. Other studies identify gay men and lesbians as having individuals from the other respective group as part of their network of friends but do not explore the dynamics and processes within particular friendship pairings (see Goldberg and Allen 2007; Weston 1991).

Historically, lesbian women and gay men have allied to provide care and support, particularly during the HIV/AIDS epidemic (Barker, Herdt, and de Vries 2006; Schneider 1992) and more recently in forging political ties in the struggle for the legalization of same-sex marriage. The work that emerges from these areas of study has not focused on the particular dimensions of friendship between lesbians and gay men.

## Same-Sex, Cross-Sexuality Friendships for Gay Men and Lesbians

As a demographic group, sexual-minority adults (in this case, gay men and lesbians) are more likely than straight adults to report having cross-orientation friendships and to having more same-sex friends than cross-sex friends (Galupo 2007b). Although cross-sexuality friendships—those between gay and straight men or between lesbian and straight women—are believed to be less common than other friendship types, they often prove to constitute significant bonds (Fee 1996; Tillmann-Healy 2001). Cross-sexuality friendships do not fit neatly into common understandings of friend relationships; rather, they challenge norms about gendered behavior.

The straight and gay male friendship dyad is one that may contest hegemonic definitions of masculinity. Nardi (1999) suggests that friendship between gay and straight men offers an alternative to heterosexist institutions and traditional forms of interaction. Fee (1996) used the term "coming over" to describe straight men's active willingness to challenge internalized homophobia by engaging in a friendship with a gay man. Coming over often allows a bond that is more emotionally intimate than other male friendships (Fee 1996).

Some cross-sexuality male friendships, however, create contexts in which aspects of homophobia may be reproduced. Price's (1999) study of gay–straight male friendships, for example, exposed a double standard; the straight man in the dyad was comfortable in the friendship so long as his gay friend did not discuss his same-sex partnership or dating life, while the straight man freely discussed his relationships with women.

Much of the past research about friendships between lesbians and straight women has been descriptive. One study noted that friendships between lesbian and straight women are most successful when the members of the dyad overcome the characterization of being fundamentally different from each other (O'Boyle and Thomas 1996). Galupo and St. John (2001) found that friendships between lesbian and straight adolescent women provided many benefits for both parties, which included increasing trust through the disclosure and acceptance of a sexual-minority identity, rejecting of stereotypes, and growing sensitivity to sexual diversity. Levitt's and Hiestand's (2004) article also discussed how butch lesbians' friendships with straight women were not uncommon, but that there was great potential for misunderstanding, primarily because straight women did not understand butch gender well enough to maintain comfortable boundaries. More recent empirical studies have found that sexual orientation was secondary to other dimensions that formed close friendships between lesbians and straight women (Galupo 2007a).

Weinstock and Bond (2002) provided one of the few empirical studies that focused on the friendship bonds between lesbians and straight women. Their research identified several positive aspects of these friendships: they broke down stereotypes and prejudice; provided support for a lesbian identity; and were free from sexual tension. In addition to these benefits, the friendships between lesbians and straight women provided opportunities to learn from each other (Weinstock and Bond 2002). The study also uncovered negative themes in these friendships that included limitations of understanding, clash of perspectives, stressors related to others' reactions to the friendship, and anxiety about sexuality (Weinstock and Bond 2002).

One area that has been researched more deeply is how friendship contact with gay men and lesbians affects straight people's homophobic and heterosexist attitudes. Straight women typically have more contact with gay men and lesbians than do straight men (Herek 1994). Those straight women and straight men that have interpersonal contact with gay men and lesbian women tend to have less homophobic attitudes than their counterparts and accordingly have more positive attitudes toward gay men and lesbians than do other straight men (Herek 2000; Herek and Capitanio 1996). Moreover, other research shows the context in which individuals have interacted with gay men also affects their attitudes toward gay men as a subcultural group (Castro-Convers, Gray, Ladany, and Metzler 2005). In particular, straight people who identify themselves as having very positive attitudes toward gay men also report having early awareness or direct and positive contact with gay men in their daily lives (Castro-Convers et al. 2005).

## Cross-Sex Heterosexual Friendships

The normative cultural paradigm in the United States idealizes same-sex friendship, which makes straight cross-sex friendships an anomaly. However, friendships between straight men and women are common among young adults and college-age individuals and in white-collar, professional workplace interactions (Rose 1985; Rubin 1985; Wright 1999). Given cultural norms of compulsory heterosexuality, cross-sex friendships often face challenges of sexual and romantic expectations, both internally and externally (O'Meara 1989). Pairings between men and women are usually interpreted as being romantic or having romantic potential—friendships exist within a system of recognized relationships and are understood within that context (Werking 1997).

Prior research shows that cross-sex friendships satisfy unmet needs of same-sex friendships and provide a unique perspective about the other sex (Rubin 1985; Werking 1997). Many cross-sex friendships provide a space where gender norms can be relaxed. For instance, both members of a cross-sex friendship often share interests and activities (Werking 1997). Such friendships permit displays of androgynous behavior, where men report feeling less competitive and women can speak in a less sensitive and more direct manner (Reeder 1996). In addition to challenging norms of gender and compulsory heterosexuality, cross-sex friendships create a context for challenging the assumption that men and women can sustain a relationship only within the bounds of a heterosexual love relationship (Swain 1992; Werking 1997).

While cross-sex friendships provide many benefits, they also face challenges, including a lack of social support, the assumption of sexual involvement, a lack of cultural models, and social inequalities between the members (O'Meara 1989; West, Anderson, and Duck 1996). Straight cross-sex friendships are also expected to be more short-lived than other friendship types (Parker and de Vries 1993). In many ways, cross-sex friendships may reinforce gender norms. Previous studies found that straight men enjoyed the nurturing support of female friends, and both men and women benefited by gaining insight into the perspectives of the friend of the other sex about the world (Werking 1997). Despite the overall comparison, distinctions between same-sex and cross-sex heterosexual friendships should not be overstated. For example, women are less likely to highlight the differences between same- and cross-sex friendship, reporting similar levels of emotional support and shared activities in both types of friendship (Werking 1997).

### Same-Sex Heterosexual Friendship

As the cultural model of friendship, same-sex friends often abide by social norms of gender and sexual orientation (O'Connor 1992).[3] Accordingly, the norms and expectations within the context of same-sex friendships for men and women have been identified as different, if only in degrees (Duck and Wright 1993; Felmlee 1999). Straight women's same-sex friendships, for example, are characterized as achieving intimacy through dialogue and providing both nurturing and emotional support (Johnson 1996; Rubin 1985). When compared with men, women report a greater degree of reciprocity in their friendships (Vaquera and Kao 2008). The character of straight women's same-sex friendships has been described as "face to face," suggesting an intimate, sharing bond (Wright 1982), though parents, peers, and the mass media also encourage girls to seek cooperation and emotional support in their relationships (Thorne 1986). Patterns of socialization seep into all social relationships, including friendships. Contemporary gender stereotypes presume that women are more cooperative and men are more instrumental in their same-sex friendships (Eagly, Wood, and Diekman 2000). Although women are socialized to be cooperative and nurturing, straight women's same-sex friendships also have been negatively characterized as competitive (Werking 1997).

Straight men's same-sex friendships are also reported as containing an element of competition (Werking 1997), which likely stems from socialization and structural factors (Myers and Raymond 2010; Thorne 1986). Some research characterizes straight men's same-sex friendships, however, as "side by side," which reflects an activity rather than an emotional basis for the bond (Inman 1996; Wright 1982). Yet there is also evidence of continuity, perceived support, and intimate self-disclosure in straight men's same-sex friendships (Grief

2009; Inman 1996). Given that both straight men's and straight women's same-sex bonds expose an enactment and negotiation of gender norms, friendships can be characterized as contexts in which gender is performed and reinforced (Werking 1997).

The differences present in heterosexual same-sex men's and women's friendships can be attributed to a variety of factors. Some point to differences in gender socialization for men and women, in which women are expected to be nurturing and men to be competitive (Felmlee 1999; Grief 2009). Others suggest that homophobia allows straight women's same-sex friendships to achieve a greater level of intimacy but keeps straight men from creating close relationships with other men, for fear of being perceived as gay (Connell 1995). This assertion reflects social expectations of the principle of consistency (Ponse 1978), which assumes that gender norms and sexual orientation are mutually constitutive. Conventional gender norms allow women, but not men, to share feelings and provide emotional support for their friends. Disregarding these norms defies the expectation of consistency in gender and sexual orientation and thus threatens straight men's claims to heterosexuality (Connell 1995). Given such factors, we would expect friendships across sex and sexuality categories to look qualitatively different from straight men's and straight women's same-sex friendships.

Much of friendship research has focused on sex and gender differences, yet some researchers have found this distinction to be exaggerated and more reflective of social norms than the activities and behaviors within a friendship (Felmlee 1999; Walker 1994). Others have argued that gender operates in conjunction with other social locations such as class, marital status, and age, and that the entirety of one's social context must be considered to fully understand the implications of any one dimension (Adams and Allen 1998). Several scholars have maintained that more overall similarities than differences are likely to exist in straight men's and women's friendships (Allan 1989; Duck and Wright 1993; Felmlee 1999).

RESEARCH ON FRIENDSHIPS

Social-psychological theories of social relationships are the theoretical foundation of friendship research. My work on friendship encompasses the symbolic interaction perspective of identity development and social interaction to consider how social structure and inequalities shape the social contexts for these relationships. The symbolic interaction perspective asserts that it is through interaction with others that we create and re-create meaning about our identities, our social worlds, and our interactions (Strauss 1959). Interactions shape our social realities so that all interactions have meaning and give meaning to our social relationships and to us as individuals.

Friendship affects social psychological processes such as identity development, the construction of social networks, and self-esteem support. In the social-psychological approach to social relationships and friendship, patterns of interactions are systematically examined and used to theorize about the individuals within them (Felmlee and Sprecher 2000). Classic social-psychological theories assert that, through our relationships and interactions with others, we learn how to think and feel about ourselves (Wright 1999). In particular, how we are treated by others, whether with regard or contempt, affects our self-perception. Classic sociological theories by Cooley and Mead address the connection between social interaction and self-perception (Cooley 1922; Mead 1934). Cooley's (1922) concept of the looking-glass self maintains that, through our interactions with others, we develop a sense of self based on the imagined reflection of others. Building on Cooley's concept, Mead (1934) theorized that individuals develop a sense of self through their interpretation of others' perceptions of them; these perceptions become integrated into an individual's self-concept.

Of particular significance for the current study are the connections between daily interactions and the effects on self-concept. Exposing a true self and having it positively reinforced by a significant friend is a meaningful way to enhance one's self-concept (Wright 1999). Moreover, an individual who feels that a new friend values her social identity is likely to form an even closer bond with that individual over time (Weisz and Wood 2005). In practice, our seemingly unremarkable daily interactions with friends have a great influence on our lives; understanding the significance of these relationships has implications for all social behavior (Duck 1999). We become socialized via our associations and interactions with other people. In particular, we learn not only social norms about relationships but also to incorporate socially acceptable behavior in our interactions with others. In addition, friendship connections are important in developing and maintaining a self-concept. Through interactions with others, we create our identity, the lens through which we view ourselves in the world (Nardi 1999; Rubin 1985; Swann and Read 1981).

## Friendships in Context

Like all social phenomena, friendships occur in a specific social context and thus are shaped by and help to reinforce structural inequalities. In the United States, social structure, stratification by gender, race, class, and sexual orientation (among other categories) is often reproduced in personal relationships (Collins 1990; Johnson 1996; O'Connor 1992). Individuals typically form friendships according to similarity in terms of race, class, and gender (Brehm 1985). Thus, the benefits and resources provided by friendships (e.g., informal employment references, social network connections) typically benefit those of the same social positions and therefore may further reinforce stratification. Yet some studies find the friendship context to be one in which oppression on the basis of gender, sex, and sexual orientation is battled (Fee 1996; Nardi 1999).

Friendship is a voluntary bond between individuals; we choose whether or not to befriend another person (Jerrome 1984; Wiseman 1986). Social-psychological theories focus on the individual, micro-level of interaction and acknowledge that friendship formation is a dynamic process that involves both individual personalities and the situations in which people interact (Jackson 1977). Yet our choices of whom to befriend and how to interact with him or her are affected by the structural, macro-social context in which they are formed (Adams and Allen 1998). Thus, to fully understand friendships, we need to examine these relationships according to the individual dimensions and structural forces that shape them.

Scripting theory is a social-psychological theory that makes context of central importance in interpreting interactions and is a useful tool in studying intersectional friendships. While typically applied to sexual behavior, scripting theory acknowledges that norms of interaction occur within specific social contexts and are guided by scripts that help individuals understand and interpret the interaction. Scripting theory thus provides a schema for interpreting social interaction. According to Gagnon and Simon (1973), whose work focused primarily on sexual scripts, behavior is enacted and interpreted according to external and internal dimensions, which constitute scripts. In the external dimension, individuals' actions are guided by mutually shared norms that allow them to successfully interact with one another. The internal dimensions of scripts are employed when individuals apply their own meanings to interactions according to the external norms of behavior (Gagnon and Simon 1973).

Scripting theory is a useful tool in interpreting not only gender, but also sexuality, norms, and expectations in social encounters.

## Theoretical Approach to Sexual Orientation and Gender Identities

Social norms and inequalities shape the context of social relationships in myriad ways. In intersectional friendships, power differences between genders or by sexuality shape interactions and experiences. One of the key ways to consider the effects of social inequality is through the lens of feminist theory. Lorber (1994) described feminist theory as the perspective that social categories such as sexual orientation and gender are social constructions that are shaped by interactions with social institutions. These constructions affect the lived experiences of all individuals and reinforce inequalities on the bases not only of sex and gender, but also of sexual orientation, race, and other social categories. Sex and gender inequalities are present in most structural dimensions of our society, including employment and the workplace (Reskin 1984) and family life (De Vault 1991; Hochschild 1983). These contrasting structural opportunities and constraints that men and women face also affect their everyday interactions and social relationships (Allan 1989).

Gendered social structures and processes may be both conserved and resisted within the friendship context (Johnson 1996; O'Connor 1992). Situated in a sexist and heterosexist social context, friends often reinforce ideas about what is appropriate or inappropriate behavior based on sex and sexual orientation (O'Connor 1992). For example, friends might communicate how acceptable one's behaviors, dress styles, or romantic partners are by these social norms of gender. Further, a stigmatized social identity such as being homosexual can shape and complicate the nature of all social interaction; as social actors, gay men and lesbians may feel the need to manage their stigmatized identity in their interactions with friends (Goffman 1963). The tone of interactions between stigmatized and non-stigmatized individuals can vary from being a context in which marginalization is reinforced to an exchange in which an empathetic alliance is formed (Goffman 1963). Friendships can in fact do either.

Social structure also shapes the context in which socialization occurs. Of particular importance is socialization into roles and identities according to gender and sexual orientation. Gender is learned, achieved, and reinforced through interactions with others (West and Zimmerman 1987), as is heterosexuality (Martin 2009; Myers and Raymond 2010). Gender socialization occurs according to categories of masculine or feminine, which correspond to a male or female identity. Yet all people, regardless of sex and sexual orientation, experience gender as a continuum, in many configurations, rather than as discrete categories (Butler 1990). A heterosexual orientation is implicit in gender socialization—that is, people learn to embody and perform masculinity and femininity based on the normative heterosexual versions of these categories. Not all individuals experience their gender identity and sexual orientation in normative ways, however. By virtue of a same-sex orientation, for example, gay men and lesbians exhibit a gender identity that is deemed inconsistent with their sex category (Stein 1997). Such individuals defy what Ponse (1978: 23–25) identified as the "principle of consistency," or the expectation that the elements of sex assignment, gender identity, sex roles (or gender roles), sexual object choice, and sexual identity vary together. Once one element is determined, the rest are presumed to co-occur. Accordingly, an individual whose sex assignment is female is expected to have a feminine gender identity, act in a feminine way, and be sexually attracted (only) to men.

The principle of consistency is based in heterosexism and emerges from the impulse to heterosexualize homosexuality—that is, to use heterosexuality as the model and to fit other sexualities into that social script (Tripp 1975) so that they resemble iterations of heterosexual norms.[4] As Ponse (1978: 24) explained: "Variations in sexual conduct, such as homosexuality are explained in terms of the assumption that same-sex sexual object choices entail a reversal of gender sex and of sex role. Thus, if a woman chooses another woman as a sex object, she is presumed to be a masculine woman and relationships between women are presumed to mirror heterosexual dyadic roles." Thus, put simply, the principle of consistency dictates that a woman who has sexual relationships with another woman (the prescribed sexual choice for men) must really be man-like or masculine, and men who have sexual relationships with men are expected to have more feminine gender identities (Connell 1992; Ponse 1978).

In actuality, the gender identities of gay men and lesbians, like those of straight men and women, are quite complex. Connell (1992), for example, acknowledges that because gay men are reared under the same social conditions of hegemonic masculinity as straight men, their gender identities often contain elements of both mainstream masculinity and femininity. Moreover, Stein's (1997) study of lesbian identities characterizes lesbian gender identity as occurring on a continuum from masculine to feminine—butch to femme. Following from such sociological discussions of sexual identity, in my analyses I acknowledge the many variations in individuals who are considered part of the same social groupings (gay man, lesbian, straight man, straight woman) and note fluidity in identities such as sexual orientation and gender. Throughout this book, I also consider how gender norms and socialization affect the overall tone and function of intersectional friendships, particularly between people differently located in these social structures of gender and sexuality.

## Additional Theories: Contact Theory and the "Darker Side"

One of the long-standing questions in sociology remains: does interaction breed greater understanding and tolerance between groups? The most widely cited study on the matter is Allport's classic contact theory of prejudice, which asserted that "prejudice may be reduced by equal status contact between majority and minority groups in the pursuit of common goals" (Allport 1954: 281). Prior research has found that straight people who have close contact with gay men and lesbians are more likely to have favorable attitudes about them (Herek and Capitanio 1996). Later work noted that this finding varied by gender and sexual orientation: even when they had close contact, straight men were reported as having more negative attitudes toward gay men than toward lesbians, and their attitudes were more negative than straight women's toward both gay men and lesbians (Herek 2000, 2002). When compared with straight women, straight men were more likely to have negative attitudes toward gay men, lesbians, and bisexual men and women and were less likely to befriend individuals from these sexual-minority groups (Galupo 2007b; Herek 2002).

People typically focus on the positive dimensions of friendships, yet a darker side to friendship also exists. Friendships end. In one study, for example, 27 percent of the individuals reported that they had experienced the end of a close friendship due to waning affection, declining interactions, and interference by other relationships (Rose and Serafica 1986). While friendship provides positive dimensions to people's lives, it also can be a source of conflict. For instance, norms for friendship and affiliation can be unclear and contradictory in some instances, which may lead to misunderstandings and disagreements between friends (Felmlee 1999). Because friendships are fraught with ambiguity and occur within the context of people's complex webs of relationships, it is unknown how friendships wax and wane throughout the course of their duration (Duck and Wood 1995). Of course, some relationships are unpleasant, irritating, destructive, and painful, though future research is needed to understand these less appealing dimensions of interaction (Felmlee and Sprecher 2000).

The body of research presented here shows us that friendships are significant relationships that provide many benefits, including bolstered self-esteem, joy, and a feeling of connectedness. Friendships can create community for groups who suffer oppression and can be used to buffer negative interactions to promote positive connections. Bridging friendships can reduce the social distance between groups to facilitate understanding and forge alliance, despite difference. Yet friendships exist in a social structure that is shaped by gender, race, class, and sexuality; these social categories provide people with different access to power, resources, and opportunity. In understanding close friendships across differences, we understand the potential of friendship to challenge inequality or reproduce it. The next chapter provides an opportunity to see intersectional friendships in action and illustrates the ways that gender race, class, and sexuality influence these relationships.

# SNAPSHOTS OF THE INTERSECTIONAL FRIENDSHIP

*I think of this friendship as something that's really steady, and even if one person's away or even if you're not seeing each other all the time, it doesn't impact if the friendship is important or not important, or strong or not strong, that even after six months or a year you can pick up and still be where you were—recognizing when . . . the other person needs help in readjusting, making a little sacrifice here or there for that person.*

*—Carrie, thirty-year-old straight white woman.*

## MING AND BEN

The friendship between Ben and Ming, who are both twenty-eight years old and Chinese, began in an elementary school in China. Ming noted that both she and Ben were latchkey kids who spent time together after school doing homework and cooking up hijinks. The friends were close through their childhood, emigration to the United States, and college, even though Ben attended a West Coast school while Ming enrolled at an East Coast university. When Ben came out as gay to Ming in college, it was an important moment in their relationship. As Ming explained:

> That was actually a very defining night for our relationship, as well, because I always felt very close to Ben. You don't know how many times I want[ed] to tell him how much I love him—just to be a great friend, I can never [say] that to him, which is kind of bad. But I really want him to know how I feel so close to him. And after that, all of a sudden, [his sexuality is] out in the open, and after that night, I remember that . . . we started to say to each other . . . , "I finally feel that I can tell you how much I love you; what I really [want] to tell you [is] I love you so much." And I think that's why I thought about this so much, 'cause . . . Ben has been so happy since he came out. And I just thought that was the greatest thing ever.

Ben's coming out as gay to Ming intensified their bond and allowed them to speak to each other more freely and express their mutual love and affection.

Now Ben and Ming live in neighboring communities in the Bay Area. Both juggle ambitious careers in business with long-term partnerships while also prioritizing their friendship. Ben was the "man of honor" at Ming's wedding, and she knows that when she becomes a mother, Ben will be the child's honorary uncle. They both foresee the bond lasting well into the future. Ming praises Ben effusively as being a solid source of support in her life: she has troubled relationships with her parents and often turns to him to vent about the most recent conflict. Since Ben shares her cultural background and has known Ming for so long, he understands the importance of her family ties while also being aware of the frustration the conflicts cause. Ming also provides support to Ben, whose biological family does not uniformly support his same-sex partnership; many of his family members do not know he is gay. Ben noted that in addition to being the sweetest friend, Ming also is a source of silly fun, making him laugh when he becomes too serious.

The pair do not spend as much time seeing each other as they would like, but both are included in extended friendship networks that participate in group dinners, parties, and other social outings. Ben and his partner are the only gay men in Ming's circle of friends; by spending time with Ben and his partner, Ming has come to understand that gay couples are not so different from her and her husband.

ALL FRIENDSHIPS HAVE A STORY. For some, the focus of the story is how the pair met by means of some twist of fate. Other friendships started more like a slow simmer but solidified when the pair encountered some hardship or dramatic event together. Still others have quietly meandered through decades together, owing their close bond to the sticking power of their connection. Intersectional friendships also have stories, and the details of the friends' meetings and weathering of tough times together vary as much as the individual personalities of each friend. Intersectional friends meet in the workplace. While some of these workplace friends clicked immediately and quickly cemented a close bond, others took much longer to develop or blossomed despite initial dislike of each other. Many intersectional friends forge bonds in childhood or adolescence, before either person is aware of his or her sexual orientation. The friendships that stick are those that fold all of the dimensions of members' identities into their mix. All of this is to say that there are common elements to the intersectional friends whose stories are at the center of this book, but they also are heterogeneous and unique in many ways.

In this chapter, I highlight the stories of three specific friendship dyads:

Emily and Patrick, Scott and Ruth, and Vanessa and Bruce. By focusing on these friendship dyads, the goal of the chapter is to introduce readers to a few of the intersectional friendships in the study and illustrate some of the most prominent themes that will be explored in the rest of the book. These stories represent specific examples of the experiences that intersectional friends reported in their interviews and as such can help us to better understand these friendships. I first provide glimpses into each of these friendships and then highlight themes present in the pair that are common to some of the other intersectional friendships in the study. One theme I discuss is how similarities and differences operate within these friendships. Because the friends are from different sexes and sexual orientations, the identities of the individuals in the friendship are a clear difference; however, in general we see that that friends typically have a great deal more in common than not. The chapter concludes by addressing various challenges that friends face in their day-to-day interactions, ranging from maintaining close ties across great distances to managing both minor and dramatic conflicts when they arise.

### EMILY AND PATRICK

Emily and Patrick have been friends for more than a decade. Patrick was the first friend Emily had when she relocated for a job nearly fifteen years ago—Patrick, her co-worker, showed her around her new city. Emily and Patrick are white and in their forties, and they work in the same office dedicated to environmental preservation. Emily and Patrick are both in long-term relationships: Emily had a commitment ceremony to celebrate her same-sex partnership with Stacy several years ago, and Patrick has been married for ten years. When I asked Emily what she and Patrick have in common aside from work, she explained, "I know we both enjoy the outdoors, so we . . . definitely have a lot of common values. . . . We're right in about the same place in terms of, like economically, so we have a lot of the same struggles, and we're very close in age, so in terms of, you know, the kinds of stages we've gone through—you know, twenties, thirties, forties— that's all pretty common, too."

Emily and Patrick both characterized their bond as a work-based friendship and described it as having a great degree of depth. When they were younger and less involved in family life, they spent more time together socially, going out with co-workers. Now they see each other every day at work and collaborate on projects but also talk about their personal lives. As Emily explained:

Sometimes I feel so close to Patrick that it feels like [having] a brother. I mean, one thing is we're very, very supportive of each other in our careers, in our lives, as individuals. He's seen me through all the relationships that didn't work until I got with someone I really loved. He's been my biggest supporter as far as my career and work, and he's always there through something I'm trying to struggle with. He's always there to listen, and I count on him to have an outside perspective that's going to help me grow, see things differently. But he's also, I think, one of the funniest people I know. I love his humor. I just love it. And I think he's really, really smart. I really, you know—I mean, it's a good thing, 'cause our desks were right near each other [in our previous jobs], too, and now we share an office.

Patrick also characterized his close bond with Emily: "I have a tendency to think, you know, outside of the context of this conversation, if you had said, 'Who are your close friends?,' I would name, you know, a friend from high school who I'm still in close touch with, my wife, maybe nobody else, and wouldn't immediately think of Emily. But again, that's kind of taking this bifurcated take on life, where work life isn't like life, and when I consciously include what I do at work, then it's really clear that Emily is a close friend."

Despite both friends' mutual descriptions of closeness, Patrick and Emily admitted that these days, they infrequently socialize with each other outside of the work setting. Patrick described the friendship as, "always amiable, but we [aren't] necessarily bosom buddies that couldn't stand to be apart, it's not really that kind of friendship." Similarly, Emily explained that they don't spend much time together outside of work and clarified, "I mean I would love to, and I love spending time with his wife and his kids. But we don't—occasionally we do, but it kinda like takes an effort. And we're not in each other's social life, we kind of have different friends."

Although they spend the majority of free time socializing with other friends, Emily and Patrick also share significant events with each other. Patrick noted such moments:

Another real high point was after [Emily] was with Stacy for a while and they decided to get married and do, like, a formal ceremony and stuff like that, and they took me and [my wife, Joanne] out to dinner to announce that. It felt really special, you know, to feel like we had that kind of intimacy, and it felt like being in her inner circle like that. That was a real highlight. I felt really privileged. Then their wedding was another real highlight. It was great to meet Emily's family and at this point to know Emily so well—to have heard about family members, and to meet them, and to see that context of her family. That was really cool.

Emily similarly recalls these events:

[Patrick] comes to birthday parties, and he came to my wedding. A number of other people I work with did, too. . . . And . . . we did this weekend thing where people who wanted to come the whole weekend, they could. In fact, his whole family did the weekend thing. He was definitely one of my, you know, special friends at the wedding ceremony. I remember when he met my brother and his wife; later, they were like, "Yeah, we could tell that you and Patrick are really close and know each other well!" . . . [W]e had a barbecue before we had the wedding, and I remember sitting at the table thinking that Patrick felt just as much like a brother as my brother—like, my brother was on my left, and Patrick was on my right. It just felt, you know, like, oh, my two brothers are going to meet each other finally!

At the time of this interview, Emily had been out as a lesbian at work for nearly as long as she had been in her line of work: fifteen years. She admitted that when she started at her latest position (the one where she met Patrick), she had tried to figure out the "right time" to come out as a lesbian. She decided to do so after Patrick strongly criticized a co-worker who was telling homophobic jokes in the office; subsequently, Patrick was the first person she came out to in her workplace. Patrick said that he was not at all surprised when Emily came out to him and recalled telling her, "Well, of course you're gay. I've known that for months." Because Patrick was already in a long-term relationship with a woman, Joanne, whom he later married, Emily never questioned his sexual orientation. Emily acknowledges that her close friendship with Patrick may be uncommon in her circle of friends. "I've noticed that a lot of the gay women I get along with don't have close friendships with straight men," she said, but she did not provide any explanation for why that might be the case.

Both Emily and Patrick identified some of the unique dimensions of their friendship that come from its being intersectional. Patrick explained the benefits he reaps from having Emily present in the workplace:

We've, I think, talked to each other about our feelings of professional inadequacy, which is something that's hard to talk about with a spouse, because a spouse is going to say, "You know, you're fine; you're really great. Just don't think about it." It's different to be able to talk about it with someone at work and to be talking at a more detailed level, saying, "You know what? My project handling skills suck. I'm good at project development, but I'm just not following through. I'm letting my deadlines slip and feeling really bad about that." That's a conversation, that's something that in [our] friendship that is safe ground. I don't know if this is one of your later questions, [but] I think that it's safer to have that kind of conversation with a woman. I don't know that I would be so ready to have that conversation with a man.

Here, Patrick explains how Emily's identity as a woman affects his ability to open up and be vulnerable with her. He describes further how their particular bond allows for a deeper friendship: "Sometimes when you've got a gender difference, a friendship has some sort of sexual undertones or whatever, and there can be like a flirtatious kind of aspect of a friendship that maybe can sometimes lead [further]. On one hand, it can be a plus for a relationship, but a lot of times it can be a negative, especially in the long run. But I think that because Emily's and my friendship really has never had that, you know, maybe there's slightly more distance in some ways at different times than there otherwise would have been."

At the core of this friendship, however, is reciprocity. Patrick described what he views as the key strength of the friendship he shares with Emily: "It's sort of this mutual admiration thing that we have going. I think it's [that] we both remind each other of our strengths, encourage each other, prop each other up. And I think if it wasn't mutual, it wouldn't feel nearly as good."

EMILY'S AND PATRICK'S friendship highlights some of the themes present in many of the intersectional friendships in this study. Most important, the friends both seem to value and enjoy their friendship, a characteristic that is true of every intersectional friendship in the study. Another key characteristic is that Emily's and Patrick's friendship is centered in the workplace, without the friends' being central to either other's broader social networks. Many of the study participants shared the workplace connection: Stuart and Cassandra, Crystal and Derek, Jill and Paul, Mitch and Danae, and Jon and Janet. As discussed in chapter 1, friendships often form in the workplace because the setting provides both proximity and similarity and allows people to connect through shared co-workers and tasks. Depending on their positions and responsibilities, workplace friends may talk every day, about anything from work projects to personal issues. Although many do not immediately think of workplace friendships as being their most meaningful friendships, often such relationships provide very intimate connections.

Emily's and Patrick's tight connection is illustrated by the important events that they share, which is a common feature of other intersectional friendships in the study. Of particular significance to both friends was Emily's marriage/ commitment ceremony to Stacy. Patrick felt honored when Emily and Stacy took him and his wife, Joanne, to dinner to announce their engagement, and Emily was impressed that Patrick and his family attended the entire weekend wedding celebration. The occasion allowed the friends to show how much esteem they had for each other and to introduce Emily's biological brother to her chosen brother, Patrick. Thus, the bond between Emily and Patrick also illustrates how intersectional friendships often serve as chosen family members, celebrating birthdays and holidays together, a topic that is discussed at greater length in chapter 3.

An additional theme present in the friendship between Emily and Patrick that emerges in other intersectional friendships is the relaxing of gendered norms. As Patrick's comment demonstrates, his friendship with Emily allows him to discuss feelings of inadequacy without threatening his claims to hegemonic masculinity, as might occur in friendships with men in which he would not want to lose face by admitting insecurity. This is also consistent with Rumens's (2008) finding that in gendered work hierarchies, gay men are more comfortable confiding in straight women than in other men, which often leads to the development of close friendships (although in this case, the sexual orientation of the parties is reversed). Moreover, because Patrick's friendship with Emily is free of sexual tension and therefore sexual possibility, he does not feel the need to present himself as virile or hegemonically masculine in the way he might if Emily were a potential sexual partner. Thus, Patrick finds some gender norms to be relaxed in his intersectional friendship with Emily, a topic that is a primary focus of chapter 4 and that is also present in a different way in the next friendship that I discuss: the bond between Scott and Ruth.

## SCOTT AND RUTH

Scott and Ruth met in 1977 when they were both twenty-two years old. Initially, they met through Ruth's husband, Tony, who was the only straight man living in a gay residential hotel where Scott also lived. Ruth and Tony divorced, but because they were musicians, they continued to hang out in the same social circles, and eventually Ruth met Scott. Ruth and Scott became friends through playing music together in San Francisco. Scott noted, "I got a bass, and she got a guitar, and we didn't really know what we were doing; we would just play. We just started playing more and more together and would do that for hours and hours, and we got to know each other musically." Scott went on to describe his initial fascination with Ruth: "She was almost this scary kind of person; she was, like, spike high heels and leather jacket and this bleached hair, and it was like, whoa, who's that? I thought she was really cool, but I thought she was unapproachable. I was really attracted to her, but I thought there was no way; I'm not that cool. She won't allow me to be in the room with her." Over time, the two developed a close bond that has endured. The friends still talk on the phone as often as possible and see each other once a month; both said they wished they could talk to and see each other more.

Ruth says that when she first met Scott, he was living in the gay hotel and she therefore took it for granted that he was gay. Similarly, Scott always assumed that Ruth was straight because she had been married to Tony. Ruth explained how her friendship with Scott was consistent with the friendships she had had since adolescence: "I've had gay male friends since I can remember. I've always gravitated towards artsy people; extending on beyond that, usually musicians and artists and then gay people are always part of trendy sorts of crowds, especially when I was young. Before I knew Scott, when I was a teenager, I had really close gay male friends. But they're all dead."

At the end of her statement, Ruth refers to the fact that she lost a large part of her friendship network during the HIV/AIDS epidemic of the 1980s, as did Scott.[1] This topic arose many times during their interviews. In one instance, Scott explained how losing many friends during the 1980s affected his life: "I've probably put too much pressure on Ruth because I don't maintain social ties with anyone. Almost everyone I was friends with died, and I have not been social since, so I haven't met a lot of people. So Ruth has to deal with the burden of me."[2]

Ruth described the great losses she endured in more detail: "The first person I knew that died of AIDS was like in '81. Yeah, so we went through this holocaust, really literally, where 50 to 75 percent of our friends died within a couple years.[3] We got numb to it. But all of his ex-lovers died. Scott found out that he was HIV-positive, and of course he thought he was going to die. That was a death sentence then. It was. Totally." She continues:

Then it was a totally different situation, so I had to prepare myself to deal with [Scott's HIV status] over and over and over again and got all neurotic about his T-cell counts, and you know. It was just horrible. And then he nursed, let's see, his best friend in the gay world, Byron, he nursed him [until his] death; his ex-lover Tim; Sammy. It was just really hard. He's the kind of person that loves to take care of people . . . so he nursed these people to the very, very end and then put up their parents for the funerals. He's just that kind of person. So it was emotionally very difficult for him. And for me, it was emotionally very difficult because I loved him so much and I thought, oh my god, he's going to die.

Scott and Ruth also both acknowledged that in addition to his HIV diagnosis being a major concern in his life, it also influenced a decision about parenting. "Me and Ruth used to talk about having a baby together until we found out I was HIV positive," Scott said, "so I've always had this sensation that [Ruth's daughter, Caroline] was mine." Ruth provided a similar but more in-depth account: "I just love him, and he loves me, and he would be the greatest father that ever existed on the planet. You know, I don't think we really wanted to have sex, but we would probably have done it or found a way to do it. The whole problem that occurred, that stopped us was, um, he got HIV. So that kinda threw a wrench in our plans."

Still, Scott has been a strong presence for Caroline, who is now a teenager.

When I asked the pair about some of the challenging times in their friendship, both Ruth and Scott discussed how Ruth's protectiveness of Scott in the past had sometimes caused friction between her and Scott's boyfriends. "I've actually had words with almost all of his boyfriends," Ruth explained. "[Scott and I have] never really had an 'I'm mad at you, I hate you' period, but we've had a couple of periods where I have been extremely jealous of his boyfriend. Jealous not as 'I want him for myself,' but just jealous in that sisterly way, I guess. I don't even know how to describe it—it's just that this person is not good enough for you; this person is taking advantage of you; this person is a loser; you need to get rid of this person kinda thing." Ruth continued:

[There was] this one very disastrous time when I moved in with him. This was probably in '85, . . . and his boyfriend lived there, too. So it was Scott and his boyfriend and me, and it got real ugly. It got real, real, real ugly. At one point, Lawrence, who was the boyfriend, and I got in this huge fight, and it escalated into a physical altercation. I got so angry I jumped on him and got him down on the floor, and I was going to choke him to death. Scott had to pull me off and throw me in my bedroom and hold the door shut so I couldn't get out and kill his boyfriend. That was a bad time. And I sorta realized that we weren't going to work out as roommates.

While Ruth and Scott were not suited to be roommates, at least during their youth, Scott noted that he views Ruth as a stabilizing influence: "I know that no matter how screwed up each of us might be, whether it's both at the same time or individually, we will come together and get ourselves together to be there for the other person." Similarly, Ruth characterized Scott's role in her life: "I think he just gives me a sense of peace and security. I think a lot of it stems from the fact that we have gone through so many life-or-death situations. It's like, you *know* he will always be there, that he's seen the worst of the worst, the most extreme situation possible, so there's nothing that I could do that would throw him for a loop." Ruth continues:

> He is always, always the same. He doesn't change; he's unwaveringly faithful. Unwavering. So I have come to sort of depend on that. I don't have any friends who are so not loopy and so just so open to whatever I throw out on the table. I mean, I could have a hysterical fit, and he'd be, like, "Oh, it's OK. Don't worry. We'll figure it out." He's always, like, "Don't worry." So I don't. Because I'm always like, "What if I can't get a job? What am I going to do? I'm going to be on the street." He's like, "No, no you won't. There's the bank of Scott."

Although the friends met each other when they were living on the economic fringes, Scott now has a well-paying professional job while Ruth is a graduate student. Ruth characterized their friendship as "ideal, despite the fact that he has, like, a million more dollars than I do." In their individual interviews, Scott and Ruth each described how they had gone from eating pancakes for a month and standing in line for free food together to taking Ruth and her daughter on a trip to Hawaii. Ruth recalled: "The whole impetus for the trip to Hawaii was that Scott wanted to pay my mom back, because a few years ago when Scott was really broke—quite a few years ago—my mom . . . had gotten some money from something, some lottery thing. Not a big thing, but she got some money, and she said, 'OK, Ruth, what do you want?' And I said, 'I want Scott.' So she flew Scott out to Las Vegas for a weekend with me and her, and he always thought that was so sweet, because he didn't have money then." Now Scott serves as Ruth's financial sounding board. "I call him and say, 'OK, I'm thinking of taking this loan,' or 'OK, I'm thinking of applying for this job,' and he is the total adviser," she said. "He is extremely successful in his field, so he makes really good money. . . . When I'm ready to do anything, he is there. Like, some people have their parents; some people have trust funds . . . Well, I have Scott."

While both friends identify many benefits of their relationship, their mutual enjoyment of each other's company ranks high on the list. "We just kind of complement each other," Ruth said. "We enjoy playing games. We enjoy, we just enjoy hanging out . . . and just the whole companionship, just the total simpatico that we have. We can hang out for hours doing pretty much nothing, just talking or playing Scrabble—just doing nothing, just walking around in the park, and feel totally comfortable. There's very few people that you can feel totally yourself with, you know, without having to manage the interaction all the time. There's no need to manage any interaction. So that's good."

Likewise, Scott described his friendship with Ruth: "I just really like Ruth. I like doing things together and working with her. She's, like, my best friend, baby sister, just, like, to do things with her. I value my friendships and family, and Ruth's one of the most important people. I'm tempted to say the most important. She's the person who's always been there. . . . When my dad died, I went back and realized how important my family is, but they're not there in the same way for me that Ruth is. They don't know me like Ruth does. No one knows me the way Ruth does. So she's the most important."

RUTH AND SCOTT'S friendship is unique in many ways, but it also contains themes present in other intersectional friendships in the study. Perhaps one of the more significant characteristics of the friendship is the comfort they provide for each other. Ruth and Scott each report that the other is a stabilizing influence on her or his life; Ruth emphasizes how relaxed she is in Scott's presence and that she just enjoys spending time with him, while Scott discloses that his relationship with Ruth is the most important in his life. The pair shares a twenty-five-year-long friendship, which is longer than that of most of the dyads in the study. These intersectional friends have shared many positive and difficult experiences, including the loss of many mutual friends to AIDS and Scott's own diagnosis of HIV. It is not surprising that they have a particularly strong bond.

One dimension of Ruth and Scott's friendship that is present in other friendships is that they include each other in their family networks, thus blending gay and straight family structures. Just as Ruth's mother once paid for Scott to join her and Ruth on a vacation, Scott has tried to reciprocate by funding a trip for Ruth's family to join him and his partner on a trip to Hawaii. Another component of the friendship is that Scott and Ruth have considered parenting together, a topic both brought up in interviews without being asked. This theme is discussed in more detail in the next chapter. However, it is worth noting that while many of the female friends in the study communicated how they expected their male friends to be present in a future child's life, Scott and Ruth were one of a few pairs who had laid out plans to have a baby together. Although Ruth eventually became pregnant by another man and gave birth to her now teenage daughter, Caroline, Scott has been a stable part of Caroline's life and stated that he has been able to experience parenting through this relationship. Thus, the family dimensions of this relationship are significant and tangible.

Another tangible thing that these friends provide for each other is financial assistance and planning for the future. Because Scott is the more financially secure friend, he is ready to assist Ruth with advice or actual funds, a dynamic that was mentioned several times throughout their interviews. Scott refers to himself as "the Bank of Scott" as a way to reassure Ruth that she has someone to back her up and bail her out if she finds herself in a financial bind; the gendered implications of this factor are discussed further in chapter 3. The dynamic of Scott's having more financial resources than Ruth is one point in a long trajectory; when Ruth and Scott met, they both lived on the financial and social fringe and, as a result, shared houses and stood in line for free food. Since that time, Scott has flourished professionally and is now financially secure and willing to share that financial security with Ruth.

One final dimension of intersectional friendship that is illustrated by Ruth's and Scott's relationship is the darker side of friendship. Ruth provides an account of a violent encounter she had with one of Scott's boyfriends. While she recalled the incident with a fair amount of humor, the reality is that at times intersectional friendships, like other relationships, are contexts in which jealousy and violence occur (Duck and Wood 1995; Felmlee and Sprecher 2000). Here, Ruth's behavior can be explained by her desire to protect Scott from what she perceives as an exploitive relationship; still, she reacted to Scott's boyfriend with violence, which heightened the tension of the situation. This darker side was not evident in all, or even most, friendships in the study, but it is important to acknowledge the presence of this element, which I will do in further detail at the conclusion of the chapter.

Vanessa and Bruce met in graduate school and have been friends for four years. Vanessa is a twenty-eight-year-old black lesbian, and Bruce is a thirty-four-year-old straight Asian American man. Before entering graduate school, Vanessa and Bruce both worked as high school teachers; one of the primary interests that they share is education. Vanessa and Bruce disagreed about how and when they became friends. Bruce remembered meeting Vanessa at a graduate-school recruitment event for minority students, but Vanessa insisted that they did not meet until the following year. "I really feel like we met in the fall once school started," Vanessa explained, "because I shaved his head." Bruce recalled, "I remember storing her motorcycle in my garage. It's still there. It's been there for, like, two years, so that may have been how, that may have been the first social capital-wise.[4] Like, I did you a favor kind of a thing; now you're my friend. . . . We had this research class together, and basically we became kind of this duo at that time. We just kind of became study buddies. And then, you know, when you start spending a lot of time with people [laughs], you don't have any choice to become good friends." While studying together, Vanessa and Bruce saw each other every day for nearly a year. Now, with different schedules, they see each other about once each week. The friends live a block away from each other in the same neighborhood. Because Vanessa stores her motorcycle in Bruce's garage, she has a key to the apartment that he shares with his long-term girlfriend, Alex.

Bruce did not know from the outset that Vanessa was a lesbian but said he figured it out very quickly: "Vanessa usually puts her identity really out there. . . . You pretty much get to know her really fast. And with Vanessa, 'I'm a black lesbian' is kinda where she's at, and she's, like, you better recognize that and see that."

Vanessa assumed that Bruce was straight, but there was some confusion because of how he referred to his girlfriend. Vanessa explained: "In the beginning, he'd talk about his 'partner,' Alex. So 'partner'—code language, right? Except he's so straight, and so I got all up in arms because I thought he was trying to perpetrate. I'm like, 'You are so not gay,' like, how can you be 'my partner, Alex?' So, I'm a little perturbed, and I was like, 'Could it be? No.' Then I found out Alex was a woman, so it was kind of funny. Like I don't think I ever really thought that he wasn't straight, but the 'partner' and 'Alex.' . . . He couldn't say 'Alexandra'; he's gotta do an 'Alex.'" Aside from studying, Vanessa and Bruce enjoy playing poker and working on cars together.

Although they share many memorable experiences, Vanessa often wishes they had more unstructured time together. "I wish we could just hang out," she said. "It feels like we're always doing something and, like, [one] morning after [a two pitchers of beer] incident, I just remember that was such a great day because we were just driving around, we were totally hung over, just . . . we had some errands to run, every ten minutes we were like, 'What should we do? OK, let's go eat.' So I think times when it's just unplanned, and they're rare, but that's—I wish there was more of that."

Bruce explained that he enjoys talking to Vanessa but that most of their conversations occur when they are doing other activities together. Vanessa explains, "I don't really call him to chit-chat. I always feel like he's busy." Bruce concurred: "Oh my god! I'm not a phone talker at all. I hate talking on the phone. So on the phone, it's just, like, 'What's up?' 'OK, good.' 'OK, see you later.' [But when we talk in person, we talk about] almost anything. I mean, we talk about anything from poker to her car stereo or my car, to her other jobs or my teaching stuff or my students or mutual friends, drama about mutual friends. You could call it gossip, I guess, but mostly it's just drama."

There are two issues that Vanessa and Bruce do not discuss: his relationship with Alex and sex. "I talk about relationships," Vanessa explained, "but he doesn't give me any info. Zero. . . . I would actually like it more if he did because I feel like that's a side of him that's just so shut down, and I don't know if he just doesn't talk about it in general or if he just doesn't talk about it with me because we're not . . . like, I'm not a guy. I'm often considered one of the guys, but at the end of the day, I'm not a guy." While Vanessa and Bruce do not discuss his relationship in detail, Bruce appreciates Vanessa's support for his relationship with Alex: "Vanessa is one of the only friends I have that encourages [Alex and me] to spend time together."

Alex and Vanessa are also friends, and Alex is supportive of the friendship that Vanessa and Bruce share. Bruce explained that the intersectional nature of his friendship with Vanessa contributes to the support: "[I think] it has to do with that sort of idea of, like, the sexual barrier. There's, like, no fear. 'What are you and Vanessa up to?' Whereas I've had other female friends where it's gotten kind of, like, you know, you think there's a boundary and then there isn't, and

[Alexandra] doesn't like that." Bruce stated that he and Vanessa are not physically attracted to each other, so they can have a more emotionally intimate friendship. Vanessa also expressed that a clear lack of sexual tension between the friends is a benefit to their relationship: "You get to have that cross-gender relationship where sex is more on the table, where it's not something you have to wonder about. So I'm a lesbian who sleeps with men, but I would never sleep with Bruce, and it's clear . . . not in a maybe sort of way, where I think if I was straight . . . I'm not certain I would have as close a relationship with Bruce or any of the guys in general."

Bruce's and Vanessa's friendship is also racially intersectional. Bruce is Chinese American, and Vanessa is black. Bruce admitted that he and Vanessa talk about identity quite often but that they have different ways of thinking about these issues. For example, Bruce commented, "[Vanessa's] like, you need to talk about what it's like to be an Asian male and, like, this kind of thing, and part of it is that I'm uncomfortable with those kind of signifiers, I guess. It's not that I don't feel Asian or I don't feel male or I don't feel straight. It's just that they're not adequate terms." He continued:

> I've been in a straight relationship forever, and it's basically one of my only relationships. . . . So does that make you straight? Does that make you therefore not part of a certain community? And so that's why if someone like Vanessa will meet me and be like, "You're straight so you don't know anything about this" . . . I don't know what to call that. In some ways, I would say being friends with Vanessa has placed my identity in relation to hers. She is, like, distinctly lesbian, black lesbian Vanessa. You know? But then it's, like, what does that leave you? And what room does that leave you to shape your identity in less fixed ways? So in lots of ways when I'm around her, my identity is very fixed in relation to hers, whereas with other people, it's very different. . . . And I'm not saying it's a black lesbian thing. I think it's a Vanessa thing.

Bruce is thoughtful about his identity and has considered how his race, gender, and sexual orientation occur in relation to those around him, particularly Vanessa. Here, Bruce also considers how his identity aligns him with others according to power relations rather than by race:

> When I think about "my people," I think about a lot of people. I think about oppressed people in general, so when I'm with Vanessa and she starts talk-

ing about her people as black people and she has, like, this possessive quality to it, it sort of excludes you from saying [anything]. . . . And I think about the students I've dealt with who are, you know, all different kinds of Asian, black, Latino; from all different parts of the Americas and Ethiopia and Bosnia. Those are my people. So to have her, like, you know, possess blackness in a way that sort of excludes you from real practices that you have and relationships that you have is really frustrating. . . . She kind of expects me to say "my people" and mean Asians. I'm not even sure that's possible. That's not to say that they're not my people, but you know what I mean?

According to both of their accounts, Vanessa and Bruce differ in their perspective about race, but these differences do not seem to harm their friendship. In fact, both clearly convey how much they truly like each other. Vanessa stated: "I just like Bruce so much, you know? He's just a really great guy. And it's one of those relationships where I still don't have any idea what he gets out of it, but I get so much out of being friends with him. He lives his life in such a way that I learn so much from him every time I'm with him. You know, he just is a really open and kind and giving person." When I asked Bruce to identify his favorite aspect of his friendship with Vanessa, he said: "My favorite thing? I don't know. I mean my favorite thing is Vanessa. I think Vanessa's just great." He then mirrored some of Vanessa's comments: "The way we go about things are so different, so I've learned so much from her as far as, like, how she deals with the world. . . . In lots of ways, it's a privilege to see somebody's life, somebody's process, and you learn so much through that about yourself. That's what I basically wrote [in a letter to her] and basically at the end, I was like, 'Through you, I learned me.'"

VANESSA'S AND BRUCE'S friendship illustrates several themes present in my interviews with intersectional friends. Both friends voiced a deep liking for each other, as is consistent with the other friendship pairs presented in this chapter. Vanessa and Bruce also discussed their mutual interests in being graduate students and educators, as well as working on cars and playing poker together. One dimension of their friendship that differs from the other friendships highlighted in this chapter is their experience of being members of racial-minority populations in the United States.

Many of the friendship members that I interviewed differed in their ethnic or racial identities, a theme that is consistent with prior research findings that gay, lesbian, and bisexual adults are more likely to form interracial, interethnic, and cross-sexuality friendships than a sample of straight adults (Galupo 2007b). It should be noted that, with a couple of exceptions, the only interviewees who mentioned race as having an effect on their friendships specifically, or on their lives in general, were those from racial-minority backgrounds. Yet not all people of color discussed how race or ethnicity affected their friendships or their lives more broadly. Also relevant is that with only a couple of exceptions, the white participants mentioned race only if their intersectional friend was from a different background or if they were in a mixed-race romantic partnership.[5]

Despite a shared status as individuals from minority-status backgrounds, Vanessa and Bruce seem to have very different perspectives about the role that race, sex, gender, and sexual orientation play in an individual's identity. Perhaps these perspectives also contribute to each friend's insistence that she or he is not sure how the other person benefits from the friendship but that they have learned from their differences.

## SIMILARITY AND DIFFERENCE
## BETWEEN FRIENDS

Prior studies have concluded that similarity is one of the greatest predictors of friendship (Brehm 1985). Clearly, intersectional friendships vary in terms of sex and sexual orientation; however, these friends share a great deal of similarity along the lines of education level, socioeconomic status of their families of origin, and age. Most of the friendship pairs were composed of individuals who both have earned college degrees and were at similar stages in life in terms of age and career trajectory; most had also grown up in homes with similar socioeconomic statuses, even if their current income levels differed. In the three dyads presented so far in this chapter, we see how similar employment, schools, or friendship circles facilitated these friendships. Yet not all dyads share these traits. In the remainder of this chapter, I provide examples of intersectional friends who navigate demographic differences in age, socioeconomic status, and geographic distance and briefly discuss how these variations influence the friendships. In doing so, I aim to provide a more complete introduction to the various dimensions of these friendships and the complexities they face.

In friendships in which age difference between the friends approached ten years, the friendship took on characteristics similar to a parental relationship. Two friendship pairs shared this dynamic: Sarah and Don and Donna and Manuel. Donna and Don, now sixty-eight and seventy-two, respectively, are a straight married couple whose daughter is a lesbian. Initially, to understand how to navigate the daughter's coming-out process, Donna and Don joined Parents, Families, and Friends of Lesbians and Gays (PFLAG).[6] There they learned that family members have rejected many lesbian and gay individuals; this upset them, and they vowed to be family for anyone who had been rejected by a natal family. Donna and Miguel, a forty-six-year-old mixed-race man, met through the local PFLAG chapter and have been friends for four years. Miguel noted that Donna has been like a supportive parent, especially when she counseled him through the terminal illness of his biological mother. Sarah, a thirty-year-old white lesbian, met Don through Donna. Sarah and Donna are classmates in a graduate program. While Sarah primarily spoke of her friendship with Don, she clearly views Don and Donna as a friendship unit. In her interview, Sarah spoke about Don and Donna as her "sub-parents" and said that if she could pick her parents, they would be Don and Donna. These friendships differ from same-age pairs in that they typically do not interact as peers; both Sarah and Manuel noted that they see their friendships as resembling *chosen* parent–child relationships.

Intersectional friends who grew up in families from different socioeconomic statuses often described stark differences in background. Some of the individuals I interviewed could not help but notice how class shaped the way they and their friend lived and viewed the world. For example, Ken, a thirty-seven-year-old gay man, compared his upbringing with that of his friend and roommate, Carrie, a thirty-two-year-old straight woman he had met in graduate school: "It's interesting to watch someone who came from such a different background than I did. Both of her parents were professionals, very much upper middle class [in the] Boston suburbs kind of thing. My mother was a single mom; she didn't marry my dad and was a secretary for my whole life, so it's a different worldview, almost, where you come from." Yet in the next sentence, Ken noted that despite the differences in status, he and Carrie had similar issues and conflicts with their families. Moreover, they both are committed to social justice and teaching, and they share interests in the outdoors. Thus, while the friends commented on how class differences shaped their perceptions and places in the world, they downplayed their present similarities.

## LONG-DISTANCE FRIENDSHIPS

Proximity is an important ingredient for friendship formation; still, some study participants maintained their friendships across great distances. Several of the individuals I interviewed lived hundreds or thousands of miles from their friend, but they were committed to maintaining a close relationship via frequent visits or phone and email contact. In each of these cases, proximity allowed the friendships to form. Consistent with previous findings, these intersectional friends have sustained an intimate friendship by working to maintain the sense of emotional closeness and involvement in each other's lives (Rubin 1985).

The future of long-distance friendships is likely a positive one. Technological developments such as cell phones and the Internet are making proximity a less important issue in the formation and maintenance of friendships. According to studies by McKenna, Green, and Gleason (2002) and Morahan-Martin and Schumacher (2003), online relationships create a sense of proximity and connection across geographic distance that promote the formation and maintenance of relationships. Some of the participants use cell phones to keep their friendship strong. Frank and Rebecca live many hundred miles apart but speak weekly by cell phone during their commutes to keep up with each other's lives. Monique, who is straight, and Jesse, who is gay, also live several hundred miles apart and have phone dates to keep up with the details of their lives, as do Zoë (straight) and Gary (gay), who live in different time zones.

## THE DARKER SIDE OF
## INTERSECTIONAL FRIENDSHIPS

Intersectional friendships clearly are important relationships to their members. Highlighting only the positive dimensions of these relationships, however, does not give a full or realistic picture of the dyads. In responding to Duck's and Wood's (1995) observation that friendships are both "rough and smooth," I address some of the more challenging dimensions of the intersectional friendship. Any relationships, particularly those that are close, will encounter rocky periods spurred by differences of opinion, personal tumult for one member or both members, and misunderstandings. In my interviews, many of the friends acknowledged that conflicts had arisen at times, though to varying degrees. The darker times range from periods in which the friends did not speak to each other because of a conflict or perceived neglect, jealousy between the friends and from participants' romantic partners, and instances of physical violence.

Misunderstandings and hurt feelings are a common occurrence in all human relationships; unclear communication or misperceived intentions often cause people to feel slighted. While most participants spent the majority of their interviews talking positively about their friendships, many admitted that the friendships sometimes had rough patches. One of the causes of conflict interviewees mentioned was feeling neglected in the face of a friend's new romantic relationship. Carl, a straight man, noted that over the course of his decades-long friendship with Debbi, there have been yearlong periods in which the two did not talk because Debbi was "too wrapped up" in a new girlfriend.

Perhaps the most common cause of rough patches in the friendships was jealousy. In the contexts of these friendships, jealousy was experienced in various ways. For example, Monique, who is straight, acknowledged that she wanted to be the most important woman in Jesse's life, which sometimes caused conflicts with Jesse's other female friends. Similarly, Jill, a thirty-one-year-old mixed-race lesbian, explained that Paul, a thirty-seven-year-old straight white man, was more likely to feel jealous of her male friends than of her romantic partners: "My experience with Paul is that he is more threatened when a male comes into my life than a female because Paul, I think, likes the idea that he's the only male in my life."

Partners also became jealous of the close bonds between intersectional friends. Justine, a thirty-six-year-old mixed-race lesbian, explained that her girlfriend felt uncomfortable about the bond she had with her twenty-eight-year-old straight Latino friend, Antonio: "The first girlfriend that [Antonio] met, I think she might have been jealous that me and Antonio bonded [about a mutual interest in playing video- and role-playing games], which she didn't know about. But then, I think she might have thought the connection was a little too deep—not that we were sexual together, but just that it was an area she didn't know about." Sometimes, the intersectional friend and the partner were jealous of each other. Leyla explained that both her intersectional friend Ethan and her boyfriend became jealous when she spent time with the other: "As long as my boyfriend does not impede on our time together, then [Ethan] is fine with it." Leyla then addressed her boyfriend's jealousy: "They get along when we're together, but, you know, I hate to say it, but my boyfriend gets kind of nervous or jealous—he feels left out when I'm with Ethan because Ethan and I have known each other for so long. We've got all of these inside jokes, so he doesn't know how to relate."

Because intersectional friends often have very intense and long-standing connections, romantic partners may not understand or may feel threatened by the relationship, often in ways that they would not if the friend were of the same sex. Likely, the threat of the close intersectional friendship is related to the unrelenting nature of the (implicitly heterosexual) romantic script that guides interactions between men and women (Gagnon and Simon 1973; Rich 1980).

We tend to view romantic relationships as the most important and intimate connection (Rubin 1985), while no such script exists for platonic friendships. In the absence of a script that dictates norms of close male–female friendships, many individuals, knowingly or not, may view the interaction through the lens of a heterosexual romantic script. As a result, a partner may feel her or his relationship is threatened by an intense connection between her or his loved one and another person. Same-sex-oriented participants are not immune to heterosexual romantic scripts. For instance, Mark's boyfriend, Jeffrey, has expressed jealousy about the time that Mark and Cristina spend together and once asked him, "Are you naked in front of her?," a comment that implies concern that the friendship might be sexual.

In some ways, the conflicts that affect intersectional friendships were like those that can color all types of relationships. Because of the long-term nature of many of these friendships, the participants have seen their friends form and break up numerous sexual and romantic relationships. Sometimes, the intersectional friend has deeply disliked a friend's choice of partner and the tone of that relationship. Mitch, a forty-two-year-old Latino who is gay, described the conflict he felt when his thirty-one-year-old straight Latina friend Danae disliked his partner: "When I first met Danae, I was going out with a guy named Tad, and yes, she talked to me a lot about why Tad was bad for me and why I should break up with him."

Physical violence rarely was noted as an issue in the intersectional friendships themselves. The only case in which the friends neared a physical altercation with each other was in what Monique characterized as one of the "darker times" in her friendship with Jesse: "We had a couple of fights that got physical when he lived with me. [We've] had some problems with physical violence—not actual hitting or anything like that, but, you know, pushing and shoving, and that was pretty awful." This instance was an exception in the otherwise close and loving friendship between Monique and Jesse, but it is indicative of the darker side that is sometimes present in friendships.

The friendship pairs I describe in this chapter highlight some of the key themes that emerged in the data while also providing a coherent picture of the details that structure each of the relationships. In the chapters that follow, I take a more detailed look at particular elements of intersectional friendships, starting with the intersectional friendship as chosen family relationships.

# 3

# WE ARE FAMILY

*I would like for Monique and I to live closer together, because we are family. We are each other's chosen family, and to me that's more significant than your biological family, 'cause we're choosing that. . . . We're implementing our power of choice. You don't choose your brother or your mother or your father; that shit is, like, handed to you whether you like it or not. . . . So that makes it even more important and meaningful, you know, that someone would choose to stick with you through thick and thin.*

—Jesse, a thirty-one-year-old gay Latino

## BRENDA AND DAN

Brenda is a thirty-seven-year-old white self-described "butch" lesbian who is the mother of a nine-month-old daughter. Dan is a forty-one-year-old straight white man who is married with two children. Brenda and Dan have maintained a close friendship for nearly twenty years. They met at John F. Kennedy Airport in 1984. Brenda was wearing her university sweatshirt in the hope that it might be a conversation starter with other travelers. Dan approached her, identifying himself as a student at the same university. After chatting for a few minutes, they discovered that they had volunteered to work on the same kibbutz (Jewish communal farm) for the summer. At some point during their flight between New York and Israel, they decided that, after their stint at the kibbutz ended, they would travel around Europe together. Several months later, the pair returned home unsure about whether or not their friendship would continue once they resumed their lives as university students. In a matter of days, however, Brenda and Dan ran into each other on campus and continued their friendship, which is based on shared intellectual curiosity and interests such as Judaic law and basketball.

When Brenda and Dan met, they both considered themselves straight. A year later, Brenda confided in Dan that she was very excited about a woman she had met and wanted to date her. Fifteen years have passed, and Dan now has trouble remembering his reaction to the news but, he says, he "definitely didn't go through a crisis." They became housemates after Brenda and her girlfriend broke up; having no place to live, Brenda took up residence on Dan's sofa. The two friends have lived together off and on since that time and have played important roles in each other's lives. For example, Brenda was the "best man" in Dan's wedding ceremony.

Five years ago, the pair bought a house together, along with an equal contribution from Dan's wife, Rosie. Thus, Brenda, Dan, Rosie, and their respective children, all currently live in a collective household and maintain a familial connection. Brenda explained the conscious steps they took to establishing a family bond:

> At the time we bought this house, it was something mutual we were buying, and [I knew] we would eventually raise our kids together. . . . I said at the time that I wanted us to think of ourselves as more like family. I used to do a lot of traveling, and I always needed rides to and from the airport, and we sort of switched to thinking of us as family, which just symbolized for me, you know, I don't want to ask my friends to take me to the airport. Like, if Dan goes on a trip, it's obvious that Rosie is going to pick him up, right? So when I go to and from the airport, one of you is going to pick me up. You know? That's family.

The trio share household responsibilities and operate as a family unit. Brenda admits that in many ways she is now closer to Rosie than to Dan; she is more likely to confide in Rosie about her feelings and difficulties. Brenda also has attended family events with Dan and Rosie, including a trip to Southern California to visit Rosie's family for the holidays.

Most of Dan's and Brenda's conversations now revolve around household matters. The only one-on-one time they spend together is during trips to buy groceries. Still, Dan characterizes Brenda as knowing him better than anyone else. Likewise, Brenda considers Dan her best male friend and declares, "He may be my favorite male on the planet."

THERE IS A PERVASIVE cultural belief that family connections are the most salient and stable bond between individuals. These beliefs are reinforced through customs, rituals, and laws that privilege familial relationships over others and determine who may be defined as family.[1] The term "family" is itself a construct that is so deeply centered in heterosexuality that disentangling heterosexist ideas from any discussion of family is a challenging task. Discussing family structures that do not abide by normative standards requires a set of qualifiers: we talk about "lesbian" families, "chosen" families, and "fictive kinship," but very rarely do we have to provide any further description beyond "family" to indicate a straight relationship network, because it is the assumed norm for relational life.[2]

As experienced, family life often occurs in varied structures, including single-parent households, households that include extended family members, and foster families, as well as countless other configurations. Intersectional friendships further expand our understanding of contemporary family life by providing an example of how lesbian, gay, and straight individuals become integrated into a kinship system. In particular, many participants in this study mutually experienced friendship as family in close intersectional friendships. Prior research about family relationships with non-kin serves as a foundation to these findings. Through discourse (Gubrium and Holstein 1990) and practice (Stack 1974), friends often are defined as family. For many gay men and lesbians, friendship and family are combined into chosen family networks (Weston 1991) that typically comprise not only other gay men and lesbians but also some straight people (Oswald 2002; Weston 1991) who presumably deem gay men and lesbians family, as well.

This chapter explores the ways in which the intersectional friends in this study enact family ties and experience their friendships as family relationships. The introductory section of the chapter discusses the definitions of friendship and family in U.S. society, with a focus on chosen families. I then use the lens of family to examine how the individuals in the study experience their intersectional friendships as family, including the roles that they play in navigating life transitions such as marriage and parenthood. At the conclusion of the chapter, I discuss how gay men in the study voice greater vulnerability in the family connections they share with intersectional friends, a point that emphasizes how heterosexual privilege differently shapes perceptions among the individuals in these friendships.

## FAMILY: FORM VERSUS FUNCTION

Considerable overlap exists in the functions that friends and family serve (Fehr 1996). Trust, respect, caring, and intimacy have been identified as attributes of friends, family, and romantic relationships (Wilmot and Shellen 1990). Friendships are less regulated than romantic relationships by social norms, receive less time, are less exclusive, and are easier to dissolve (Wiseman 1986; Wright 1985); thus, friendship is at once the most flexible and most tenuous of social relationships. In contrast, family is a regulated social institution that is expected to provide material and social care and connection to its members (Cherlin 2002). Although definitions of family are socially and legally contested, the functions that families serve are similar regardless of who performs the tasks. That is, various forms of work, including emotional support, financial assistance, and care throughout the life course, lie at the center of family life (Carrington 1999; Hartmann 1981; Hochschild and Machung 1989). These functions are important to the extent that people who lack or are alienated from desired family support often build fictive kinship networks (Weston 1991).

The pervasive notion that there is only one definition of family has been challenged by contemporary studies of kinship (Stacey 1996, 1998a; Weston 1991). For instance, chosen family structures of gay men and lesbians typically comprise partners, former partners, and friends and may also include biological family members (Nardi 1999; Weston 1991). These structures provide social and instrumental support in a reciprocal and voluntary manner (Carrington 1999; Nardi 1999; Stacey 1998a). Chosen family networks are important for gay men and lesbians, who historically have had compromised access to families of origin because of rejection or geographic distance resulting from a move to live in lesbian, gay, bisexual, and transgender (LGBT) communities (Chauncey 1994; Nardi 1999). Gay men and lesbians also have constructed alternative family forms to challenge normative conceptions of "the family" (Weeks, Heaphy, and Donovan 2001) in favor of kinship structures that promote a more progressive egalitarian connection (Clarke 2002; Clarke and Kitzinger 2005). Moreover, restrictive laws limit gay men's and lesbian women's full participation in legally sanctioned forms of family life that emerge from marriage and parenthood, which often leads to the construction of chosen family relationships.

Prior studies show that straight people also form chosen family relationships when their ties to nuclear family are limited (Lindsey 1981). The previous research focuses on communities that are marginalized with regard to age (MacRae 1992), race (Chatters, Robert, and Jayakody 1994; Stack 1974), or country of origin (Ebaugh and Curry 2000). For example, in black and recent immigrant communities, fictive kin often are added to an extended family unit, which increases the number of people who participate in a family network (Chatters et al. 1994; Ebaugh and Curry 2000; Stack 1974). Fictive kin and chosen families have in common an expansion of resources through informal support. In general, non-marginalized straight people who have access to nuclear families are not expected to rely on chosen family bonds, despite wide historical variations in family life (Coontz 1992; Lindsey 1981). Similar to gay men and lesbians, however, straight individuals who are alienated or geographically distant from their families of origin, as well as lifelong straight singles, sometimes turn friends into chosen families (Rubin 1985; Stein 1981). Changing demographics also contribute to straight adults' contemporary creation of chosen families. Many people remain single well into adulthood; in the year 2000, one in four individuals age thirty-five and older had never been married (Egelman 2004). Similarly, single and widowed older adults often rely on support from friends whom they view as family members (MacRae 1992). Hence, many singles form networks to fulfill family functions.

Research about chosen families has focused either on gay men's and lesbians' networks (Carrington 1999; Nardi 1999; Stacey 1998b) or on straights' fictive kin arrangements (Chatters et al. 1994; Ebaugh and Curry 2000; MacRae 1992; Stack 1974). As a result, there appears to be little overlap in these networks. The fact that straight friends are identified as part of lesbians' and gay men's chosen families (Weston 1991), however, suggests that choosing kin may bring gay, lesbian, and straight people, same and cross-gender, together in family networks (Oswald 2002; Tillmann-Healy 2001). Prior research also does not address potential feelings of tenuousness in chosen family bonds. In the idealized cultural perceptions, family ties are unconditional and indelible, even though we know that alienation, estrangement, and divorce regularly occurs in family life. The participants in this study showed not only that intersectional friendships were contexts in which friendship and family became one and the same, but also that these ties felt more tenuous for some individuals than for others.

A TRUE FAMILY

Throughout the course of the interviews, individuals defined their friends as family, indicated the ways that their intersectional friends were better or truer forms of family than their families of origin, and used the family vocabulary as a means to characterize their friendship. In fact, many of the interviewees used the term "chosen family" to describe an intersectional friend and named a gay male or lesbian friend as family in reference to their inclusion in important life events, such as holidays and celebrations.[3] As Rubin (1985: 16) notes, "The idea of kin is so deeply rooted within us that it is the most common metaphor for describing closeness." Indeed, many straight, gay, and lesbian participants characterized their intersectional friend as family as a way to denote importance. Monique, a thirty-one-year-old straight white woman, discussed her relationship with Jesse, her thirty-one-year-old gay Latino friend: "[It's] as important as my relationship with my husband and more important than my relationship with both of my parents, who I'm not very fond of anyway. If I lost him, I would be devastated. It would be the same as losing a spouse, or a brother, or something like that."

Bruce, a thirty-four-year-old straight Asian American man, also explained the importance of his chosen family: "Well, I think my friends are closer than my family. It's not that my family is not close, but I feel like my friends are the family I've chosen for myself. And in some ways, my commitment to them is a little greater." Bruce's recognition that he is more committed to and has closer relationships with his friends than his family of origin suggests that he subscribes to a definition of family that resembles the chosen family networks more common among gay men and lesbians.

Other participants distinguished the differences between their chosen families and biological families. For example, Patrick said of Emily: "I totally would invite her to Thanksgiving, and it would feel like having another family member. Probably more. I'd probably be happier to see her than some of my blood-family members." On a similar note, Jill, a thirty-one-year-old mixed-race lesbian, illustrated her complex understanding of family in relation to her friendship with Paul, a thirty-seven-year-old straight white man: "I definitely consider him part of the family—part of the family that's a non-judging person. My family is very, I think, judging, and he's not that way. He's very open-minded. So, yeah, he's definitely part of the family." In her statement, Jill identified Paul as a part of her family but in a way that differentiated him as a more desired family member than those in her bio-legal family. Both Patrick and Jill classified their intersectional friend as family in a way that simultaneously characterized the friendship as being superior to biological family ties and used the language of the natal family to imply the ultimate level of closeness.

Many participants defined their intersectional friendships as being the truest form of family. Ruth described her relationship with Scott: "I really think that close friends are a deeper bond for me than even family. And I think most people, if they really thought about it, would say that, too, because you can't choose your family. You can choose your friends . . . but you cannot choose your family. I mean, I love my family, but a lot of that is culturally prescribed. You have to love your grandmother. You have to love your brother. You know, if I knew my brother on the street without being my brother, I wouldn't even interact with him at all, ever. So, you know, it's interesting, I think of Scott as a true family member." In his interview, Scott said that he also considered Ruth and her daughter his family. Ruth's comments acknowledged the complex understanding of family shared by many participants. On the one hand, Ruth accepted that friends, not family, are determined by choice. On the other hand, Ruth recognized that family is a socially constructed institution, and despite the cultural prescriptions that define families of origin as the most authentic form of connection, she insinuated that Scott is a truer family member than biological kin. Such contradictory perceptions were voiced throughout the interviews.

The identification of these significant friends as family likely was, in some part, related to strained relationships with families of origin. This aligns with Townsend's (1957) principle of substitution, which notes that when people lack traditional family bonds, they create chosen family members of their friends. Many participants reported alienation from families of origin or a lack of access to a traditional family unit. There were no clear differences in the tendency to create families from close friends with respect to sex and sexual orientation. In other words, the gay men and lesbians in the sample did not construct intentional families because they were alienated from families of origin any more than straight participants did.

The characterization of intersectional friendships as a more significant or truer form of family was also common among all types of participants. In fact, chosen family was described as being more important than family members of origin for a large portion of the sample. This shuffling of the traditional hierarchical ordering of friends and family might reflect unmet expectations in immediate family connections. According to Rubin (1985: 22), "Friends *choose* to do what kin are *obliged* to do." In situations where biological family members were perceived as shirking their kinship responsibilities or not meeting the idealized image of family, a chosen family member's willingness to perform familial duties was even more meaningful.

### Chosen Parents and Siblings

Another way that the participants characterized their bonds as familial was to compare friends to sibling, parental, and other family relationships, as is consistent with prior research (Nardi 1999; Rubin 1985; Werking 1997; Weston 1991). Some participants characterized aspects of their friendships as parental. Cristina, a thirty-year-old straight Latina, stated that her friendship with her gay friend Mark, who is mixed-race and twenty-one, provides her with the opportunity to act maternal. And although he is five years older than his thirty-year-old roommate, Carrie, Ken described Carrie as being like a "stabilizing mom."

Another common characterization of intersectional friends was to identify them as like siblings, especially when they were age peers (born within a few years of each other). For example, Debbi, a thirty-nine-year-old white lesbian, described her forty-three-year-old straight white male friend Carl as a brother. Often, participants described their friends as siblings at least partly to emphasize the platonic nature of the bond. Cassandra, a twenty-nine-year-old white queer woman, employed this strategy when asked whether she had ever had sex with her thirty-five-year-old white friend Stuart: "That would be a big N-O. [Stuart's] like my brother." Ethan, a twenty-three-year-old Latino gay man, was very surprised to be asked whether he and his Iranian American friend, Leyla, twenty-four, had ever been sexually involved: "That is so far from where our friendship is. . . . I kind of view her more as a sister, so I'm more protective of her in terms of, you know, people that may want to make advances on her and things like that. So I would never go down that road with her, just because [she] is just like my sister, and that would just be wrong."

Likewise, Leyla said that her future children would know her friend as "Uncle Ethan."

FUNCTIONS OF CHOSEN FAMILY

Many of the participants stated that their friends served the functions that are expected of family. In particular, they provided financial and emotional support.

*Financial Support*

One element that distinguishes friendship from family is the provision of financial support. In particular, lending money and negotiating the feelings in such lending, is typically considered kin work, which is a responsibility of family members (Carrington 1999). Connor, a thirty-seven-year-old white gay man, previously provided financial support for his thirty-year-old straight Iranian American female friend, Nadia. "Connor has gotten me out of some binds," she said. "He's been like a lifesaver to me at times. I really owe him a lot that way. He really, really has, better than any brother or dad I could have come up with or any friends. I wasn't working once for almost eight months and stuff like that, and he's really helped me out." In other cases (e.g., Carrie and Ken, Brenda and Dan,

Crystal and Derek), the friends who provided kin work were housemates who shared resources, such as food, cars, and professional advice, which also is consistent with previous findings about chosen families (Weston 1991).

It should be noted that the act of giving and taking financial support was gendered for intersectional friends in the study, with the gay and straight men in these dyads assuming provider roles, at least in an economic sense. This pattern is noteworthy because in many cases, being housemates suggests that friends equally rely on each other financially—perhaps not in the lending of money, but in the sharing of resources. Such actions would not seem to invoke gender differences, yet they did in the context of these relationships. Ruth and Scott recalled leaning on each other in leaner years, but Scott currently assumes the male provider role because he is the more fiscally secure member of the pair. He described his concern about Ruth's well-being: "I'm always trying to get her stable in her life. I'm always worried about her finances and everything and worried about her getting a [retirement plan] going. I'm worried about her when she's seventy and all that stuff, so I want her to own real estate. . . . The scheme was OK: I'll sell this condo, and we'll use all that money for a down payment on a bigger condo, and [Ruth and I] can get a condo together, and [she'll] have real estate."

## Emotional Support

Although financial support was normatively gendered in these friendships, the conditions of emotional support were more complex. Many of the gay men in the study identified their straight female friend as a crucial source of emotional support. For instance, Ethan described his reliance on Leyla: "I can literally say that without our friendship, I probably would not be alive today, 'cause she's helped me through some really, really dark times. And she's the only person, [of] even my very, very close friends, [who] I feel 100 percent comfortable with. I don't have to worry about, you know, how I come off. I don't have to worry about how I act or what I say. She'll always be there, and she'll always stand behind me." Ethan's comfort with Leyla illustrates what Rubin (1985) describes as the ability for friends to share a level of self-disclosure and an anticipated acceptance that greatly differs from immediate family relationships. In her interviews, she found that "almost all talked spontaneously and at length about the issue of self-disclosure—about how much more easily they can share important parts of themselves with friends than with kin, about how much less judgmental friends are about how they live, what they think, indeed even who they are" (Rubin 1985: 18). This finding is notable because it contradicts previous research, which showed that the more extensive and personal help that is required, such as Leyla's role in maintaining Ethan's feelings of stability, the more likely people were to use primary kin for assistance (Allan 1989). In terms of gender, emotional support was not the sole domain of women in these friendships. Monique, who is straight, said that Jesse is the first person she calls to discuss relationship problems. And Ming often turned to Ben to talk about issues with her parents.

Financial and emotional support intertwined several years before the interviews took place when Paul, who is straight, convinced his friend Jill to make dramatic life changes. "[Paul said,] 'Don't worry about it, go for it, we'll figure it out, you can move in with me,'" Jill explained. "And everything sort of happened so quickly. Next thing I know, I'm living with Paul. I broke up with my girlfriend, and he was so supportive. I didn't have any money; I was scared to death of starting [a] management position and had never been a manager before. He was just a solid person in my life, and that was a really tough time, and he made it . . . a good experience. I had no worries. I mean, basically he paid the bills for a really long time until I could get things figured out. . . . He was totally there for me." Here, Paul's financial and emotional assistance provided the security that helped Jill take personal and professional risks and, ultimately, make positive changes in her life. These two types of support—financial and emotional—are benchmarks on which the chosen family connection is built.

NAVIGATING LIFE'S TRANSITIONS TOGETHER

A variety of issues emerged in how the dyads navigated or planned to travel through life transitions together, another process in which family support is expected. The specific transitions that arose throughout the interviews were growing old together, heterosexual marriage, and parenthood. Only rarely did the intersectional friends express attitudes that critically challenged traditional ideas about family; rather, throughout the interviews, the straight participants described attempts to modify their friendships to fit the standard meanings and practices of family. Yet the participants' intentions to incorporate friends into family provided evidence that in their eyes, the family does not have a fixed definition but is pliable according to individual and community needs and desires.

*Growing Old Together*

Many of the participants described their plans to grow old together. Even though they are only in their mid-twenties, Leyla and Ethan, who have been friends for thirteen years, cannot imagine growing old without each other. Leyla characterized their bond: "Thirteen years is just a small step; I think it's going to be going on probably until the day we die. I have no doubt—we talk about long-term stuff all the time. [We talk about] getting old together. And he says I'm gonna wear those flashy muumuus, and it's gonna be his job to tone it down!" Although Leyla may not have considered the realities of aging, she clearly views her friendship with Ethan as enduring. Bruce also discussed his desire to continue his bond with Vanessa: "That's one of the things I wrote in [a] note to her is like—that I would like to grow old with [her], and we'd sit on the porch and scare all of the little kids on the block and play dominoes and just be loud old people." Both Leyla's and Bruce's ideas of older people relied on stereotypes, with Leyla envisioning herself in muumuus and Bruce sitting on the porch with Vanessa being loud and scaring children. Still, both communicated a clear intention and desire to maintain the closeness of their friendship bond throughout life's transitions.

In addition to providing company through the twilight years, families are the most likely individuals to provide care to aging and ailing adults (Wolff and Kasper 2006). Most individuals expect spouses or other family members to provide care and companionship as they age, a finding that is consistent with prior work about the social networks of older adults (Adams, Blieszner, and de Vries 2000; Antonucci and Akiyama 1987). Those in intersectional friendships adopted the expectation that their friendships would persist and fantasized about plans to grow old and retire together much in the same way married couples do. Interestingly, these dreams of growing old together rarely incorporated any discussion of a potential spouse; rather, the friendship was imagined as a self-sufficient and insular dyad. Such plans may have been situated in the myth that older people are not interested in romance and sex (Calasanti and King 2005). Thus, intersectional friendships—most of which were intimate, but not sexual—were thought to mimic the perceived marital relationship of older people. In any case, intersectional friends discussed their mutual plans for old age.

An example of intersectional friends who plan to retire together are Ruth and Scott, both forty-six years old. This pair uniquely identified a romantic partner's role (Scott's longtime partner, Bradley) in their retirement plans, as Scott and Bradley own their retirement property together. Ruth and Scott mutually supported each other during financially difficult times and cared for dying friends at the height of the AIDS epidemic in the 1980s. This history of providing financial and emotional support appears to have influenced their future plans. "We do have future plans for when we're old," Ruth said about the plans she and Scott had to retire together someday. "He bought this place in [a nearby riverfront town]. It's this beautiful place; it's on this hill and right below it there's this little cottage [laughs]. That's where I'm going to live." Ruth's and Scott's plan for the future seemed feasible. Their long-standing friendship of twenty-five years, combined with understanding of illness and other life challenges, seemed to provide them with a clear perspective about caregiving as part of their family connection.

*Heterosexual Weddings*

Another life transition poised to affect intersectional friends in a tangible way is heterosexual marriage. In heterosexual weddings, social and familial roles are clearly articulated and highly gendered (Oswald 2000); the way that these established roles might be adopted or altered as same-sex marriage is legalized and becomes more commonplace is unknown. Typically, those who are invited to participate in the wedding ceremony are family or close friends of the couple (Rubin 1985); thus, being asked to serve as part of the wedding party is an act of inclusion (Oswald 2000). According to Ingraham (1999: 4), a wedding is also "one of the major events that signal readiness and prepare heterosexuals for membership in marriage as an organizing practice for the institution of heterosexuality." Hence, in both the practices within the ceremony (e.g., a bride being "given away" to a groom by her father) and the broader act of legally marrying, heterosexual weddings reinforce norms of gender and sexuality.

While weddings and marriages are heteronormative,[4] they also are significant and meaningful events for the individuals involved; hence, many of the participants incorporated their intersectional friends into their wedding ceremonies. In some cases, the desire to include a gay friend in a heterosexual wedding ceremony caused familial conflict because of the challenge it posed to conventional norms. Ming was determined to have her gay best friend Ben as her "man of honor" in her wedding ceremony, which caused a battle with her future in-laws:

My mental picture of our wedding ceremony is me; Adam, my husband; Ben on my side; and somebody else. So Ben has always been in the picture, you know? But he's a guy, Adam's family is Catholic, so being man of honor, that might be a problem. When I talked to Ben, of course he wasn't too happy, and I cried, but he supported me through this whole hoopla. Ben was still supportive throughout the whole thing, but I just felt so uncomfortable for quite a few months. And I finally decided, you know, I was fighting with Adam every day about this, I was just not happy. So after a few months, I finally said, "You know, we can't do this without Ben." Because the first image was me and Ben and Adam, you know, I can't shake it. Basically, I just need this guy to be my man of honor.

The man-of-honor conflict also had an impact on Ben, who recalled: "She was under pressure from the groom's family side—they wanted to have a female maid of honor. So originally she said she felt most comfortable on her wedding day having me stand right beside her, but then somehow there was a big discussion, and she decided to have someone else. I was sort of hurt by that, and she was very hurt, and she was having fights with her fiancé. I'm like, 'Don't fight.' I didn't want to ruin the friendship and the rest because of this. . . . But eventually, things worked out. I became her man of honor again." By insisting that Ben play a role in her wedding that is generally occupied by a (presumably) straight woman, Ming challenged convention. In this instance, the argument against Ben's being the man of honor appeared in both accounts to lie more in his gender than his sexuality. Ben's being gay was not discussed as an issue in his standing up with Ming in her Catholic wedding; only his being male.

Several straight interviewees discussed the role that a gay male or lesbian friend had played in her or his heterosexual wedding ceremony without mentioning controversy. Nadia, who is straight, asked her gay best friend Connor to walk her down the aisle and give her away during her wedding ceremony. Dan's heterosexual wedding featured his lesbian friend, Brenda, as his "best man." In each case, the straight interviewee asked her or his gay male or lesbian friend to play a significant and symbolic familial role in their wedding ceremony. Still, a wedding is arguably a cultural tradition that serves to reinforce the family as a heterosexual institution based on legal marriage, to which same-sex partners have been denied equal access. Weddings connect the personal decision to marry with heterosexual privileges, such as social, legal, financial, and religious benefits (Oswald 2000). For example, because they cannot legally marry in most states in the United States, same-sex couples are not eligible for Social Security survivor and spousal benefits and tax protections on shared property and inheritance from partners (Cahill, South, and Spade 2000).[5] Hence, straight members of these friendship dyads include their gay and lesbian friends in a ceremony that, by virtue of formalizing marriage in its currently exclusionary form, reinforces heterosexuality as a social norm. Yet none of the straight interviewees who planned weddings to include their gay male or lesbian chosen family members in the ceremony recognized (or, at least, acknowledged) that such an action equated to asking the friend to participate in an activity that reinforces heterosexual privilege.

Some study participants planned to subvert social norms in their wedding ceremonies by including an intersectional friend. Monique, who at the time of her interview was planning a formal wedding in the Catholic church, expected Jesse to play an important role in her ceremony: "It's going to be a riot, because here's gonna be this big fag walking me down the aisle." Monique recognized that Jesse's walking her down the aisle in the Catholic church (a faith that condemns homosexuality) is a transgression of cultural norms. Yet she failed to recognize the irony in having Jesse stand beside her in a ceremony that reinforces her heterosexual status and the accompanying privileges and, as such, actively participating in and reinforcing the institution that excludes him as a gay man.

Monique's and Ming's insistence that their gay male friend play a central role in their weddings is not entirely without consequence. Symbolically, the inclusion of gay male and lesbian friends in straight weddings subverts the ideal of the family as heterosexual by definition. Unfortunately, this inclusion occurs within the context of a social institution that reinforces traditional heterosexual norms about family.

## Links to (Compulsory) Parenthood

Along with cultural rituals that regulate the family, family life is often defined by the expectation of raising children (Morell 1994). Although increasing numbers of lesbians and gay men are parenting, they still face many obstacles in their efforts. For instance, to follow strict legal terms, a lesbian who wants to inseminate artificially is urged not only to find a donor to become pregnant, but also to use a medical intermediary to limit the donor's paternity claims (Arnup 1994). In addition, laws are already in place that limit adoption practices for gay men and lesbians. States such as Mississippi and Utah have laws that explicitly prohibit gay men and lesbians from adopting children (Human Rights Campaign [HRC] 2011). Only nine states and the District of Columbia have made second parent adoption available, a practice that provides gay men and lesbian couples the equivalent of stepparent adoptions, allowing both members of a couple to become the legal parents of any children they may raise together (HRC 2011).[6] Even with the passage of laws that facilitate adoption for same-sex individuals, gay men are reliant on either a surrogate or on adoption to have a child.

Gay men most frequently said that their friendship with a straight woman increased the possibility that they would have a close experience with children and heterosexual family life. Specifically, several gay men in the sample noted that they anticipated being part of the lives of children born to their straight female friends; there were no similar discussions in the lesbian–straight man dyads. Scott explained that, through his twenty-five-year friendship with Ruth and her daughter, who is now a teenager, he was able to experience childrearing: "I mean, I felt like [Ruth's daughter] was kind of like mine. Me and Ruth used to talk about having a baby together until we found out I was HIV-positive, so I've always had this sensation [that her daughter] was kind of mine." Similarly, Seth identified his straight friend Shayna as his primary connection to straight family life: "I've been thinking about this lately, too. . . . She's also my connection to like to kids—to, like, families. You know what I mean? . . . She's gonna be the person in my life that's going to set up a family—it's just the closeness with her, the fact that our friendship can be so close—I'm going to be part of her little family, which I don't think other friendships would give."

Several straight women in the study recognized the challenges that their gay male friends would face in becoming parents; understanding their potential capacities to assist them, they indicated willingness to serve as surrogates for their close gay male friends. Interestingly, most of the gay male participants had not asked about surrogacy or even expressed interest in being parents. Such was the situation for Crystal, a thirty-year-old straight Latina, who explained that she would consider having a baby for her white gay friend Derek, age thirty-two: "I don't really necessarily want to have children, but I'm not ready to tie my tubes or anything, and I've thought about the possibility of having a child for someone else. I have other gay friends, and I thought that maybe I would do that for them." In his interview, Derek explained that he has briefly thought about becoming a parent but is still too busy raising himself to give it serious consideration. Cristina, a straight woman, also commented that she has considered having a child for her gay male friend Mark and his future life partner. In his interview, Mark discussed wanting to become a parent but indicated that he wanted to adopt and did not consider co-parenting with Cristina or asking her to have a baby for him.

Marriage also influenced the ways that straight women thought about having a child with or for a gay male friend. One married straight female interviewee, who asked not to be identified with this comment, stated: "Even though [my gay male friend] has never asked, I've actually thought about this before but don't tell him. If he ever asked, 'Can you bear my kids?'—like, if he and [his partner] wanted to have kids of their own—I would say yes. I don't know what [my husband] would think about the whole thing, but I would have no problem with it." The interviewee's comment suggests that, while she still considered having a baby for her gay male friend a possibility, her marriage has altered her ability to discuss whether or not she would serve as a surrogate freely.

Expectations of normative family life seemed also to color thoughts about serving as a surrogate. Nadia explained how being married complicates her thinking about bearing a child for Connor:

> Now that I'm married, it is different, but I always told both him and [another close gay male friend] that if they wanted a baby, I'd have one for them. When I would say, "I'd have a baby for you," it was because I would assume they were with a partner and they have their life and they want a baby. I always assumed that if I was going to have children, I would be married and this and that, because I do not want to raise a child alone, so I never really thought of it that way—co-parenting, I mean. I would be a part of the baby's life, . . . but I wouldn't be co-parenting, really. I have no idea what my husband would think if I wanted to have a baby for Connor. He'd probably not go for that very well, you know?

Nadia's statement reflects a dual-parent, heterosexual model of ideal parenthood; she expected to have her own children within a heterosexual marriage and would act as a surrogate for Connor if he and a partner wanted to parent a baby. Now that she is married, Nadia recognizes that having a baby for Connor is complicated by the expectations of marriage. Historically, marital customs were founded on expectations of monogamy for the purpose of knowing the rightful parent of a child (Ingraham 1999). These customs persist into contemporary family life, with laws enforcing parental support of biological children and marital fidelity (Ingraham 1999). Marriage presents a challenge to becoming a friend's surrogate because our social norms place the marital relationship at the top of a relationship hierarchy. Marital status affected these women's thoughts about having a child with or for their gay male friends; however, the women still indicated potential willingness to have children for their friends, despite being married. At the same time, the women consistently prioritized their marital relationships over their friendships, which reinforces normative family life. The straight women in the study indicated that they had a degree of freedom to build non-normative family structures so long as they were not married.

A second issue inherent in the straight women's comments is that they appeared to universalize the desire to have children. For instance, Nadia thought that Connor might someday want a baby; however, in his interview, Connor stated that he had no desire to become a parent. This was true for many of the gay male participants. In assuming that their gay male friends would want to parent, many of the straight female participants placed onto their gay male friends the desire to parent. The voiced willingness of straight female participants to bear children for gay male friends is both generous and transgressive in that it not only challenges traditional gender norms of motherhood, which equates procreation with parenthood, but also contests beliefs that gay men should not be allowed to parent. Yet in assuming that their gay male friends aspired to the same family constructs that they do, the straight women falsely conflated the familial desires of gay men and straight women—or, at least, assumed that their friends' family lives would align with their own perceptions of family.

In the cases of both heterosexual weddings and surrogacy, the actions or attitudes of the straight women challenged the cultural norm of family being defined by blood ties. Most of the straight women in the study, however, were never overtly critical of social regulations that dictate who can be a legally recognized family; rather, many appeared wholeheartedly to accept the primacy of the heterosexual family structure, including marriage and parenthood within marriage, and to view it as ideal. This is not to say that the act of forcing the intersectional friendship into a normative family frame had no effect; doing so suggested that the family is a pliable construct. In addition, by viewing gay men as potential parents, straight women divorced conceptions of gender and family as mutually constitutive and grounded in reproduction within a heterosexual union. While this does not necessarily challenge the norms of gay male identity, it poses a challenge to accepted definitions of family.

Despite the clear indications of how important they are to their straight female friends, some of the gay men I interviewed expressed concerns that the bond would change once their intersectional friend settled into a traditional family life. Rubin (1985: 23) addressed the unsettled dimension that creates anxiety in constructing family structures out of friends: "It's this very quality of friendship that is at once so powerfully seductive and so anxiety-provoking, indeed that is both its strength and its weakness. To be able to choose is to be free; to be chosen is to feel loved and admired. But in this, as in other arenas of living, freedom exacts its price in our sense of security and certainty. For what is given freely can be taken away with impunity as well. If we can be chosen, we can also be 'unchosen.'"

It is important to note that only the gay men articulated anxiety about the possible dissolution of their chosen families. Connor, who walked his friend Nadia down the aisle at her wedding, voiced his concerns: "[Nadia's] going to make me an uncle one day—well, depending on where they're living, although that's what I worry about, too, just because people change. Being gay in a gay relationship, you sort of stay the same as your other gay friends, but when you're married, things are different. Then you have kids, and your life goes in other directions." Here, Connor identified his anxiety over his chosen family status as being rooted in Nadia's heterosexual marriage, which he viewed as qualitatively different from a gay relationship. While Connor's comment suggests that he welcomed being an uncle to Nadia's future child, he simultaneously braced himself for the possibility that heterosexual married life would stand in the way of his continued chosen family relationship. Likewise, Ben, the man of honor at Ming's wedding, also expressed concern about what would happen to his role in Ming's life once she had children. At the time of their interviews, both Connor and Ben were very satisfied with the current state of their friendships, but they understood that the roles that heterosexual family demands from mothers could interfere with their chosen family relationships.

Such fears may be well grounded. Previous research shows that when a woman marries, her friendships become more peripheral to her romantic relationship (Pogrebin 1987; Werking 1997). Cultural scripts determine that the romantic relationship is the most valued (Rubin 1985), particularly in heterosexual relationships that have the possibility of childbearing (Nardi 1999). This may be one of the primary ways that a chosen family differs for heterosexuals and gay men or lesbians: a straight person may not be as reliant on his or her chosen family to meet familial needs and can live normatively, marrying legally and having the potential to procreate without intervention. Although a straight friend may never intend to dissolve her chosen family, the possibility that she will enter into heterosexual family life may cause the gay male friend perpetually to question whether or not a bond will remain familial. The same may also be true for friendships between lesbians and straight men, although the possibility of lesbians' being able to bear children in a way that is not equally available to straight men may alter the dynamic. In any event, straight men and lesbians did not discuss the tenuousness of their friendship bond vis-à-vis heterosexual coupling, marriage, or childbearing.

In this context, the gay man occupies the role of what Collins (1991) described as the "outsider within," or the position of an oppressed person experiencing a situation in which dominant cultural norms are acted out and insiders fail to notice, much less question, the subjugation (Collins 1991; Ebaugh and Curry 2000; Oswald 2000). Thus, both Ben and Connor were active participants in their friends' family lives but recognized that their position might be supplanted by the norms of straight married life and eventual parenthood. According to Collins, as the outsider within, an oppressed individual understands the power relations behind those rules and what alternative realities they obscure. Just as Ben and Connor acknowledged that they saw their positions in their friends' families as tenuous because they counter normative family life, Nadia and Ming, the straight female halves of each dyad, were unaware that their participation in normative family life could jeopardize the chosen family connection they have with the gay male friend. While the straight friends did not voice any intention to alter the chosen kin relationships, the pressures toward normative family life may be difficult to resist. Indeed, in this sample the intersectional friendships that sustained the longest and most rewarding familial-type bonds were those in which the straight friend remained unmarried or committed to a life that defied heteronormative conventions, such as residing in communal households or maintaining radical political ideologies about gender and family.

TRANSGRESSION OR CONVENTION?

Almost all of the interviewees described either the overall character or particular aspects of their friendship as familial. This finding begs the question of whether the conceptualization of friends as family was more a metaphor than an actual feeling of kinship. In his study of gay male friendship, Nardi (1999: 59) investigated this point and concluded that "for most [gay men and lesbians] friends are like their ideal families and on a daily basis are more likely than is a biological family to provide material and emotional assistance, identity, history, nurturing, loyalty, and support." Whether the same is true for straight individuals is difficult to ascertain. The word "friend" can encompass a wide range of relationships of varying intensities, from casual bonds to the most significant relationships. Hence, the interviewees' use of family terms to describe their bonds is a way to identify the importance of the relationship, as others have suggested (Ibsen and Klobus 1972; Nardi 1999). The use of metaphor also addresses what is unstated in this situation—that is, there is no sufficient social script to guide or characterize non-biological and platonic, yet emotionally intimate and socially reliant, relationships between close friends. This being the case, individuals involved in such bonds may default to characterizing their friendships in terms of family relationships, which are easily understood as being a meaningful connection.

The assumption that participants characterized friendships as family simply as a metaphor, however, is a disservice to their strong connections. Such an assumption reinforces the idea that family is limited to bio-legal ties, which thus denies many individuals' experiences. Indeed, in acknowledging that family is a largely constructed phenomenon (Carrington 1999), it would seem that, to a certain extent, acting as family would be sufficient criteria to be classified as family. While not all close friendships necessarily approximate a familial connection, Carrington's (1999: 5) suggestion that "any family is a social construction or set of relationships recognized, edified, and sustained through human initiative" allows the definition of family to include a multitude of experiences. Such a perspective is consistent with Thomas's (1967: 331–36) conceptualization of the "definition of the situation," which asserted that circumstances perceived or defined as real to the individual are real in their consequences. In the case of close intersectional friends, the individuals who defined their friendships as familial have experienced and defined their relationships as real, rather than metaphorical, family ties.

Another important issue to address is the theoretical usefulness of comparing gay and lesbian chosen families to straight families. Weston (1991) cautioned against the assumption that gay male and lesbian chosen families represent variations of traditional kinship structures. A more useful theoretical model required viewing such chosen families as historical transformations rather than derivations of heterosexual family structures. Such a perspective reflects the argument that chosen kinship is transformative rather than derivative of other kin relationships. As Rapp (1987: 129) explained: "When we assume male-headed, nuclear families to be central units of kinship, and all alternative patterns to be extensions or exceptions, we accept an aspect of cultural hegemony instead of studying it. In the process, we miss the contested domain in which symbolic innovation may occur." Indeed, based on the interview data, my suggestion that intersectional friendships often constituted chosen families aligns well with Rapp's position that the chosen kin relationship may be transformative of family life. The degree to which intersectional friends transform normative conceptions of family, however, remains to be seen. Including straights, gay men, and lesbians in one's family structure certainly challenges heterocentric definitions of the family. Yet ultimately, reinforcing the heterosexual family as the ideal norm fails to adequately revolutionize meanings of the family to incorporate the experiences of lesbians and gay men, as well as those of other people who do not have access to traditional family ties.

Another issue to consider is whether or not, for political reasons, friendship and family should be viewed as separate entities. Some have argued that because common conceptions of the family are based on an oppressive dimension of relational life that historically negates homosexuality as a viable identity, viewing friendship as family undermines the role of friends in the lives of gay men and lesbians (Weeks et al. 2001). Moreover, some individuals construct chosen kinship structures to contest normative definitions of family by placing non-romantic and non-bio-legal ties at the center of relational life (Weinstock 2000); the conflation of friendship and family negates this challenge. Conversely, expanding the definition of family to include a multiplicity of relations can also be a political act, as it offers an alternative to the monolithic ideal of family life as nuclear and bio-legal.

The participants in the study present a complex understanding of family life. Despite some of the individuals' strained relationships with families of origin, for example, they persisted in identifying their friendships in familial terms. Simultaneously, this strategy reflected the intimacy and importance of friends and overlooked the inconsistencies in identifying the "family" relationship with chosen kin as positive and that with natal family as negative. Perhaps the distinction lay in favoring the families they chose over the ones they were born into, at least discursively.

While most of the participants identified their intersectional friends as chosen family, the occurrence of the chosen family for straight people differed from that of gay men and lesbians, because in many cases it lacked the same sense of necessity. Although the degrees of privilege that heterosexuals experience with regard to family structure varies, family life still is not equally available to lesbians and gay men through laws, policies, and practices. Nonetheless, these friendships exist as mutually beneficial and meaningful chosen families. Contrary to conservatives' allegations that gay men and lesbians threaten family life, it seems that family life may be growing through the voluntary bonds of friendship and reflect the state of the postmodern family arrangements as various and fluid (Stacey 1996). Indeed, the contemporary family, bio-legal or chosen, may be in a constant state of flux, adding and losing members while adapting to the social context at hand.

**4**

# GENDER

# COPS AND

# ROBBERS

*I feel like Guy is one of a handful of men I know who I feel like—I guess I'll just be extreme about it: he's one of a handful of men who I know who's not a shit head. I grew up kind of with men who weren't great. . . . He's emotional and communicative and real and you can talk to him, and I don't know a whole lot of men like that. So he's really special in that way.*
*—Wallis, a thirty-year-old white lesbian*

## MARK AND CRISTINA

*Mark met Christina at work a little over a year ago. At the time, Mark was working as a representative for a fragrance company at a large department store in San Francisco, as was Cristina. Theirs was not a "love at first sight" friendship: Mark thought Cristina was snobby and "bitchy" when he first met her; Cristina thought Mark was a "prissy little bitch." The story goes that when Mark heard Cristina talking to someone else in Tagalog, a Filipino language, he approached her because he was surprised to hear her speaking in a language dear to him. Cristina is Latina; Mark is half-Filipino. They started talking and quickly developed a deep friendship. Mark says he knew that Cristina was straight when he first met her because they both are attracted to the same type of men. Cristina never had to ask whether Mark was gay. She just knew.*

*Now Mark and Cristina are inseparable. They talk to each other on the phone several times a day and discuss topics that range from makeup and sex to what they are having for dinner or buying at the grocery store. They both enjoy going out, drinking, clubbing, and shopping together. They also like to travel together. Both Mark and Cristina fondly spoke about a recent trip to Miami, where they both had their bodies waxed by a skilled aesthetician. They were so impressed by the experience that they purchased the aesthetician's wax and used it to wax each other back in San Francisco.*

*Since they met, Mark has moved to a town an hour east of the Bay Area and now works as a hairstylist. Still, he visits Cristina in San Francisco every weekend. Mark is several years* younger than Cristina—he is twenty-four to her thirty-two—and he explained that she is like a big sister "leading me and guiding me." Cristina and Mark have met each other's families and have spent major holidays together. Both have very close family bonds. Mark's mother refers to Cristina as his "auntie." Cristina admits that she treats Mark in a very maternal way, tucking in his shirt and giving him advice.

Both of the friends admit that one of the reasons they get along so well is that they both have strong personalities. They think this makes them intimidating to others. Mark explained that his relationship with Cristina makes him a more confident person.

WE CANNOT TALK about intersectional friendships without addressing how gender shapes and influences expectations and interactions. The common media depiction of gay men and straight women being the best of friends, while true for many of the interviewees in this study, is largely based on gender norms. Often gay men and straight women are presumed to be a variation of "girlfriends" who talk about men, go to clubs and bars together, shop together, and overall have very superficial relationships. There is no comparable expectation for lesbian and straight male friends. Many people were skeptical that I would find such friends to interview in the early stages of researching this book because of the common perception that such friendships do not exist. Both of these perceptions stem from conventional gender norms for men and women of all sexual orientations.

The goal of this chapter is to focus on how gender norms and identities operate in intersectional friendships. I examine both how gender norms shape expectations about these friendships and how the intersectional friendship context (to a degree) serves as a space in which individuals are able to enact less traditional gendered behaviors. Also, I address two significant ways that gender is regulated within the intersectional friendships in this study: participants both act as gender police and encourage their friends to be gender outlaws. Gender policing refers to the subtle and not-so-subtle ways that intersectional friends reinforce conventional gender expectations; through their actions and expectations, all categories of friends in the study police and are policed by others. The same is true for gender outlaws, a term introduced by Bornstein (1994) that refers to a non-traditional gender identity. Those who serve as gender outlaws both encourage and embody gender-nonconforming attitudes and behaviors. Both processes occur side by side in intersectional friendships and thus highlight how gender operates in this context.

The existing expectations for gay–straight friendships are based, in part, on our society's binary gender norms, in which individuals are viewed as either masculine or feminine (West and Zimmerman 1987) and are hierarchical, where masculinity is valued over femininity (Schilt and Westbrook 2009). Hegemonic masculinity, which is based on men's dominance over both women and other men, is the social norm of masculinity under this binary system (Connell 1995). Gender norms are organized around the assumption of heterosexuality for both masculinity and femininity, as well (Connell 1995; Myers and Raymond 2010; Thorne 1986). These norms do not reflect the actual ways that individuals experience or identify with either masculinity or femininity; rather, they define ideals that are difficult, if not impossible, to live up to (Fee 2000). Hegemonic forms of gender are reinforced through everyday social interaction; gender norms are informally and formally enforced by rewarding conforming behavior and punishing nonconformity, which limits gender variation (Corbett 1999; Halberstam 1998; Lorber 1994). For example, informal enforcement of a gender norm takes place when people stare at an individual whose gender cannot be easily identified; formal enforcement occurs when a person is asked to leave a women's restroom or risks arrest because she or he does not appear sufficiently feminine to be perceived as female.

Friendships are also subject to a social context of heteronormativity, which is defined as the "mundane, everyday ways that heterosexuality is privileged and taken for granted as normal and natural" (Martin 2009: 190). The lens of heterosexism is applied to gender in such a way that gay men and lesbians are viewed by society at large as being inherently different from heterosexuals not only in their sexual practices, but also in their gender identities—that is, sex and gender are coupled (Connell 1995; Pharr 1988). Yet gender identities are complex for all individuals: lesbian women, gay men, and straight men and women all have myriad gender expressions and identities. Scholarship about transgender issues and experiences is useful in highlighting strategies to disentangle gender, sex, and sexual orientation. In particular, transgender female-to-male individuals understand that a male body is not necessary to masculinity and, by extension, that a female body is not necessary to femininity (Vidal-Ortiz 2002). Instead, according to Green (1987), masculinity and femininity can be found in body language, behavior, occupation, speech, inflection, and cultural stereotypes for appropriate actions, which ultimately become incorporated into an individual's personality.

While sex, gender, and sexual orientation do not neatly coincide, gay men and lesbians may be more likely to display gender nonconformity than straight individuals. Previous research has found that many gay men reject traditional displays of masculinity in favor of a range of masculinities that vary from hyper-masculine to effeminate (Kimmel 1996; Nardi 2000). Likewise, many lesbians reject traditional forms of femininity and instead identify their gender identity on the continuum of butch to femme (Butler 1991; Levitt and Hiestand 2004; Stein 1997). Presumably, these varying forms of gender identity affect the social relationships of all gay men and lesbians, including those with straight men and women. In fact, throughout my interviews, the participants' comments implied that their gendered behavior was influenced by and negotiated within intersectional dyads. The friends demonstrated an ongoing tension between the reinforcement of gender norms and the encouragement of gender noncon-formity in these friendships. In these ways, these intersectional friendships are both unconventional and traditional.

GENDER POLICING

*Policing Straight Women's Appearance*

One of the ways the gay men and straight women I interviewed police gender is by reinforcing the appearance norms for straight women. Many straight female participants indicated that they value the attention their gay male friends pay to their appearance, in addition to other aspects of their friends' personalities. "They're the best friends," said Nadia, a thirty-year-old straight Iranian American woman. "They are complimentary; they'll tell you when something doesn't look good on you; they're polite; they're courteous; they're kind. . . . They're just good friends." An emphasis on appearance was also present in the friendship between Mark, who is gay, and Cristina, who is straight. Mark identified some of Cristina's positive qualities: "A lot of my gay friends say, 'You're living vicari-ously through Cristina. You want her height, you want her boobs, her body, figure.' . . . She's very much a woman. Very much a girl. . . . She shaves every day. We call Sundays 'pedicure Sundays.' We get them every Sunday. There's not a masculine bone in her, honestly."

In the next breath, Mark focused on Cristina's gender-nonconforming be-havior: "But she does things for herself. She can check oil and do stuff like that, but her mannerism, her nails, everything—she's just a girl. She's every gay man's fantasy of being a woman."

Here, Mark praised Cristina's accomplishment of conventional femininity (West and Zimmerman 1987) and noted the cultural cachet that comes with it. While Mark also commented that he admires Cristina's independence and values her opinion on career matters, on balance he characterized Cristina according to her feminine traits throughout the interview.

In turn, Cristina discussed why gay men and straight women make good friends: "Well, sometimes the gay man wants to be a woman; perhaps some of the physical attributes. . . . Sometimes that brings a gay man and a straight woman together." In this case, Mark and Cristina serve as mutual gender police: they both reinforce straight femininity as essential. Moreover, Cristina's comments imply that she views Mark through the principle of consistency, a cultural construction that understands sex, gender, and sexual orientation as synonymous and consistent (Ponse 1978), with heterosexuality being normative; as such, a man who is sexually oriented toward men defies these norms. By extension, under the principle of consistency, because he is sexually attracted to men, Christina infers that in some capacity, Mark must want to be a woman.

In their interviews, gay men sometimes focused on conventionally feminine aspects when describing their straight female friends and glossed over the ways the women defied gender expectations. Simultaneously, many straight women applied a feminized set of attributes to their gay male friends without acknowledging the shades of gender identity that exist for gay men. Both tendencies appear to be related to internalized heterosexism, where norms related to sex, gender, and sexual orientation are interconnected so that straight women are expected to embody only femininity and gay men are viewed as a stereotype of gay masculinity. According to Szymanski (2004: 145), internalized heterosexism includes *sexism* as an important component in the oppression of sexual minorities. Internalized heterosexism was present in some of the generalizations by gay men and straight women in the study, who connected sexual orientation and sex to a set of limited and fixed characteristics. Exposing this aspect of intersectional friendships is significant because it underscores the tension between gender convention and resistance in intersectional friendships.

## Gay Man Trapped in a Straight Woman's Body

One of the primary ways that straight women in the study policed gay men's identity was by describing themselves as a "gay man trapped in a straight woman's body" as a means to explain their own personal identity. Monique, a thirty-year-old straight white woman, provided the most multidimensional explanation:

> I call myself queer in a way because I'm very, very queer-identified, and I know what it's like to have it hard—you know what I mean? To be told that there's something fundamentally wrong with you?—and I think maybe that's something [gay men] identify with.[1] [I also have] the ability to code switch: the affinity for music, for urban life, but also a certain refinement. You know what I mean? There's a difference between being street smart and being able to code switch and being ghetto—you know what I mean? Like, I don't identify with being ghetto, and to me that's a state of mind, not a place. And I like men, so that's another way of saying a fag in a woman's body.

Monique's identification as a "fag in a woman's body" encompasses her ability to move in and out of marginalized identities. In her interview, Monique indicated that she had worked as a stripper in young adulthood and was raised in an unstable home; both experiences made her feel socially marginalized. In adulthood, she relates to and values gay men's culture, partly because she relates to the aesthetics and partly because she understands the marginal place it occupies in society. Throughout her interview, Monique described gay culture in purely positive ways, yet she also applied stereotypical and homogeneous characteristics to gay men, which are not universal experiences that all gay men share.

Jesse, Monique's thirty-one-year-old gay Latino friend, provided a description that similarly relied on the essential nature of what it means to be a gay man: "I always tell Monique she is a gay man trapped [in a straight woman's body]. She's more of a gay man than I am sometimes! . . . Just the shit she says, just her orientation toward life. I mean, when I say that, that's kind of a gross stereotype, because Monique doesn't necessarily flow with the established paradigms of acceptable behavior and notions. She's very liberated. She's sex-positive, you know; she fucks three guys in one week. She would be OK with that."[2] Jesse's description of Monique is similar to Nardi's (1999) discussion of women being described as "gayer than gay," a label used to connote a woman who acts in instrumentally masculine ways with regard to sexual behavior. This label differs from the colloquial term "slut" that typically is applied to women perceived as overtly and actively sexual. Although it was Jesse who directly attributed Monique's being a gay man trapped in a straight woman's body to her views on sex, Monique also characterized her past sexual life: "I don't like to use the term 'big 'ho,' but I was, definitely. You know. [I] didn't spend any time in steady relationships and, you know, chronic monogamy." Monique also identified her behaviors as more common for gay men.

The "gay man trapped in a straight woman's body" label is shorthand that both Monique and Jesse used to describe Monique's feelings of marginality and her gender-nonconforming behavior, which is indicative of gender outlaw behavior. However, this characterization also reinforces an essential identity of gay men as hypersexual. Doing so presents a paradox in some of the straight women's understanding of gay men: gay men are thus stereotyped as both feminine and hypersexual, which are generally viewed as mutually exclusive characteristics. An open attitude toward sex and sexuality is an element of gay male culture that many straight female interviewees valued in their gay male friends, yet the assumption that gay men are not just sexual, but hypersexual (Gross, Green, Storck, and Vanyur 1980), also inhibits the potential resistance of gender norms.

Other straight women relied on different stereotypes to describe themselves as gay men trapped in straight women's bodies. Zoë, a thirty-year-old straight white woman, was straightforward in acknowledging some of her traditional beliefs about gay men: "I feel like I am a gay man inside. I'm completely anal-retentive. I mean, I know that these are totally essentialist categories that I'm creating, but for the most part they're true. I'm totally anal-retentive and very keyed up. I like things very pristine in my environment. I love show tunes, I'm just—I'm not entirely glamorous enough to be a gay man, but, you know, other than that, I feel like we are pretty much right there." Zoë's characterization of what it means to be a gay man focused primarily on the aesthetics of gay male culture as a means of self-identification rather than on sex and sexual-object choice.

Another way the straight women identified themselves as "gay men in straight women's bodies" was with respect to their gender identity. This was the case for Crystal, a thirty-year-old straight Latina, who said, "Because I identify with gay men, I feel like inside I am a gay man. I feel more masculine than some other women." Crystal adopted this descriptor because she identifies her feelings as "more masculine" or insufficiently feminine. Again, a contradiction about gay men's expected gender identity surfaces, with Crystal's attribution of being a gay man centered in feeling "more masculine than other women," as gay men are often stereotyped as feminine. Still, in adopting the "gay man" label, Crystal articulated her own feelings of gender nonconformity.

The straight women who described themselves as "gay men in straight women's bodies" relied on their interpretations of the (often stereotypical) social identities of gay men. Interestingly, some gay men in the sample voiced frustration because their straight female friends perceived them as virtually indistinguishable from, and largely interchangeable with, other gay men. One gay man, who asked that his comment remain anonymous, noted the discomfort he sometimes feels:

> I think maybe she sort of buys into the kind of the gay stereotype a little too much. . . . Sometimes I get the feeling that she sort of sees me almost [as] not identical, but, you know, as stereotypical, sort of having more in common with her other gay friends than I actually do. So that's kind of been an issue on occasions in the past; just certain assumptions she's made. There have been instances where she's thought, you know, just because something is gay or other gay guys like it or thought it was cute or funny that I would [laughs], and I haven't. I think sometimes she doesn't always get that. . . . Like, every time she meets a gay guy, she tells me how much I would love him, and of course I don't at all. And you know, that makes me wonder about our friendship. Does she really know me?

Other gay male participants recognized that their straight female friends expected them to embody gender identities that did not feel genuine. For example, Seth, a twenty-seven-year-old gay white man, commented: "It seems like [Shayna's] friends are all straight, [and sometimes I feel] a little out of place . . . unless it's with her straight girlfriends. Then I can just be, like, their little gay boy, you know, and that's fine. I can play that role for a little while." Seth acknowledged his willingness to play "little gay boy" but also that this is a role and not his genuine identity. Both of these men's comments indicated that they feel uncomfortable with the friend's expectation that they embody a prototype of gay maleness rather than being valued for their individual personalities. Thus, in characterizing themselves as gay men trapped in straight women's bodies, many straight women reinforce gender stereotypes. Moreover, some gay men indicate that their straight female friends sometimes see them as caricatures of stereotypical gay men and expressed different degrees of discomfort with that perception.

Realistically, when going about daily life in our heterosexist society, it is unlikely that being a "gay man in a straight woman's body" is a consistent identity for these straight women, though they may be conscious of the ways in which they do not embody traditional femininity. The straight interviewees' use of the gay man label, however, should not be disregarded as merely a symbolic means of expressing affinity or connection with their intersectional friend. According to Strauss (1959: 15–21), language is essential to the realization of identity. Furthermore, the way one feels in relation to one another depends on what is singled out, what is given a name, and the connotations of those names.

The label "gay man trapped in a straight woman's body" appears to be related to these straight women's perceptions that they are not successfully performing or accomplishing gender (West and Zimmerman 1987) and heterosexuality (Schilt and Westbrook 2009) because they do not successfully accomplish heterosexual femininity. In describing themselves as gay men, these straight women were commenting on the rigid and limiting gender expectations surrounding heterosexual womanhood. The women's use of such language implies that the existing gender categories they occupy are too limited to encompass their felt identities to such an extent that they feel marginalized and instead relate better to alternative gender identities. Yet with the exception of Monique, many straight participants choose to use the "gay man trapped in a straight woman's body" label instead of calling themselves "queer," an identity that would place them in a more known, marginal, and broad identity category. In so doing, they reinforce their identities as straight women and thus, to some degree, maintain the heterosexual privilege that allows them to discard their "gay man" label, meaning that in most interactions the women are simply viewed as straight women—albeit, straight women who do not see themselves as able to fully accomplish femininity.

## Unconditional Love

Gender also was policed in the study by both gay and straight men, by reinforcing the social expectation that women are nurturing, which has positive and negative dimensions. Being nurturing is one of the essential qualities often assigned to women because of their potential for procreation and motherhood. In discussing their friendships with straight women, the gay male interviewees focused on the emotional benefits they gained from the friendships. Many gay men pointed to a lack of sexual tension as a purely positive quality, as it facilitated a deep connection with straight women. Manuel, a forty-two-year-old gay white man, commented on his friendship with Barbara, a fifty-nine-year-old straight white woman: "There's definitely a safety. The whole sexual tension thing is gone, you know, does not exist. And therefore I think there can be an intimacy between a gay man and a straight woman that can't exist otherwise."

The fact that both interviewees were in midlife and nearly twenty years apart in age also could have prompted the perception of safety in this bond.

Other interviewees focused on security, comfort, and stability as key benefits of the friendship. Frank, a thirty-two-year-old white gay man, explained the comfort he found in his friendship with Rebecca, a thirty-two-year-old straight mixed-race woman: "No matter how I screw up or bottom out or what horrible things I say or do or how horrible I feel about myself, I know she will always be there for me. Even in the worst situation, I know I can count on her to come help me out." Similarly, Pete, a gay Asian American man who is thirty-two, stated that his straight female friend Karyn, thirty-one, provides a sense of "comfort knowing that she'll always be there for me."

From these friendships, many gay men receive unconditional emotional support and stability, an ideal characteristic of all friendships; yet simultaneously, some equated this nurturance with motherhood. Mark described Cristina as "very maternal. That's the main thing about her. Like, she helps tuck in my sweater. I think that's not necessarily a uniqueness, but it's something that draws me to her." Hence, in some cases the emotional support is taken to the extreme, where straight female friends are viewed as embodying a mother-like role. On the one hand, this dynamic may create a positive and equal way for women to express nurturance without all of the responsibilities of motherhood, because they choose to nurture a peer. On the other hand, the characterization of the straight women as motherly or maternal seemingly equates nurturance to motherhood in an essential way. At stake here is the potential to challenge gender norms for straight women within friendships with gay men. Hence, while these intersectional friendships are contexts in which some gender expectations are relaxed, other norms are reinforced.

A related dynamic exists for lesbians in the study, but with different gender norms in place. Many of the straight men identified the benefits of their lesbian friends' emotional support in terms of their own freedom from masculine gender norms rather than describing the women as motherly. As I discussed in chapter 2, Patrick and Emily have a workplace friendship in which he discusses his perceived shortcomings because he does not worry about her judgment of his masculinity. This bond also is emotionally safe because of the lack of sexual tension between the friends. Patrick's description of his friendship with Emily, discussed in detail in chapter 2, illustrates how sex and sexual orientation regulate the tone of their friendship. As a straight man constrained by heterosexual masculine norms, Patrick is able to share his feelings of self-doubt with Emily without compromising his masculinity, because this is gender-appropriate behavior, particularly for a cross-sex friendship situated in a work context (Fine 1986; Werking 1997). What makes the intersectional friendship an even safer context for such admissions is that neither member mistakes this intimacy for romantic or sexual attraction, because, as Patrick said, the friendship lacks sexual undertones.

The preservation of gender norms is complicated in friendships between lesbian women and straight men. Many of the straight men in the study treated their lesbian friends gender-atypically by talking freely about their need to treat all women, except the lesbian friend, as sexual objects. In their interviews, many of the lesbians suggested that in their company the straight male friends had explicitly admitted to feeling released from pressures to embody masculine norms. Debbi, a thirty-nine-year-old white lesbian, explained that Carl, a forty-three-year-old straight white man, articulated this sentiment: "He actually told [me] one time that it was easier for him to hang out with lesbians because he said that he doesn't feel that need to try to figure out where he stands on the 'man meter.' He's said before that it's also a safe place for him because he doesn't have to feel like he has to puff up or act different or whatever. He can just be himself." Debbi further explained that she perceives Carl as sizing up every woman he meets in terms of either having or lacking sexual potential and commented, "I think it's sad for him." Charlene, a twenty-eight-year-old white lesbian, similarly characterized her straight male friend, Alec:[3] "More than anyone else I know, he's interested in every woman he meets, in a sexual way. He either dismisses them immediately or is interested in them. There's not a whole lot of in-between, and I think I was the exception: . . . 'Here comes one who won't sleep with him.' I'm the one that's going to stick, right? Everyone else is ruled out." These passages illustrate the complicated gender norms that lesbian and straight male participants play out in the context of their friendships and help to illustrate the strong pressures that hegemonic masculinity places on straight men more broadly.

In these examples, the straight male participants assigned a dual identity to lesbian friends, which constituted gender policing. On the one hand, the lesbian friends are viewed in a traditional feminine role, which allows the male friend to discuss his feelings of frustration about masculinity and be vulnerable without threatening his masculinity. On the other hand, the lesbian women are simultaneously viewed as inherently and essentially different from the straight male interviewees' objects of desire. To some extent, these men have it right: lesbian women experience different gender roles than straight women (Levitt and Hiestand 2004). Yet these same straight men often turn to their lesbian friends for insight into romantic relationships with women. Jill, a thirty-one-year-old mixed-race lesbian, explained how this surfaces in the friendship with her thirty-seven-year-old straight white friend, Paul: "He's asked me advice about being in a relationship with a woman. 'What do they want?' I'm trying to figure it out, too, and I'm a woman. [Women] want to talk a lot; they want to, you know, talk about their feelings, and, you know, it's like its maintenance, you know. Give me the oil change on the car, you know. It's like you have to maintain it. . . . They just want you to listen; they don't want you to solve the problem." Paul also admitted to asking Jill for advice about having sexual relationships with women and said he often says, "OK . . . come on—give me some pointers."

This aspect of the relationship does not work in the reverse; none of the lesbians in the study said that they ask their straight male friends for advice about relationships with women, even though many of the straight men were in long-term relationships and marriages. Specifically, Vanessa explained that she never talked about sexual relationships with Bruce; instead, she talked to her lesbian friends. The lesbian participants likely understand that there are differences between lesbian and straight women's experiences and embodiments of gender, which affects their romantic relationships, and which therefore makes asking men about how to behave with lesbian partners illogical. In particular, lesbian gender expressions include femme and butch identities, which position women differently in terms of appearance and how they engage in romantic relationships with other women (Levitt and Hiestand 2004, 2005). While we may try to heterosexualize the lesbian genders of femme and butch by viewing them as equivalent to masculinity and femininity, they are not the same (Levitt and Hiestand 2004, 2005).

For many of the straight men I interviewed, however, the friend's sex was sufficient to confer authority about women's desires in relationships; the men did not necessarily recognize the gender distinctions among lesbians as being potentially different from those of straight women. Antonio, a twenty-eight-year-old straight Latino in a friendship dyad with Justine, a thirty-six-year-old mixed-race lesbian, aptly characterized the dynamic: "With a lesbian, you have the benefits of you get to talk to this woman, you get to know [the] inside and see the world that women have. At the same time, since you know there isn't that sexual tension there, you might be willing to be more open with her than with someone who you might consider a potential girlfriend or something." Hence, in this context many straight men indicated that they felt freed from some constraints and expectations of hegemonic masculinity in terms of needing to impress women as potential sexual partners. The perception that hegemonic masculinity is somewhat relaxed in these contexts allows straight men to be more open and honest about their feelings than they are with straight women. Antonio's statements indicate that having a lesbian friend allows him to know women and their worlds more fully, yet in their behavior the straight men do not consistently view their friends as female and lesbian—at least, in terms of viewing their sex as distinct from their genders and orientations.

Many of the lesbian participants' comments suggest that through their intersectional friendship they gain benefits of association with a straight and male perspective. For example, Debbi remarked that when she is with Carl, she feels a sense of personal safety:

> There have been times that I was really glad that he was with me or us because I felt safer, because he's, like, six foot three or six foot four. He's a little on the thin side, but he's very athletic, so I do kind of feel safer. So there's kind of that escort thing going on, and I think that there's kind of a sense—I'm not a small person, but I think there is kind of a sense that it's nice to have a big guy around. . . . There is also—I mean, if I were to go someplace with him, you don't have to worry about being approached by other guys, because they think you're with him, whereas if you're with a group of girls, it's kind of like open season.

Debbi thus enjoys the security of being in public without having to worry about her safety and being approached or leered at by men when she is with Carl.

Other participants noted that their friendships with straight men allow them to gain insight into men's lives. Cassandra, a twenty-nine-year-old queer white woman, relied heavily on her friendship with her thirty-five-year-old straight white friend, Stuart, when her transsexual partner transitioned from female to male. "I probably would have had a really hard time with Leo's transition, whereas I didn't so much," Cassandra recalled. "I mean, there were issues, a lot of them I talked to Stuart about, because he's a bio[logical] guy.[4] . . . I made him answer all these questions about puberty, because Leo's going to go through it. I'm like, 'How often did you think about sex when you were this age? OK, so how fast did your penis grow?' Do you know what I mean? I was asking all of these crazy questions. And he would answer all of them. So I think Leo's transition would have been really difficult for me and maybe even impossible [without Stuart]."

While a transitioning female-to-male (FTM) individual likely will experience gender and sexual development very differently than a straight person born male, a FTM physical transition includes a period of puberty. Cassandra turned to Stuart to coach her through what she could expect of Leo's body during this period because she felt comfortable asking him about his experiences in puberty.

Debbi's and Cassandra's accounts illustrate another paradox in intersectional friendship. As previously discussed, many straight male participants benefited from relaxed hegemonic masculine norms through friendships with lesbians. Yet the lesbian women in the study also identified access to male privilege and traditional masculinity as an asset of their intersectional friendships. Clearly, there are benefits of maleness and masculinity, one of which is men's privilege to be able to walk in public without fear of harassment or violence. Unlike the other friendship compositions in the study, some lesbian participants situated the unique benefits of having a straight male friend as centered in the intersection of the social and physical experiences of being a man (i.e., the meanings and experiences of safety and puberty in male bodies). Perhaps, the lesbian participants focused on their straight male friends' essential elements of masculinity because they were more likely to expect emotional connection elsewhere—from women, in particular. What is distinct in the friendships between lesbians and straight men is that the level of emotional support does not appear to go both ways. Justine explained that she and her straight male friend, Antonio, "don't get emotional. I save that for my female friends." In any event, some lesbians in the study served as a respite from, and reinforced, some traditional aspects of masculinity in their intersectional friendships.

To summarize, in these friendships, gender is policed in various ways, according to the sex and sexual orientation of the dyad members. Gay men in the study reinforce straight women's femininity by focusing on their appearance and expecting nurturance. Straight men who were interviewed also expect their lesbian friends to be nurturing and reported that their intersectional friend-ships are contexts with relaxed expectations of masculine norms. Yet these straight men see their lesbian friends' sex as their primary status while also viewing them as fundamentally different from straight women. In particular, these straight men look to their lesbian friends to provide insight about women and overlook the possibility that there are differences between lesbian and straight women in general, as well as in their expectations about relationships. Many of the lesbian interviewees noted that they value straight men's physi-cal contributions but do not seek emotional support from their intersectional friends when they are having problems; rather, they seek out other lesbians for emotional assistance. This dynamic reinforces the stereotype that straight men are not as emotionally adept as women and, particularly, lesbians. Finally, straight women in the study police gender by reinforcing the stereotypical expectation that gay men are hypersexual and effeminate and by treating gay men as a homogenous group.

## GENDER OUTLAWS

In these friendships, gender outlaw behavior co-occurs with gender policing. To promote or embrace gender outlaw behavior is to encourage and embody gender-nonconforming attitudes and behavior. This is to say that intersectional bonds in the study have elements that promote both gender transgression and convention. One challenge to gender norms is present in the shared activities of the lesbians and straight men. Many of the lesbian and straight male partici-pants share interests and engage in various activities that, arguably, are related to hegemonic forms of masculinity (though these norms are changing rapidly). Debbi listed the activities she participated in with Carl: "We used to play basket-ball together; we've actually run together; we swim together." Likewise, Char-lene stated that she and her friend, Alec, "play pool a lot. That's the fundamen-tal common interest." I am not suggesting that playing sports is fundamentally not feminine, but in terms of normative gender, activities such as playing pool are associated more with masculinity than femininity. When men and women participate in sports together free of the presence of potential romantic or sexual interest, the behavior constitutes gender transgression because it chal-lenges normative expectations of male–female interaction, given strong social pressures toward compulsory heterosexuality (Connell 1995; West and Zim-merman 1987).

The lesbian interviewees also challenged social norms that require being female to coincide with conventional forms of femininity. For instance, Antonio described his friendship with Justine: "[She] sort of fills the male niche in my friends here. I share the interests with her that I would share with other [guys]." Charlene discussed her affinity for male friends: "More of my friends have been straight men than anything else. . . . My best friends were always boys, partly because I was a tomboy, [though] I don't think that was all of it. . . . I never liked the doll stuff and just wasn't into that sort of thing, so I could play better games with boys. I think that was mostly what it was about. So maybe that's the basis for it now. I don't know." When men and women perform the same activities together, particularly if the activities they mutually perform are marked by gender, they disrupt the essential nature of these activities and thus constitute a radical gendered act (West and Zimmerman 1987). By participating in activities socially coded as male, a lesbian friend challenges the male domain of activities as masculine. In such contexts, lesbians participate in—and, perhaps, create—a female form of masculinity, which Halberstam (1998: 9) described as "a queer subject position that can successfully challenge hegemonic models of gender conformity." The friends themselves do not seem to recognize themselves as challenging gender norms in these contexts, however. Consistent with prior research findings, these friends enjoy similar activities and report their friendships to be full of camaraderie (Levitt and Hiestand 2004).

## A Woman in a Man's Body

Gender and gender expression were sometimes confounded in the lesbian–straight man pairs. The lesbians in the study enjoyed the masculine-coded activities in which they engaged with their straight male friends at the same time that they valued their male friends' gender-nonconforming behavior. While not as common a characterization as a "gay man trapped in a straight woman's body," some straight men in the study were described as being women or lesbians in men's bodies. This label was invoked not by the straight man but by his lesbian friend. For example, Vanessa characterized the differences between herself and Bruce: "He watches films, and I watch movies. Something's got to get blown up for me to be interested [laughs]. I think maybe he's really a lesbian and I'm really a straight guy. It would explain so much." Here, Vanessa playfully comments more on their inversely gendered interests than on Bruce's sexual orientation; but she also jokingly refers to herself as a "straight guy." The humorous way that Vanessa describes both her own and Bruce's behavior seemingly reflects her awareness that she is applying stereotypes rather than questioning gender identity in an authentic manner in this instance.

Straight men who freely display emotions are seen as breaking gender norms. For instance, Jill described her friend Paul: "He's so nurturing, and I always say that he's very in touch with his feminine side; he's a woman in a man's body." Jill is not the only one who has noticed Paul's gender-nonconforming behavior. Paul explained: "I definitely understand [Jill] and try to understand the things I don't understand, and people tease. Like I said, I have some [jock friends] who call me a woman in a man's body or stuff like that. . . . I've been hanging out with [Jill] for so long. I've [also] been single for a lengthy period of time, so friends who aren't used to seeing that ask me if I'm gay, that sort of thing." Paul's defying of gender expectations and showing of emotional characteristics typically associated more with femininity thus has caused his sexual orientation to be questioned, a common example of social sanctioning for acting as a gender outlaw (Kimmel 2000). Many of the lesbian participants attributed the closeness of their intersectional bond to the straight man's tenuous relationship with conventional masculinity. As Margaret said about her affection for her straight friend, Guy: "The thing I love about him so much is that he has no insecurities about stuff, and there's nothing macho about him. And he's totally a guy. He's very much a guy's guy, but . . . we were hanging out one time, and he ended up trying on this dress, kind of hippie-ish, and he totally tried it on and said, 'I don't know, it's a little airy.' He is just so cute."

Other lesbians in the study explained that their straight male friends had played important roles in helping them to trust men. Cassandra identified one of many ways that her friendship with Stuart has affected her: "[Stuart] changed how men could be in my head because he's gentle and loving and we have absolutely no weird sexual anything. You know, I grew up thinking that men were fucked up sexually—I guess, really not thinking that intellectually, but kind of knowing it and knowing that I was a sexual something for them to consume. There's never been anything like that with him, so he really did help me kind of accept that there could be men who were sexual but were not disgusting." In their friendships with lesbians, straight male participants who countered expectations of hegemonic masculinity were supported and valued for their transgressions. This process contradicts the perception that masculine behavior (and gender) corresponds with sex and thus exposes the friendship's potential to challenge gender norms.

## The "Fag Hag"

Many of the straight women I interviewed noted that in their friendships with gay men they experience a relationship that has a different set of expectations from bonds with straight men. Karyn explained how she views gay masculine norms: "I think just the behaviors and encouragement that you get in the gay culture to sort of cultivate connections and sort of being verbal—you kind of get to drop a lot of the masculine walls for things that I think just benefits relationships. And [gay men] get to sort of not feel like they have to hold back, and they're sort of encouraged by one another to do that, so I think that just makes you closer." Some of the straight female friends seemed to idealize gay men as a substitute for heterosexual relationships. Crystal identified the benefit of having a close gay male friend: "I think that it can be really, really good for a woman like me, who's single, to have that kind of a male energy and that male relationship in my life, because I don't feel . . . deprived of male companionship, even though I'm a single woman." Women like Crystal who seek out the attention of gay men are often considered "fag hags," a derisive term used to characterize women who associate with gay men (Moon 1995; Nardi 1999). The fag-hag characterization has varying meanings, from straight women who simply like the company of gay men to women who want to date and be sexually involved with gay men (Nardi 1999).

An alternative meaning of the term "fag hag" is that a woman is acting in gender-non-normative ways (Maddison 2000). Both Ruth and Monique referred to themselves as fag hags, but almost as a term of pride. Zoë shared her insider perspective: "I know all the terms. I hate 'fag hag,' but I do like 'fairy princess' and 'queen bee.' I don't like 'fruit fly.' There are all these terms. I can be down with some of them; some of them I find really offensive. I kind of typify [these labels] not by any kind of conscious choice; it just kind of has happened." Zoë's description that such relationships just "kind of happen" does not account for the possibility that she and other straight women in the sample actively promoted gender outlaw behavior through their friendships. In fact, some of the straight women in the sample seemed to seek out men who act in gender-nonconforming ways and who encourage the women to do the same. Maddison (2000) identifies such behavior as acts of "gender dissent," because these women dis-align themselves with heterosexual patriarchy.

The intersectional friendships between the gay male and straight female participants allow women to express and be appreciated for gender-atypical behavior. Zoë described the significant benefits she reaps in friendships with gay men:

> You get to be a whole person. Back when I was younger and more concerned with these things, I didn't have to be feminine. I could be myself, and I could be loud, and I could be funny, and I could be bawdy, and all of those things would be totally embraced. That's what people would think was great about me, as opposed to [being considered] unfeminine. . . . I think I gave up that whole concept, but earlier in my evolution, I think I thought I had to be a certain way—how you're supposed to eat like a bird and all that stupid stuff; do aerobics; be a certain size and all of those things. None of that mattered. And, you know, my gay friends certainly will aesthetically appreciate that perhaps in somebody, but it wasn't going to be a part of my being in their life, because they thought I was great, and I could take up space and be myself.

The benefits of being a gender outlaw that Monique, Zoë, and other straight female interviewees have experienced draws attention to the gender policing to which they are subjected on a daily basis. Through intersectional friendships, these straight women are encouraged to "take up space" and be themselves by gay men who also act as gender outlaws.

Earlier in the chapter, I discussed how gay male interviewees police gender with respect to a straight women's embodiment of conventional attractiveness. Yet gay men also urge women to be gender outlaws by accepting and celebrating their bodies. Jesse explained that he encourages Monique to reject social pressures about appearance and feel good about her physique: "Monique hasn't always been as confident as she should be. I think I've played an essential role in helping her to feel more confident. You know, 'cause she's beautiful, and I think a lot of times, especially with women, they don't realize their own inherent worth. 'So you've got a big ass. Be one with it!' That's what I told her. That's a quote. She's like, 'My ass is so big. I can't wear this.' I'm like, 'Be one with your big ass! Ain't nobody want a fucking bone but a dog, and he buries it!'"

Monique agreed that Jesse has had a positive influence on her self-confidence: "My friend and I are more like big, strapping Amazons, not VIP house music club-type girls, and he's always been like, 'Girl, you're a queen. Go with it.' You know what I mean? He's always encouraged us to be one with our hips." From Jesse, Monique receives positive male attention that simultaneously encourages her to buck gender norms by feeling confident about herself, whatever her size.

## Sexual Liberation

Another expression of gender outlaw behavior in these friendships occurs in relation to sex. Friendships between gay men and straight women in the study were contexts in which sexual behavior and desire were frankly discussed and encouraged, which counters norms of conventional femininity but reinforces expectations of gay masculinity. Karyn considered the effect of gay male sexuality on straight women:

> [Gay men] talk about sexuality so much, and they're just so open and you share things, so it sort of elicits that from you in a way that I don't think I would ever literally talk about my sexual habits with my straight male friends. Even though they'll occasionally make jokes or innuendos or whatever, we sort of stay at that level, where at times, when we [Karyn and her gay male friends] have all gone skiing or are drinking wine or whatever, it gets very literal, and I [don't] mind that as much, and I think it's like I will never sleep with any of you; therefore, I can actually say this stuff in a way that I won't worry that it's going to come back to haunt me at some other point.

In the company of gay men, Karyn feels free to discuss her sexuality and sexual behavior without fear of reproach. This enables her to act outside normative expectations for women and freely acknowledge sexual aspects of her life.

According to the interviewees, many gay men advocate sexual activity and satisfaction for their straight female friends. Leyla explained that Ethan has encouraged her to be more willing to see herself as a sexual person and to be physically intimate (as far as her comfort level allows) in her relationships: "So [Ethan] helped me become more comfortable with my own sexuality, so there you go. . . . But I'm more comfortable now; I mean, I decked a guy once for trying to kiss me, and now I don't do that. Well, number one, [if I hadn't met Ethan] I probably wouldn't be so open to this whole idea of, like, physical intimacy. In all honesty, I probably wouldn't be dating. He's really opened my mind to that." During the course of her interview, Leyla reported that she was in a relationship with her first boyfriend, a development encouraged by Ethan. For Leyla and other straight women in the study, gay male friends urged them to be open and positive about sex and claim sexual agency.

What the gay men gained from these intersectional friendships with respect to being gender outlaws was less apparent overall, but particularly in discussions about sex, as they reported turning to other gay men to discuss sex and relationships. Candid conversation about sex is a gendered expectation of men, and even more so of gay men. Thus, they may be less reliant on their straight female friends for such discussions. Gary, for example, said he does not share intimate details about sex with Zoë: "Certainly I'll talk with other friends, or especially other [gay] guy friends. You know, I'll talk [about sex] in much more detail. . . . I mean sexually 'cause other guys are having sex with other guys, so they sort of get it."

Seth held a similar view: "It just seems like it's a lot easier for me to talk to my gay male friends about sex and relationships than it is to talk to [Shayna] because they relate [better]." Thus, straight women in the study value the context of their intersectional friendship as a space to talk freely about sex and sexuality, while the gay men I interviewed turned to other gay men to talk about their own sexual behavior. In this example, the norm-breaking potential of intersectional friendships is realized for straight women, but not for gay men.

In general, the gay men in the study placed less emphasis on the opportunity for intersectional friendships to encourage gender-nonconforming behavior, perhaps because norms of gay masculinity consider a broader range of emotions and activities to be acceptable than do norms of hegemonic (straight) masculinity (Nardi 1999). Thus, gay men are less likely to turn to intersectional friends for gender outlaw support. Moreover, as Nardi (1999: 117) discussed, gay and lesbian social movements often have been a source of redefining traditional gender roles and sexuality: "So, for example, when gay men exhibit more disclosing and emotional interactions with other men, it demonstrates the limitations of male gender roles typically enacted among many heterosexual male friends. By calling attention to the impact of homophobia on heterosexual men's lives, gay men's friendships illustrate the potentiality for expressive intimacy among all men." In their interviews, gay men rarely identified support for gender nonconformity as an asset of their intersectional friendships. However, the straight women in the study consistently named this as a valued part of relationships with gay men. This finding suggests that many intersectional friends in the study positively reinforce gender-nonconforming behavior, even though gay men do not identify this practice as an asset unique to relationships with straight women.

The support of gender outlaw behavior and identities is evident in each type of intersectional dyad in the study. The gay men I interviewed encouraged straight women to be comfortable with their bodies and to claim sexual agency. They also provided straight women with male company that felt free of sexual expectations and full of acceptance. Many straight men in the study reported that their relationships with lesbian friends allowed hegemonic gender norms to be relaxed. As a result, in their friendships with lesbians, they felt able to share feelings of personal weakness, a dimension that counters norms of hegemonic masculinity. The lesbians in the study acted as gender outlaws in their friendships with straight men by engaging in mutually enjoyable activities. In addition, the lesbians I interviewed gained insight and developed a greater understanding of the heterogeneity of straight men's lives through these friendships, which results in a greater degree of empathy toward men.

Gay men and lesbians in the study did not benefit as gender outlaws to the extent that straight individuals do vis-à-vis these friendships. This is not to say that the straight friends do not value the gay men's and lesbian women's gender nonconformity; rather, it likely reflects support of gender nonconformity by other gay men and lesbian women. Overall, the straight men and straight women I interviewed reaped the greatest benefits in terms of support for gender nonconformity in intersectional friendships. The lesbians and gay men in the study appeared to have greater support for gender nonconformity or outlaw behavior within their lesbian and gay communities, so they may have been less reliant on their connections to straight people to provide this avenue for acceptance.

## GENDER COPS AND ROBBERS

In my critique of gender policing and gender outlaw behavior, my intention is not to downplay the benefits that gender policing can sometimes have in bolstering individuals' esteem. When gay men value and praise straight women for their appearance, they make the women feel good about themselves. Given the social context, in which women's appearance is regulated informally, receiving compliments about one's comportment can provide a very real ego boost and promote self-acceptance. Likewise, being someone to whom friends turn for nurturance and unconditional emotional support can make an individual feel valued, which is an important part of belonging to communities. On a related note, many straight men are proud of their male bodies and gain esteem from providing a sense of security to their female friends. My scrutiny of each of these dynamics is not intended to downplay or disparage the positive benefits that some individuals reap from gender policing; indeed, these cases represent successful accomplishments of gender (West and Zimmerman 1987). My intention is to critique the gender norms that exist and show the durability of gender within our social context. The benefits that arise from successful performances of gender reinforce social inequalities based on the ways that men and women "do" traditional forms of gender, so that they emphasize the cultural norms that men and women are inherently and essentially different. That many of the interviewees valued the dimensions of intersectional friendships that allowed them to act as gender outlaws illustrates the limitations that exist in the traditional gender norms that are policed in various ways.

My emphases on the incomplete gender transgressions in intersectional friendships are connected to broader scholarship about intergroup relationships. According to prior social psychological studies, close contact between people from different social locations is expected to increase tolerance of social differences (Herek and Capitanio 1996). Hence, we expect intersectional friendships to challenge social norms. By forming close friendships across sex and sexual-orientation categories, intersectional friendships challenge compulsory heterosexuality (Rich 1980). Indeed, intersectional friends who participated in this study encouraged gender outlaw behavior; however, they also policed gender within the friendships. All categories of interviewee (gay men, lesbians, straight women, and straight men) both reinforced and challenged gender norms by policing and encouraging gender outlaw behavior. This tension exposes the strong structural aspects of gender; even in friendships that challenge social norms, it is nearly impossible to escape conventions. In revealing this tension, the intersectional friendships I studied demonstrate how people create and re-create gender in everyday interaction. Specifically, in the moments in which individuals acted as gender outlaws, they disrupted social expectations that dictate an innate connection between sex and gender. Within these intersectional friendships, individuals do not "do" gender in a traditional sense, because their behavior does not easily align with predictable sex and sexual-orientation categories (West and Zimmerman 1987). Instead, they reinforce the idea that masculinity does not need to coincide with a male body, and femininity does not need to coincide with a female body (Green 1987). Still, the interactions within these intersectional friendships are not wholly transgressive or conventional. Rather, they have the potential to transform men's and women's interaction within a structural context that closely regulates gender and sexual orientation.

# 5

# WHAT'S SEX GOT

# TO DO WITH IT?

*Our sexuality is just a small part of our lives, and people need to drop that issue. I think gender and sexuality both shouldn't be a factor. And the more the close friendships occur, the less those things matter.*

—Janet, a thirty-five-year-old white lesbian

## JUSTINE AND ANTONIO

Justine and Antonio met in a comic book store in Miami in the early 1990s. Antonio is a twenty-eight-year-old straight Latino, and Justine is a thirty-six-year-old mixed-race lesbian. One afternoon more than a decade ago, Justine rode into the store on her skateboard and met a group of guys who were role-playing game regulars. Antonio was part of that group. Justine sat in on the game and before long she started showing up regularly to role-play. Shortly thereafter, Justine and Antonio strayed from the group, playing games and going to movies together. Antonio recalls that he knew that Justine was a lesbian when he met her because of her appearance (she had a shaved head and wore baggy clothes), but he did not know what to say to her about her sexual orientation. About a month into their friendship, she came out to Antonio by introducing him to her girlfriend. Justine always assumed that Antonio was straight, though she did not say why that was the case.

When asked to chronicle the development of their friendship, each has a different recollection about how it progressed. What is clear is that after a couple years of intensive time together, Antonio and Justine started spending less time together. Antonio attributes these gaps to changing interests; Justine attributes their drifting apart to rebuking Antonio for making a romantic overture toward her. Justine recalls that at some later point, they talked about the incident; he apologized; and their friendship resumed, stronger than before. The pair lost touch when Justine moved to the Bay Area in 1997. When Antonio relocated to the Bay Area a year later, Justine contacted him through a mutual friend, and they rekindled their friendship. Now they see each other at least once a month and talk on the phone weekly.

When Antonio and Justine spend time together, they most often play videogames. Some of their favorite times together have been sleepovers when they played games into the early morning hours. They also go to amusement parks and gaming conventions. Justine notes that they have cruised women together at these conventions but usually are unsuccessful because people assume they are a couple.

While they share interests, Antonio and Justine are not always equally on board with sharing intimate details about relationships and emotions. Antonio is more likely to share his feelings than Justine, who talks to other lesbians about what is on her mind. They also do not talk about politics or religion because they have dramatically different and conflicting views: Justine is the more politically progressive of the two and practices a pagan religion, while Antonio is admittedly more conservative and was raised Catholic. Yet Justine's friendship with Antonio provides a unique space for her to be genuinely herself because she does not feel judged by him. She views Antonio as a respite from what she calls the politically correct lesbian culture of the Bay Area. Justine likes that she can say whatever she wants to Antonio without having to process the meaning of her comments, as would be necessary if she were talking to other lesbians. At the same time, Antonio credits Justine with helping him to become more open-minded.

While they share many interests, Justine's and Antonio's differences limit the scope of activities they do together. For example, Justine often balks at the conventions of straight relationships that are the backbone of much of mainstream popular culture. For example, they went together to see the opera La Boheme but found that they experienced it in vastly different ways. Antonio describes this and similar incidents as "culture clashes." These clashes keep Antonio from inviting Justine to events that are considered more mainstream or cultured, such as going to high tea or a fine restaurant. As a result, Antonio's and Justine's lives are not enmeshed. Instead, Antonio and Justine compare their bond to that of Bert and Ernie on Sesame Street or Han Solo and Chewbacca from Star Wars. They are each other's sidekick, partner in crime, or playmate, but not each other's primary support.

ONE OF THE guiding themes in the film When Harry Met Sally was the much pondered question, "Can men and women be friends?" Presuming universal heterosexuality, Harry claims that men and women cannot be friends because the man always wants to have sex with the woman, which limits the extent to which they can truly be friends. Sally argues the counterpoint but develops romantic feelings for Harry after they have sex. While Harry and Sally had been platonic friends for many years before having sex, the film culminates with their wedding and thus answers the question with a resounding "No!" Indeed, in the movie, sex intervenes and confirms that friendship between men and women is possible only within marriage. Sociological research, however, has determined otherwise and concludes that straight men and women maintain meaningful, long-term friendships (Allan 1989; O'Meara 1989; Swain 1992; Werking 1997), although they often endure conflict in the defiance of social norms that dictate that such relationships should be romantic pairings.

What happens when men and women from different sexual orientations come together? Can they be friends? Presumably, such friendships would be characterized by the absence of sexual tension and possibility. Would that not open up the possibility that men and women could unproblematically maintain a friendship? While these questions have infused the entirety of this book, in this chapter I focus specifically on the complex ways that sexuality and emotional intimacy shape intersectional friendships into "queer relationships" that provide connection and commitment in defiance of norms of compulsory heterosexuality.

Given representations in popular culture, it appears that the ideal friendship exists between gay men and straight women. If we look to television's now defunct *Will and Grace*, for example, the answer to the question "Can men and women be friends?" changes to an unquestionable "Yes! Gay men and straight women are the *best* of friends." Yet even in this simplified portrayal, all is not what it seems in terms of sexuality and sexual tension. Through flashbacks and discussions, we learn that Will and Grace had been romantically involved in the past, even though the story's arch clearly shows that, despite Grace's best efforts to seduce Will, they never had a sexual relationship. Still, in the show the friendship was often portrayed in sexualized terms, as one episode had Will fantasizing about Grace, while another had the pair share a romantic kiss amid wedding decorations. Although these dimensions of the show have been (very appropriately) attributed to efforts to heterosexualize it (Quimby 2005), they can be read as depicting a more complicated relationship than one that is entirely free of sexual tension. Instead, the show hinted at the complicated negotiation of both sexuality and intimacy that many people navigate in intersectional friendships. This is not to say that all intersectional friendship dyads experience sexual tension; rather, it acknowledges that like sexuality itself, desire, attraction, and identity are experienced on a continuum, where meaning is not necessarily fixed.

## RESISTING ROMANTIC SCRIPTS

Complex social identities such as sexual orientation exist within a society that holds heterosexuality as the norm and in which the only acceptable context to experience sex and intimacy is marriage between a man and a woman. As a result, expressions of sexual orientation and attraction rarely manifest in consistent ways, both in society at large and, particularly, within the intersectional friendships I studied. The intersectional friends I interviewed negotiated sexual boundaries and struggled with and against fitting these friendships into accepted heterosexual relational norms. While earlier chapters showed the unique dimensions of intersectional friendships in resisting social norms and expectations, we have yet to fully explore how these friendships often resemble heterosexual romantic pairings, even as the participants struggle to define themselves differently. Typically, these relationships are platonic, and participants do not view them as having romantic potential, but as these friendships assume the tone of intimacy and commitment that is commonly understood as the domain of romantic couplings, the meanings of such relationships become less clear.

Society is built on norms of compulsory heterosexuality—that is, the expectation that women will be oriented toward men as sexual and romantic partners and men will likewise be oriented toward women (Rich 1980). Due to the cross-sex nature of these friendships and the existing norms of compulsory heterosexuality, the line between what constitutes a friendship and a romantic relationship can become blurred, both for those in the relationship and for those who interact with the pair. Furthermore, similar to friendships between cross-sex heterosexuals (Allan 1989; O'Meara 1989; Swain 1992), these relationships are scriptless, meaning that there are no commonly understood norms for how gay men and straight women and lesbians and straight men who maintain close ties (and are not biologically or legally related) are to behave. In some instances, sexual tension or attraction, imagined to be impossible for someone identified as attracted to people of the same sex, complicated the intersectional friendships in this study and sometimes obscured the fact that, while sexuality is imagined to be a fixed identity, it is in fact more fluid than we often acknowledge.

Scripting theory can elucidate why intersectional friendships are subject to expectations of romantic coupling. According to Gagnon and Simon (1973), sexual behavior is enacted and interpreted according to external and internal dimensions, which comprise scripts. With respect to the external, individuals' actions are guided by mutually shared norms that allow them to interact successfully with others. The external dimension encompasses the cultural definitions of sexual behavior, from language to actions. The internal dimension of sexual scripts occurs when individuals apply their own meanings to interactions according to the external norms of sexual behavior. Gagnon and Simon (1973: 19) illustrated how sexual scripts guide behavior: "It is . . . our collective blindness to or ineptitude in locating and defining these scripts that has allowed biology to explain sexual behavior. . . . Without the proper elements of a script that defines the situation, names the actors, and plots the behavior, nothing sexual is likely to happen. . . . Combining such elements as desire, privacy, and a physically attractive person of the appropriate sex, the probability of something sexual happening will remain exceedingly small until either one or both actors organize these behaviors into an appropriate script." In organizing behavior into scripts, social actors decode ambiguous and overt sexual behavior, define boundaries for their own sexual responses, and link nonsexual to sexual aspects of life. Sexual scripts thus drive sexual behavior and help individuals to learn social and sexual roles.

Sexual scripts help us to identify circumstances as potentially sexual so that we know how to interact with and give meaning to social exchanges and relationships. Scripts serve as a guide for understanding behavior and circumstances. For example, when I interact with another person, I may assess the sexual potential of the interaction in various ways. Is the person I am interacting with an "appropriate" sexual partner for me? Do I feel sexually attracted to this person? Is the context of the interaction imbued with sexual possibility? Why? If I go to dinner and a movie with a man, as a straight woman, how do I know that this is or is not a romantic interaction? How should I interpret strong feelings of affection for a man? How about for a woman?

Most of us have had interactions that deviated from our known sexual or romantic scripts. We know that our interaction has been guided by a defective script when we question why we perceived an individual's actions as sexual when they were not or when we were oblivious to another's sexual come-ons. This occurs because we rely on sexual scripts to outline expectations and decode behavior. However, sexual scripts are not "one size fits all." Norms of compulsory heterosexuality guide sexual scripts so that we often deem interactions between all men and women as having sexual potential and ignore the possibility of same-sex sexual scripts: this practice occurs in the segregation of men and women into same-sex bathrooms and college dormitories. Furthermore, the same actions have different scripted meanings depending on who is doing the acting. When I spend the evening drinking and dancing at a bar with a female friend, I am having a "girls' night out." When I spend the evening drinking and dancing with a man I just met, I am abiding by a sexual script that says we may end up having sex. Conversely, a lesbian who is following a same-sex script likely will view these behaviors in a different light.

Sexual scripts are significant in how we, and the members of the friendship dyads I am discussing, understand intersectional friendships. Because they exist outside compulsory heterosexuality norms, the available scripts may be inadequate; we may not understand how to interpret intersectional friends' actions in the way that we more readily understand the scripts in other cross-sex relationships. As a result, some intersectional friends who share intimate bonds may find themselves unable to distinguish how these bonds of friendship differ from sexual and romantic bonds, since the behavior and feelings may resemble those in other relationships, even as the context remains different. For instance, Jill discussed her decision to stop sharing an apartment with Paul because their relationship had begun to resemble a heterosexual romantic relationship:

> One of the most difficult times I'd say would be deciding whether or not to move out, because we had lived together for about five years. . . . I just felt like I was overly dependent on him. I had been with him for five years, and I just felt like I really needed to be independent, separate from him, just find my own identity, because it just became enmeshed. It was just such a—You know. I cleaned the house; he did the grocery shopping. It just felt too couply, you know? And I just really felt like it would be stronger if we just took some space from each other and did our own thing, and I think it was a really good thing, because now we have separate identities, and we come together and be separate people and still are really solid friends. . . . It just became confusing, and people were just telling me from the outside—I mean, I sort of felt that way—but people from the outside were saying, "Jill, you know, you guys are boyfriend and girlfriend without having sex." And that didn't feel good to me, because I felt like I was blocking other people out of my life because he was such a big part of it.

Here, Jill was uncomfortable with both her own and others' observations that she and Paul were essentially acting as a heterosexual couple. Arguably, their behavior, division of household labor, and interdependence could be identified as those of friends or roommates helping each other. However, the social expectations of male–female interaction scripted their behavior as that of a romantic couple. With that powerful lens, no other interpretations were as viable.

Overall, the participants described their friendships in three distinct ways with respect to their perception of romantic feelings, sexual tension, and expectations of emotional intimacy within the relationship. The majority of participants articulated that their friendships were free of sexual tension, a feature that was presented as strengthening the friendship. A second group of participants acknowledged hints of sexual tension or sexualized behavior within their friendships and, perhaps, some feelings of unrequited romantic attraction by one or both of the individuals at some point during the tenure of the relationship. The third, least common group of participants had ongoing, sexual relationships or had experienced a degree of sexual tension or romantic interest that influenced the overall relationship. In the next section, I address the unique aspects of each grouping of individuals and highlight the benefits and challenges of friendships in which sexuality is actively and passively negotiated.

## NO SEX EQUALS CLOSER FRIENDSHIP

For most friendships in the study, sexual interest and attraction were not issues that needed to be negotiated or managed. In fact, a lack of sexual tension and possibility benefited many friendships by allowing close relationships to flourish, according to the participants. That is, to the participants in these dyads, removing the possibility of a sexual component in the relationship allowed the close relationship to develop. One way that a lack of sexual tension influences these friendship dyads is by removing the possibility of a sexual component in the relationship. According to the participants, this allows close and uncomplicated friendship interactions to develop. Karyn, a thirty-one-year-old straight white woman, described the lack of sexual tension between her and her thirty-two-year-old gay Asian friend, Pete, as "completely liberating," allowing for the closeness of their friendship.

The gay men in the study uniquely noted how a lack of sexual tension differentiates their intersectional friendship from gay male friendships. For instance, Ethan, a twenty-three-year-old gay Latino, discussed gay male–straight female friendships more generally: "I think that there would be no element of, you know, sexual frustration there—at least, not on the gay man's part. I don't know about the straight woman. But I think that there is probably more of a freedom there, just because there's not that way that straight men and straight women would interact." Ben, twenty-eight, similarly explained how the lack of sexual tension with Ming, who is also twenty-eight, has enhanced their friendship: "If anything, [my being gay and her being straight] probably got us closer. Had I been straight, there might have been a weirdness. There could be jealousy from her partner's side, and there might be some sort of tension, you know? Knowing that there will be no possibility of any personal—you know, couple-type—relationship, it's really broken down all barriers. So that's probably gotten us closer."

Intersectional friendships also provide a context in which sexual expectations can be relaxed. For example, Scott, forty-six, explained the benefits of his friendships with straight female friends such as Ruth, also forty-six, particularly in contrast to his friendships with other gay men in which sexual tension has existed: "I would think for a lot of gay men, [friendship with straight women] would be a good thing, because for gay men there's a lot of sexuality involved, and if you want to remove the sex question—It's just like a man and a woman in a straight situation that are friends. Is there sexual tension there? And if you act on that sexual tension, will it make things so awkward that things crash? So you don't have to deal with that. You can just have a friendship beyond question." Scott appreciated the asexual nature of his friendship with Ruth, contrasting it with previous experiences of having sexual friendships with other gay men: "I can say with my friend Todd, who I said I felt very much the same way [as I do about Ruth], there was that sexual tension, and there was a time when we had to ride through [trying to have a sexual relationship] . . . after knowing each other fifteen years and then finding out that this doesn't work and the awkwardness that it builds when you hurt someone going through that. It makes you not want to do it in the first place. I think it's comforting to know that [Ruth and I] don't have to deal with that. We just are friends." While many gay men sustain satisfying same-sex friendships that include a sexual component (Nardi 1999), Scott's account is representative of other interviewees who value their friendships with straight women because of the absence of sex. Straight women in the study also voiced appreciation of gay male friends because they could be emotionally intimate with them without worrying about how to negotiate sexual tension and expectations.

Several partnered interviewees recognized that the intersectional nature of their friendship provided a measure of freedom because the presumed lack of sexual tension alleviated the potential jealousy a spouse or partner might otherwise feel. James, a thirty-five-year-old straight white man, acknowledged the effect that Melissa's lesbian identification has had on their friendship while referring to his wife's friendship with a gay man:

I can't help but wonder, if Melissa was straight, [would our relationship] be an issue? . . . I mean, Kent is a friend of mine, and he's gay. [My wife] Sheila and I see him a lot, and Sheila and Kent click really well, and I think if he wasn't gay, I wouldn't feel comfortable, but as it is . . . I only feel that mild kind of jealousy that goes with the fact that they get along so well. They click in a way that Sheila and I don't all the time; they click on a different level . . . So, I'm just saying, if he was straight, it might be an issue, so if Melissa were straight, you know.

Because Melissa is a lesbian woman, she and James can maintain a very close friendship without causing Sheila to feel jealous of a potential sexual or romantic attraction. James also recognized that his wife's friendship with Kent posed no threat to their marriage because Kent is gay.

Interviewees in committed romantic relationships were cognizant of how their friends' sex and sexual identity made their partners feel comfortable. For example, Jill acknowledged that Paul's identity as a straight man allowed them to have a strong connection without suspicion or jealousy from her partner: "The person that I'm with now is very cool with Paul. I mean, she's glad that [he's] a guy and not a woman, because . . . I think she'd feel threatened by it. [She's] like, 'Who are you hanging out with? Paul? Oh, that's OK.' You know, 'Paul spent the night.' 'Oh, that's OK.'" Hence, these friends are given the freedom to forge close connections without arousing a partner's suspicions of infidelity.

Even as a friend's sexual orientation is liberating to many participants and provides reassurance to partners and spouses, some interviewees described their efforts to speculate about how their relationship would differ if they or the intersectional friends were of a different sexual orientation. Pete stated: "I'm glad with the way things are because we've got such a strong bond, but then I wonder, if I were straight, would I be attracted to Karyn, and would that have changed things? I'm guessing that would have changed a lot. She's a beautiful woman, and she's got a great personality, so I don't know." Similarly, Frank, a thirty-two-year-old white gay man, pondered how his friendship with Rebecca, who is thirty-two years old, straight, and of mixed race, might be different: "It's difficult to speculate. If I were straight, would we still have the same sort of relationship? I tend to think probably not, just because I don't think you could maintain the kind of intensity and duration of a relationship . . . if there was a sexual underpinning or undercurrent to that relationship. It would be difficult, if not impossible, I think, to maintain the kind of closeness that we've had."

Both Pete's and Frank's comments express an awareness of the difficulties that men and women often encounter in the face of strong norms of compulsory heterosexuality. In each hypothetical exploration, the interviewees defaulted to discussing how their friendship might differ if the gay male or lesbian person in the dyad were straight, rather than questioning how their friendship might be affected if the straight person were another sex or sexual orientation. This was evident in both Pete's and Frank's questioning of how their respective friendships with Karyn and Rebecca might differ if they were straight (instead of gay) men, rather than considering how changing either woman's sex might also alter the dyad. This finding reflects heterosexuality's normative social position; changing a straight person's sex or sexual orientation to be in accordance with a same-sex object of attraction appears inconceivable. Such a perception also reflects the persistence of sexual and romantic pairing as the dominant social script for male–female interaction.

## SEXUAL TENSION EQUALS COMPLICATIONS

Sexual orientation, like gender, occurs on a continuum. The spectrum of sexual orientation occurs between heterosexual and homosexual, with variation according to an individual's behavior and identity (Kinsey, Pomeroy, and Martin 1948, 1953). For straight men and women in particular, an intersectional friend's sex is consistent with that of his or her other-sex orientation; thus, it would seem more likely that sexual or romantic feelings might emerge from the straight friend. Yet because sexual orientation is experienced on the continuum, feelings of sexual attraction, both fleeting and enduring, can emerge on both sides of the intersectional friendships. Some friends in the study admitted that there are times when sexual desire, both unrequited and mutual, has arisen. Many referred to it as part of the history of the friendship. For example, while their friendship was free from any sexual tension at the time of the interview, Frank recalled the sexual tension between him and his straight friend, Rebecca, during high school: "We kind of avoid talking about one particular event. . . . It was right before we were both leaving for college, and we were both kind of considering whether we wanted to have sex and decided not to, and we've never really talked that out." Others discussed random events as "sexualized." For example, Guy, a twenty-nine-year-old straight white man, remembered one sexually charged situation with his lesbian friends, the partners Margaret and

Wallis, who are thirty-seven and thirty, respectively, and white. Guy recalled that they were washing his hair and he was undressed to his boxers, "and I'm not sure why I was dressed in my boxers to get my hair washed."

Even though the participants identify as sexually incompatible according to fixed social definitions of sexual orientation, sexual tension sometimes exists. Were sexual orientation an absolute dichotomy with fixed meanings and preferences, intersectional friends could be entirely free from sexual tension in their friendship. As many interviewees explained, this is not the case. Furthermore, sexual tension is not considered a positive attribute by the interviewees. In fact, the participants reported that when either sexual tension or unrequited romantic interest was present in a friendship, complications arose. Pointing to the complexity of sexual attraction and desire, Ken, a thirty-five-year-old mixed-race gay man, explained, "I think the easy thing that people can look at is the sexual tension aspect and say in that kind of relationship, it's not there, but as human beings, it is."

Some of the participants reported having unrequited crushes on their intersectional friend at some point in the past. Zoë, a thirty-year-old straight white woman, for example, recognized that her feelings had origins in the friend's being a safe object of her affection and did not expect reciprocation:

> I mean you can be attracted to somebody. . . . [My gay friends] tend to be really attractive, wonderful, sensitive men, so sometimes it's hard to keep, kind of shut down, what may be natural heterosexual feelings, especially if you're not having an outlet in some other way, which I tend to not have. So it becomes very easy for me to kind of take all the feelings that normally would go into a relationship, and put them on a friendship. It puts too much pressure on a friendship, and I'm getting certain needs met, but I'm not getting them met with the same intention on the other side, and that can be really hurtful. Even when you know it intellectually, it doesn't mean that you don't still want more. So, yeah, you get to have that closeness, and in some ways it does feel like a relationship, and yet it's like the pro and the con. . . . It doesn't feel good, . . . and you don't want them to be other than they are, so it's not like you want them to be straight, either, so that part is really hard.

Part of the difficulty that Zoë expressed may be related to the difference in scripts that she and her thirty-year-old white gay friend Gary each used to guide their friendship. Since intersectional friendships are scriptless, one or both of the friends may have used a common social script, the sexual script, as a guide for intense feelings of love, intimacy, and loyalty as a means for understanding their relationship. As Gagnon and Simon (1973: 23) explained, sexual scripts are complex: "The sources of arousal, passion, or excitement (the recognition of a sexual possibility), as well as the way the event is experienced (if, indeed, an event follows), derive from a complicated set of layered symbolic meanings that are not only difficult to comprehend from the observed behavior, but also may not be shared by the participants." Because Zoë does not always have an outlet for her romantic feelings, the pieced-together script that guides her friendship with Gary becomes blurred with more traditional sexual scripts. She clarified that she does not want him to be different but is aware that the available script of love and intimacy involves sexual attraction.

Both Zoë and Gary stated that they had never wanted to have a serious romantic or sexual relationship together. Nonetheless, available social scripts of heteronormativity altered how others perceive them and could be differentially frustrating. This was a source of discomfort when they took a long road trip together, according to Zoë:

> It drove him crazy when we were in the heartland driving across country. They were like, "You kids married?," and I would find it really funny. I didn't find it completely problematic in the same way he did. So it was hard when we were driving across country, because I could still have, you know, crush-type feelings for him. He was a very safe receptacle for that because, of course, he was never going to be interested and yet, you know, we could have the closeness that you could have with a partner and not have it be remotely threatening at all, you know, physically or anything like that.

Zoë's recognition that she was able to view her relationship with Gary as a "safe" way to meet her needs for intimacy illustrates how she assumed and then discarded scripts as they fit the context of the friendship and her desire for emotional intimacy. She was able to wear the script placed on her by strangers and try out a heterosexual coupling but also recognized that the script did not, and would never, fit. This temporary role-playing may be more easily available to straight members of intersectional friendships because their friend is the same sex as their sexual object choice and of the script.

Other interviewees reported unrequited sexual or romantic interest as an issue in their intersectional friendship. Justine recalled how Antonio's overtures nearly ended their friendship: "We lost touch. . . . He basically tried to pick up on me, and I didn't like that. It wasn't the act of picking up [but] the context of the situation that really pissed me off, so I stopped contact for a couple of months, and then [our interactions] became very superficial." After several years, Justine and Antonio resumed contact, discussed the incident, and rekindled their friendship. Neither suggested that sexual tension has been a recurring issue in the relationship during their interviews.

SEX AND SEXUAL TENSION

Few participants in the study acknowledged that they had acted on sexual tension or had a sexual relationship with their intersectional friend. Those friends who had acted on their sexual tension admitted that it had shaped their friendship in both positive and negative ways. One such case was Janet, a thirty-five-year-old white lesbian, and her straight friend, Jon, a thirty-eight-year-old white man. After meeting at work, Janet and Jon became friends and then began a sexual relationship. "We had a relationship, . . . an affair for eight months, something like that," Janet said. "That was obviously a great time. . . . Our worst time perhaps was right after [we broke up]. There was no reason for it, because it wasn't a bad breakup. [Our relationship] was an unrealistic thing—we both knew that's where it was going, but it just, you know, it wasn't comfortable. Suddenly we had been so close, and now we weren't." Jon's recollections provided a different perspective: "We had a huge crush on each other, and . . . it turned out to be intimate. [It] very shortly materialized into this short-lived relationship, which was a good thing. We were very attracted to each other, playful. . . . One of the things that wasn't right, you know, the physical element; there just wasn't chemistry. It was on every level except for the sexual part. I didn't, I don't have a sexual attraction to her, and, you know, really, really, there wasn't a spark there."

Janet and Jon's romantic relationship ended, but the friendship continued. Both friends explained that the period between breaking up and resuming the friendship was difficult but that they were glad to have such a close relationship now. Though both Janet and Jon are involved in long-term relationships with other people, Janet continues to feel some measure of lingering sexual and romantic interest. "It flashes through my mind; it still does, you know, like, to be together," she said. "I mean, it was a long, long time ago, but our sex life was great, and . . . I'm sure we would do really well. . . . There's still an attraction there, at least on my part. So, you know, when Jon's around, I light up. I have a great time and I feel very close to him and, you know, not in an obnoxious way, because I wouldn't want to make [his wife] uncomfortable." Despite the challenges, the friendship between Jon and Janet has remained strong, and they and their partners got along well and regularly vacationed and spent time together. Their friendship exposes a rarely discussed aspect of intersectional friendships: sexual attraction does arise and is negotiated by one or both members of some intersectional dyads.

The interviewees who indicated that they had felt attraction also reported that they had been able to mitigate sexual or romantic tension. They acknowledged feeling it but believed they managed it in ways that did not affect the friendship. Others described the ongoing challenges that unrequited attraction presented. Mitch, a forty-two-year-old Latino gay man, voiced his frustration with his straight friend, the thirty-one-year-old Latina Danae: "We've had a few challenges, . . . mostly around that whole issue of this whole romantic thing, and me kind of saying, 'No, I'm gay. It can't happen,' and her kind of wanting a little more from the relationship, so much so that when gay friends have come around, she'll be very jealous of them. . . . That was more so in the beginning, and I think now we've had seven years to deal with it, so now I think we've both just accepted that it's a good friendship."

Mitch feels that over time the issue has become less pressing. However, he recognized that Danae's ongoing jealousy and possessiveness has negatively affected their friendship, in part because of her unwillingness to initiate other relationships: "Sometimes I actually feel a little constricted, like maybe some of my freedom is gone because of the friendship . . . and she doesn't ever want to be in a relationship. [She says] that she loves our friendship and with our friendship she doesn't need a relationship. I try to convince her, 'No, no, no! We're friends. You still need a relationship.' . . . If I were straight, I would definitely consider Danae as a partner, but I'm not straight."

Mitch and Danae each described the tension present in their friendship during their individual interviews. It also became clear that the tension was rooted in something more than mere unrequited feelings from Danae. Of all of the interviews, Danae's was the only one that ended abruptly, after I asked whether she and Mitch had ever been sexually involved. In his interview, Mitch had responded sheepishly, "Well, not really." I asked him to clarify, but he repeated his response, offering no further detail. When I asked Danae the same question in her interview, she told me to go with whatever Mitch had said. I probed further, trying to assess whether or not she was merely joking, but she became steely and refused to answer any further questions. The issues of unrequited (or possibly shared) attraction were clearly not resolved for Mitch and

Danae and seemed to present a serious challenge to their friendship—or, at least, to their ability to characterize their relationship.

## CONSTRUCTING NEW SCRIPTS?

The difficulties that these intersectional friendships encounter as they navigate the available heterosexual scripts for cross-sex behavior are informative. Many interviewees pointed to a lack of sexual tension as a beneficial aspect that allowed for the formation of a deep emotional connection with friends. However, as these examples show, not all intersectional friendships are free from sexual tension. It is, in fact, the presence of these tensions—imagined to be impossible, given the limited scripts available for sexuality—that illustrate the fluidity of sexuality and sexual attraction in intersectional friendship. Ranging from moments of sexual tension to long-term sexual relationships, sexuality (like gender) has shaped interaction within these dyads in complex and dynamic ways.

The emergence of sexual tension and behavior in intersectional friendship serves to underscore the idea that relationships are situated in a particular historical and structural context (Stryker 1980). Heterosexuality is a valued social institution that shapes and limits individual identity development and interaction. Within our contemporary social context, interaction between men and women is prescribed to be a romantic or sexual connection (Rich 1980). The intersectional friendship challenges this construct but is not wholly successful in expanding the confines of structural influences and therefore struggles against norms of compulsory heterosexuality. This is an important element in exposing the construction of sexual orientation as a social category. By existing within a social structure that imposes false binaries on gender and sexual orientation, intersectional friendships provide evidence that such identities are neither entirely fixed nor essential.[1]

Yet the general tendency to presume that sexual orientation is fixed seems to serve these friendships well. Put simply, sexual orientation matters in these friendships. A gay man is expected to be free from sexual thoughts about his straight female friend; thus, this friendship is presumed to be platonic in the past, present, and future. As such, the romantic partners and spouses of the friends are able to tolerate, if not celebrate, the intersectional friendship because they, too, perceive the friendship as free from sexual possibility. Whereas a close, emotionally intimate relationship between a straight man and his straight female friend may cause his spouse to feel jealousy and suspicion that he is cheating; when the friend is a lesbian, any possibility of a sexual relationship seems off the table and the friend is rendered non-threatening. Furthermore, the sexual impossibility of the relationship to the friends themselves appears to have facilitated the formation, intensity, and longevity of the intersectional friendship. In other words, despite the evidence that some intersectional friendship pairs navigate sexual attraction, the majority of the friends themselves view the friendship as free from any sexual possibility, which, in turn, is noted as a benefit to the friendship.

Even as attraction points to the fluidity of sexuality, most interviewees viewed sexual tension and attraction as both a nuisance and a threat to friendship. Such notions suggest that friendship and sex are antithetical—as the phrase "just friends" suggests. This further demonstrates how these relationships are situated in a social context (Stryker 1980). The current social and structural context in which these intersectional friendships exist is one that values sexual monogamy and treats sexuality without it as taboo, while identifying friendship as the very absence of sex. In other words, given cultural norms about both friendship and sexuality, non-romantic expressions of sexuality within friendship are viewed as anomalies. Previous studies also find instances in straight cross-sex friendships where the individuals have had sex but characterize the sexual dimension of the relationship as difficult to negotiate (Rubin 1985; Werking 1997). On the rare occasions that such intimacies occur, the friends are culturally referred to as "fuck buddies," a term that downplays the strength of friendship and the potential intimacy of sex or "friends with benefits." In both cases, the friendship is given a qualifier that clarifies the sexual component of the friendship. This demonstrates the acceptance of available scripts that insist that friendships are platonic and, if they cease to be platonic, they must be re-classified as a different type of relationship.

Participants were aware of these scripts and positioned themselves in relation to them. They did not question them. Perhaps, then, the inability of the intersectional friendship to fully defy compulsory heterosexuality lies in the near-erasure or denial of sexual attraction in all relationships except socially sanctioned dyads—romantic, monogamous relationships. Such social mores were evident throughout these friendships. Of the interviewees, gay men most openly addressed the positive aspects of sexuality, a finding that is consistent with other research. As Nardi (1999) found, in gay men's friendships, not only were friendship and sex not mutually exclusive, but it also was common for men to have ongoing sexual friendships within gay male communities. Even with this more flexible understanding of friendship, gay men repeatedly denied sexual attraction to their straight female friends and attributed this absence as facilitating close and stable bonds. This difference between gay men's friendships having sexual potential that is absent in the intersectional friendships I studied may reflect a difference in sexual scripts based either on sexual orientation or on gender. One interpretation is that the scripts of those who have same-sex orientations may identify relationships with men, but not with women, as having sexual potential. A more likely explanation is that heterosexual scripts are highly gendered so that men are viewed as seeking love relationships for sex, while women engage in sex as a way to achieve love relationships. In such scripts, friendship does not include sex unless the bond will become a romantic relationship.

Most interviewees in this study—of all sexualities and genders—insisted that sexuality and sexual tension were disruptive to the friendship rather than something that they negotiated (e.g., Werking 1997). The acceptance of these mores without cultural interrogation is surprising, as these friendships' very existence holds the potential to call these values into question. Moreover, the fully transformative effects of intersectional friendship are limited to those that exist within the bounds of our contemporary social context. Hence, while the intersectional friendship serves as an unconventional relational form in some respects, it also reinforces social norms about sexuality, sexual orientation, and friendship so that sexual tension or activity in friendship is viewed negatively.

The data also illustrate the complexity of sexual orientation. Sexual attraction and behavior are generally the determinants of sexual orientation; however, as the data suggest, identifying as a gay man or lesbian does not alleviate the possibility of experiencing sexual feelings with a friend of the other sex. This complexity is also what makes it possible for friendship dyads of straight men and straight women to exist without sexual tension. Thus, the data serve as an example of how sexual orientation, like gender, is a socially constructed identity that is not necessarily absolute or fixed. Rather, when sexual tensions arose, the participants navigated the situations and generally found ways to keep the friendship intact. Thus, the intersectional friendships can serve as a model for how men and women can navigate sexual attraction in intimate but not sexual relationships.

# 6

# THE PERSONAL IS

# POLITICAL

I think straight people don't get a chance to experience life outside their own little sphere unless they meet one of us. . . . You can have those little atomic relationships between straight people and gay people and you really break open the barrier between those two worlds by doing that.

—Sarah, a thirty-year-old white lesbian

## LEYLA AND ETHAN

Leyla and Ethan met in Miss Beecher's sixth-grade math class some thirteen years ago, but it was not until high school that they started spending more time together. Leyla, who is Iranian American, and Ethan, who is Latino, were both members of the debate team and were part of a clique who ate lunch together and took all of the classes for smart kids.

Ethan and Leyla are best friends. They speak on the phone nearly every day and see each other several times a week. The pair enjoys doing the same things; even though they have busy schedules, they find time to travel together once a year and often go to movies and the theater. They make even the most mundane aspects of life more enjoyable for each other. For example, they often accompany each other while running errands. Leyla has gone with Ethan to hair appointments and has given him rides to his mechanic, while Ethan has taken Leyla to the doctor and to manicure appointments.

Leyla was the first person Ethan told he was gay. Three years ago, Leyla acted as a facilitator when Ethan came out to his family, because he was very nervous about coming out to them. In addition to being an important part of his coming-out process, Leyla "dragged" Ethan to gay clubs, gay bookstores, and gay pride events because he felt shy about being gay. In time, Ethan helped Leyla to be more comfortable with her sexuality by being very open about his own sexual activity. Leyla explained that Ethan told her how to kiss men; he explained, for example, that in most cases you should not bite a man while kissing him. (Leyla once decked a guy for trying to kiss her, so Ethan had his work cut out for him.) But Ethan sometimes withholds details about his sexual activity from Leyla because she is squeamish about physical affection. For example, Leyla covers her eyes when actors kiss in a movie.

While Leyla's and Ethan's friendship is solid, other people in their lives sometimes take issue with their close bond. Leyla's boyfriend, for example, becomes jealous when she spends a lot of time with Ethan. And when Leyla, her boyfriend, and Ethan spend time together, the two men often jockey for her attention in what she calls "power plays." The tension between Ethan and Leyla's boyfriend is ironic, since Ethan played a key role in encouraging her to get into her current relationship.

The pair's personalities balance each other out. Ethan helps to bring Leyla down to earth; she often has her head in the clouds, while he is more likely to have his feet firmly planted on the ground. Leyla is the optimist to Ethan's pessimist. When Ethan is in a bad mood, Leyla is usually able to make him laugh and forget about feeling grouchy.

The friends clearly enjoy and value each other for all of their quirks. Leyla characterizes their friendship as being like the show I Love Lucy, where she is like Lucy and Ethan is like Ethel. Even though he swears that her ideas are harebrained, he goes along anyway. At the same time, the friendship allows Ethan to show his darker side and let down his guard. Leyla has been on the "front lines" in dealing with him when he has been depressed, and he feels less inhibited around her than around anyone else. Ethan admits that he is a much happier person because Leyla is a part of his life.

THE PREVIOUS CHAPTERS show the intersectional friendships in this study to be significant relationships that shape people's lives. Intersectional friendships are meaningful bonds that in many cases constitute chosen family relationships and allow individuals to act outside prescribed social norms. According to the interviewees, the interaction within these dyads also serves to educate its members about each other's social locations,[1] which has outcomes that range from lessening prejudice to motivating activism. This chapter examines the extent to which intersectional friendships are bonds that can (but do not always) foster tolerance and acceptance, as well as politicize their members to challenge heterosexism. Following from Mills's (1959) discussion of personal troubles as public issues, I address the extent to which the intersectional friend relationship reflects and propels larger social transformation.

The assertion that intersectional friendships are to some extent political is supported by previous research, which found that interaction between individuals is a context in which social inequalities can be resisted through contact. Prior studies have concluded that close contact between people of dominant and oppressed groups reduces prejudice and perhaps promotes tolerance and equality, as well (Allport 1954; Crosby, Bromley, and Saxe 1980; Dovidio, Gaertner, and Kawakami 2003; Herek and Capitanio 1996; Miller 2002; Sherif, Harvey, White, Hood, and Sherif 1961; Stephan and Finlay 1999; Taylor 1999). Simultaneously, friendship interactions influence social identities and inequalities, in some instances reinforcing and in others challenging oppression based on sex and sexual orientation (Johnson 1996; O'Connor 1992; Swain 1992; Weinstock and Bond 2002).

As discussed in previous chapters, the data suggest that within the intersectional friendships I studied, men and women interact in a context in which normative expectations of heterosexuality can be relaxed. Hence, in their very existence, intersectional friendships potentially constitute a political connection as they pose a challenge to normative expectations about bonds between men and women. The potential of these friendships to promote social change goes beyond challenging the norm of compulsory heterosexuality.[2] Many gay men and lesbians in the study, for example, attributed their sense of comfort interacting with straight people and their expanded social network beyond homosexual ghettoization to their intersectional friendship. However, given the social and state regulation of same-sex intimate relationships (e.g. laws prohibiting same-sex marriage), gay men and lesbians are likely aware of the politicization of personal choices and are not reliant on friendships with straight friends to create this awareness. The straight members of these friendship dyads were more radically influenced. Straight participants credited intersectional friendships with a range of transformative elements, from changing their individual awareness and perceptions of the effects of heterosexism to motivating direct political activism. Hence, the intersectional friendships highlighted in this book constitute not only a significant bond, but also a political partnership.

## BRIDGING WORLDS AND EXPOSING HETEROSEXISM

Intersectional friendships allow gay men and lesbians to experience aspects of straight life that may not be readily available to them otherwise. Previous studies of gay men and lesbian communities show their friendships to consist primarily of other gay men and lesbians who shield each other from a largely unwelcoming straight society (Nardi 1999). The limited access to various aspects of straight life is a result of the pervasive inequality based on sexual orientation vis-à-vis heterosexism. Such inequalities persist at the institutional level, while social repression is waning at the personal and interpersonal levels, meaning that symbolic and social boundaries between gay men and lesbians and straight people have lessened (Seidman, Meeks, and Traschen 1999).

Institutional forms of heterosexism are present in employment, as well as in state regulation of family life. Twenty-nine states do not have legal protections against employment discrimination based on sexual orientation (Human Rights Campaign [HRC] 2011). Many employers do not offer domestic partnership benefits for same-sex couples, although 41 percent of Fortune 500 companies have enacted nondiscrimination policies that include gender identity or expression (HRC 2011). As discussed in previous chapters, heterosexist laws also limit the possibilities for family life among gay men and lesbians so that gay men and lesbians are largely prohibited from legally marrying and therefore do not receive the social, legal, financial, and religious benefits that come from participating in this institution (Oswald 2000).[3] Hence, while tolerance with respect to sexual orientation may be increasing, lesbians and gay men are in many ways still second-class citizens (Seidman 2002).

One of the ways that social boundaries are relaxed in the intersectional friendships discussed in this book is by straight friends' acting as informants for gay men and lesbians, which allows the counterpart to experience the world from a different perspective. For example, Ben, a twenty-eight-year-old Asian American gay man, explained one such contribution that Ming, a straight twenty-eight-year-old Asian American woman, makes to him: "It's a window to see into a straight couple's world of the same generation, people my age. It's given me some perspective on how a couple functions, how they bounce off each other, what role they play in their relationship. Sometimes it's interesting to make that comparison with a gay relationship."

Other interviewees commented that the straight friend allowed them access to interactions with straight life and straight people. Connor, a thirty-seven-year-old white gay man, described this aspect of his friendship with Nadia, a thirty-year-old straight Iranian American woman: "Well, instead of just staying in the gay clubs, which I still did, we'd be in her apartment, and some guys would come over, and they'd be straight. It would give me a chance to talk to straight people and not be so gay, because you can get too gay, you can get too comfortable, and then you feel uncomfortable leaving [the gay community]." Connor's explanation illustrated that, through his friendship with Nadia, he became more at ease interacting with straight people, which is consistent with prior research showing that straight women sometimes are perceived by gay men to serve as their bridges between the gay and straight world (Grigoriou 2004). This is not to say that Connor did not have other connections to heterosexuals through his family, with whom he is close, but his connection with Nadia allowed interactions with straight peers with whom he otherwise might not have been comfortable interacting.

Many lesbians and gay male participants recognized that the intersectional friend provided a connection to larger society. As Sarah, a thirty-year-old white lesbian, explained: "[Hanging out with straight people is] new for me, at least since coming out. I came out when I was eighteen, and probably from eighteen to twenty-eight, I hung around nothing but gay people." For the gay men and lesbians in the study, having positive contact with straight people broadened their perspectives. Melissa, a thirty-five-year-old Latina lesbian, explained the rewards she gained from the close friendship with her thirty-five-year-old straight white friend, James: "I think it gives me another perspective on the world, because I think sometimes we tend, in our lesbian and gay culture, [to] think that this is the right way or this is the only situation and blah, blah, blah. We kind of forget that there are other people outside the gay and lesbian culture, that there are some empathetic, thoughtful people. I know that my friendship with James has reminded me that there are conscious straight people who do care about justice, who care about people." Thus, her friendship with James reminds Melissa that straight society is not just a place of oppression.

While many of the gay male and lesbian interviewees identified increased affiliation with straight communities as one of the perks of their intersectional friendship, some voiced concern that straight members of the dyad might disproportionately benefit from the friendship. Bruce, a thirty-four-year-old straight Asian American man, explained: "I think, based on heterosexist society, [that] straight guys would benefit more from the relationship with lesbians than the other way around. I don't know if that's the case with me and Vanessa. [I mean,] to what point does this lesbian woman become this informant for the straight guy about, like, this other world? And [is it a context] for him to come to terms with both [his] privilege and [his] role in society?" Here, Bruce raised the important issue of the gay male or lesbian friend acting as an informant for the straight friend. This is decidedly different from straight people acting as informants to straight society, given that lesbians and gay men are oppressed relative to the social positions of straight people. Such a perspective is related to those of hooks (1984) and Collins (1990), who explained that a position of marginalization in society based on identities such as race, gender, class, and sexuality provides a perspective obscured from those who occupy more dominant positions. Stated more simply, being oppressed provides an understanding of the social world that is not available to those who are not similarly oppressed. Thus, individuals who are part of an oppressed group are in a unique position to know and understand inequality; within intersectional friendship, knowledge is shared across groups with respect to an individual's social location (i.e., knowledge of marginalization is shared with straight people).

In the particular case of Bruce's and Vanessa's friendship, Bruce is a straight Asian American man and Vanessa is a black lesbian. Thus, there were additional influences of marginalization from dominant society at work. Bruce referred to this power differential and the possibility that, in her position as someone who experiences race, gender, and sexual oppression, Vanessa served as an informant who teaches him about his heterosexual and male privilege. In some ways, such a function can be viewed positively as a means to foster a greater understanding across groups. Yet Bruce's insight resonates with a larger discussion of intergroup contact as a context in which the marginalized person is called on to educate members of the dominant society about experiences of inequality (hooks 1984). As a result, not only do members of dominant groups enjoy heterosexual and sex privilege, but members from marginalized groups are given the added responsibility of exposing this privilege.

Alternatively, the particular subject position of the marginalized individual may offer knowledge that provides her or him with advantages in particular situations. For example, in his study of urban life, Anderson (1999) found that black male youths occupy a superordinate position vis-à-vis middle-class blacks and whites in certain interactional contexts because they have "street wisdom." In such instances, there is a reversal of privilege, in which the normally subordinate becomes superordinate because he has inside knowledge about a particular subculture or situation. Applying this theoretical framework to intersectional friendships, it is likely that within interactional contexts that are coded as gay or lesbian, (e.g., gay or lesbian bars and neighborhoods), the lesbian or gay male half of the dyad may be at a greater advantage to navigate the experience.

This situation is further complicated with regard to intersectional friendships because a variety of dimensions of identity operate simultaneously within the dyad. In the pairing between straight men and lesbians, the power differential is obvious. Straight men occupy the highest positions in the social hierarchy, especially if they are white, middle-class, and able-bodied, while lesbians are oppressed by virtue of sex and sexual orientation, as well as by race and class in many instances (Collins 1990). The case of gay men and straight women is more complex.

Inequality affects gay men and straight women in different ways. Gay men experience inequality because of their homosexuality and therefore have been denied many aspects of sex privilege. Straight hegemonic masculinity, which is based in a model of domination, is constituted in relation to and against other forms of masculinity and femininity (Connell 1992). Antagonism toward gay men is used to define hegemonic masculinity, which results in the oppression of gay men (Herek 1986; Connell 1995), both socially and legally. However, within these discussions, scholars caution against equating gay men's challenges to the gender order with challenges to sexism (Ward 2000). Despite straight women's access to heterosexual privilege, sexism at the societal level persists, with men (gay and straight) experiencing some degree of male privilege vis-à-vis women. Hence, sexism can be reinforced by gay men as well as by straight men (Ward 2000). Still, in being allowed to participate in institutions such as marriage and parenthood in a normative way, straight women are provided heterosexual privilege that is denied to gay men. Both gay men and straight women experience and enact oppression and privilege.

## THE CONTINUUM OF STRAIGHT POLITICIZATION

The previous section addressed how heterosexism influences the lives of lesbians and gay men and teased out some ways in which power and privilege affect intersectional bonds. The straight members of intersectional friendships also are powerfully affected by these strong connections. The following sections address how intersectional friendships in the study have advanced the politicization of straight people along a continuum from shifting attitudes to inspiring activism.

### The Role of Contact

Many straight interviewees identified intersectional friendships as fostering a better understanding of, and promoting greater tolerance for, gay men and lesbians. This is consistent with previous studies that found social interaction to be a context in which prejudicial attitudes can be reinforced or reproduced. One particular theoretical perspective that informs how the intersectional friendships influence discriminatory attitudes is the contact hypothesis of prejudice described by Allport (1954). The contact hypothesis responded to the claim that ignorance is the cause of prejudice (specifically, between racial groups) and proposed that intergroup connection between dominant and oppressed groups is a means to lessen intolerance.

Contact alone, however, does not reduce intergroup prejudice; in fact, in some cases, more contact is associated with increased prejudice (Taylor 1999). Instead, the type of contact is an important determinant of reducing prejudice. According to Allport (1954), contact can reduce intergroup prejudice under five different conditions: casual contact, acquaintance, residential contact, occupational contact, and the pursuit of common goals and objectives (Allport 1954; Sherif et al. 1961). Other types of contact also lead to reduced prejudice and more favorable attitudes toward members of an out-group. For example, those individuals who have personal acquaintance with individuals whose characteristics defy stereotypical group expectations, as well as those who maintain a friendship with a member of an oppressed group, are less prejudiced (Miller 2002).

Findings about intergroup contact between whites and blacks are similar to studies about heterosexual intergroup contact with gay men and lesbians.[4] Straight people who have interpersonal contact with gay men or lesbians, for example, reported more favorable attitudes toward same-sex-oriented individuals than those without any contact (Herek and Capitanio 1996). The effect of contact differed by sex; straight men indicated that they were significantly more uncomfortable around gay men than around lesbians, and straight women revealed that they were significantly more uncomfortable around lesbians than around gay men (Gentry 1987; Herek 2000, 2002). This suggests that straight people's biased attitudes about same-sex lesbians or gay men may remain, despite contact with other-sex lesbians or gay men.

Many of the interview data support the contact hypothesis, with straight participants reporting that the close contact provided by their intersectional relationships has promoted a greater acceptance of lesbians and gay men. Before he met Jill, his thirty-one-year-old mixed-race lesbian friend, Paul, a thirty-seven-year-old straight white man, recalled that he had a limited understanding of homosexuality: "[I saw] San Francisco and all those extreme [images]—black leather—that's what I always saw as gay. Then I met her, and she was no different than I am. Her dreams and desires are no different than mine." Beyond challenging his stereotypes, Paul credited his friendship with broadening his perspective:

I used to see things that I interpreted as strange, or I'd be quick to say, "OK, they're freaks," or something like that, whereas [Jill] has a talent for, whoever it is or whatever it is, kind of finding the good in that, and, you know, really looking at that rather than anything else and being intrigued by it and learning more about it. So I think I learned that piece of, like, everything I do now, even with work I notice it. Where I used to be quick to judge, now I'm like—I kind of look at it from a different angle.

Although Paul may never have held overtly prejudicial attitudes prior to his friendship with Jill, his comments expressed a limited understanding of the varying identities and experiences of gay men and lesbians. Such outcomes provide an example of how contact can positively influence attitudes in intersectional friendships even if to a somewhat limited extent (Herek and Capitanio 1996; Miller 2002).

Many of the straight interviewees identified their intersectional friend as their only close gay male or lesbian friend. As such, intersectional friends provided these straight individuals with their primary connection to lesbian and gay life. Antonio explained: "I had a few gay male friends before, and I had known lesbians before that, but [Justine] was the first one I got to know really well." The closeness of the intersectional friendship bond has had a significant effect on how the straight participants understand lesbian and gay life. Accordingly, Patrick described how his friendship with Emily has influenced him:

Having an intimate relationship with a lesbian, and a lesbian couple, is another thing that I don't have elsewhere—well, certainly not at this level of, you know, intimacy and history. I think it probably has helped to defuse whatever uncertainties or questions or presumptions about, you know—Like if that was totally unknown, and when I ran into other lesbians, say at the school or just in like general, I am probably, you know because of the friendship with Emily, more comfortable with all that. . . . [I] just wouldn't have a sense of, well, how would this person feel about x because [she's] a lesbian? You know? I wonder if [she] would feel different about this.

Patrick believed that his long-term, close friendship with Emily has made him more comfortable with lesbianism in general, something he carried with him into his other social interactions. According to several straight male interviewees, close contact with just one lesbian substantially and positively influenced attitudes about lesbians more generally, which is consistent with prior research (Herek and Capitanio 1996; Miller 2002). This illustrates one facet of the contact hypothesis, which states that greater knowledge of oppressed groups can reduce both avoidance of interactions and uncertainty and discomfort in these interactions (Crosby et al. 1980).

In some cases, having one significant lesbian or gay male friend provided an opportunity for contact with extended networks of gay men and lesbians. Through her best friend, Ben, Ming (and her husband) had had opportunities to counter myths about gay men and lesbians:

> [My husband and I] get to meet a lot of people who are gay. When I was [a student] at Sarah Lawrence, people around me, a lot of them [were] lesbians, but I don't think I ever got to be their friend. But when Ben's having a party and we're invited, we get to meet a lot of gay people, who are just like us. I mean, they're nothing different than what we are. They have the same problems, the same everything. So I just thought that was good to know, and that it's very—In a way, it's very comforting to know that they're not weirdoes. It's sort of confirming my belief that they're . . . not weird and nobody he knows is weird.

By participating in Ben's social circle, Ming recognized that she had commonalities with gay men and lesbians. This exposure debunked Ming's interpretation of social expectations that gay men and lesbians are "weird." Recognizing this potential of intersectional friendships, Cassandra, a twenty-nine-year-old white woman who self-identified as queer, explained, "It's building bridges because straight people are socialized to be afraid of us and think that we're going to affect their life or something, that there's something abnormal about us." In building the bridge between gay men's and lesbians' and straight people's lives, some intersectional friendships provided an example of how straight people's views of gay men and lesbians have changed beyond what they think only about their particular friend. In such cases, the one friend could have been viewed as the exception to the norm of same-sex-oriented individuals (Herek and Capitanio 1996). Instead, these contacts generated greater tolerance for and acceptance of difference.

Another aspect of the contact hypothesis is that it associates the reduction of intergroup bias to an increasing recognition of injustice (Dovidio et al. 2003). Learning about the discrimination suffered by oppressed groups while empathizing with members of those groups leads to the perception that those in the oppressed groups do not deserve to be the targets of prejudice (Stephan and

Finlay 1999). Attitudes developed within the context of friendship, however, do not necessarily motivate people to behave in ways that would lessen social inequality based on race or sexual orientation. Studies of whites' attitudes toward blacks, for example, complicate the connection of friendship with reduced prejudice and discrimination. Such research found that with intergroup contact through friendship and acquaintance, whites' feelings of closeness or warmth toward blacks changed more easily than negative character assessments of qualities such as dependability and intelligence (Jackman and Crane 1986). Such attitudes extended to the realm of social policy. For example, one study found that between two-thirds and three-quarters of white individuals with black friends persisted in opposing government measures to promote racial equality (Jackman and Crane 1986). Thus, while contact may cause whites to have more positive feelings about blacks, it does not necessarily inspire whites to advance structural change.

In fact, maintaining friendly relations among dominant and subordinate groups may reproduce inequality. According to Jackman (1994: 10), affinity is not antithetical to domination: "Affection, far from being alien to exploitative relations, is precisely the emotion that dominant groups wish to feel toward those whom they exploit. The everyday practice of discrimination does not require feelings of hostility, and, indeed, it is not at all difficult to have fond regard for those whom we subordinate, especially when the subject of our domination accedes to the relationship compliantly. To denote this phenomenon of discrimination without the expression of hostility, I use the term paternalism." In turn, subordinates are kept complacent by the coercive love of the dominant group.

Jackman did not address how such intergroup relationships might affect sexual orientation, but the potential implications of her argument are that intersectional friendships could serve to reinforce social inequalities. In other words, it is possible that this coercive intergroup process of paternalism is one by which heterosexism may be reinforced. There was no clear evidence in the data that suggested paternalism influenced these intersectional friendships as individual entities, which was Jackman's unit of theoretical focus. Yet, the tone of inter-group relations across sexual orientation may indeed lead to the perception that social inequalities are less significant because individual straight people and an individual gay man or lesbian carry on amicable, if not emotionally intimate relationships. Given that gay men and lesbians still do not enjoy many of the benefits of full citizenship in our society (e.g., same-sex marriage, equal employment protection), the use of such relations as a barometer for a shrinking gap in social inequality is spurious.

Intergroup relationships, according to Seidman et al. (1999), have had positive outcomes for gay men and lesbians. Positive interpersonal relationships that cross categories of sexual orientation are key elements that enable gay and lesbian people to be open about their sexuality. As a result, gay men and lesbians, as a group, are more willing to disclose their same-sex identification to others, date and form relationships, and make their intimacies public. Yet as with race, these interpersonal gains do not always translate to the level of structural change (Seidman et al. 1999).

## The Wisdom of Friendship

According to Goffman's (1963) discussion of stigma, interaction links issues of interpersonal prejudice to larger social inequalities. Goffman theorized that a stigmatized identity such as a same-sex orientation shapes the nature of all social interaction, which extends to those enacted within the bonds of friendship. Because homosexuality is socially stigmatized, individuals who are same-sex-oriented experience their stigma through the process of interacting with others. Goffman based the majority of his discussion of stigma on "mixed contacts," or interactions between those with a stigmatizing condition and those without, whom Goffman termed "normals." This perspective is particularly relevant in the case of intersectional friendships, where, using Goffman's characterization of identity, the gay male or lesbian member of the friendship is stigmatized. In such case, the straight half of the dyad is what Goffman (1963: 28) calls "wise," which he defined as "persons who are normal but whose special situation has made them intimately privy to the secret life of the stigmatized individual and sympathetic with it, and who find themselves accorded a measure of acceptance [in the stigmatized group], a measure of courtesy membership in the clan." Thus, the wise are individuals who do not carry the stigma of the individual with whom they are sympathetic, but their close connection to a stigmatized person causes them to be accepted to some extent by the stigmatized subgroup. A wise status emerges from this sense of understanding, empathy, and inclusion.

In reflecting on their intersectional friendships, straight women and men can be characterized as assuming the position of the wise. The straight interviewees' comments suggested that the straight friend perceived himself or herself as having gained insight into lesbian and gay male life and felt a sense of empathy with and connection to large gay male and lesbian communities. Carrie, a thirty-year-old straight white woman, discussed how her friendship with her gay roommate Ken, a thirty-five-year-old mixed-race man, has influenced her both personally and professionally:

> I think I've learned a lot about what it would mean to be a gay male living in the Castro [district] in San Francisco and what comes up with how he's had to position himself at [work]. I've definitely gotten, you know, just him talking through that. He taught middle school for a number of years and high school and [made] choices [about] coming out or not coming out to faculty and staff, and I think . . . [I] have more of an understanding of what goes on inside his head. . . . I mean, it's probably made me a better teacher or better able to address the needs of kids who are gay or lesbian or questioning in terms of what they are going through or maybe what they need.

In being intimately privy and sympathetic to Ken and the challenges he has faced, Carrie occupied the position of the wise.

Other straight interviewees assumed a wise status in a broader sense by participating in social networks that included large numbers of lesbians and gay men. These relationships influenced their perceptions of and reactions to the intersectional friendships. For example, Dan, a forty-one-year-old white straight man, explained, "The culture and that kind of thing I know fairly well, and there's a certain level of normalcy that has occurred with just sort of being accustomed, being used to, being exposed to it. . . . There was a period of time when one of my friends who was a lesbian worked on sets for plays in San Francisco venues. . . . I wanted to invite Brenda to these lesbian types of shows, and that was very ironic." Dan's comment illustrated how his network of lesbian and gay male friends has given him access to lesbian social life that Brenda did not have. Such contacts have also served to normalize lesbian relationships and culture for Dan.

Another straight male interviewee who felt very connected to and comfortable within LGBT communities was Stuart, a thirty-five-year-old straight white man. Stuart's friend Cassandra characterized him as having a queer survival mentality (meaning that he creates community with others based on his feelings of having an outsider status) and a chosen family, both of which reflected his connection to lesbian and gay male community. Stuart partly credited his history of political activism with influencing his understanding of lesbian and gay male life:

I came from a political background of doing organizing and activism and examining a lot of stuff about myself, as well as society, and I think that I was able to—I mean, I've always had queer friends, but I think that because I have examined my own heterosexuality, I think that's one thing that makes it easier to be friends with queer people. I think I know queer culture to some extent. You know, there are references that I get, whatever. I'm used to it. I also had a women's studies minor when I went to college, so I know all that lesbo talk. I do know the history of dykes in the women's movement, for instance. . . . I think that it's hard to be friends with people if you don't know the history they're coming from. . . . I think there are also a lot of un-examined queers out there who would be happy to hang out with unex-amined straight people, so, you know, it's not like a prerequisite.

Stuart's participation in queer communities, in addition to his awareness of his own relationship with heterosexual privilege, has given him an insider view into gay male and lesbian life. Thus, he recognized that, just as some straight people are not self-reflective about their positions, some gay men and lesbians also do not look at the world in a critical way. Occupying the role of the wise allowed for such an insider understanding.

Another way that intersectional friends in the study became privy to the lives of stigmatized individuals was through their own family lives. Barbara, a fifty-nine-year-old straight white woman, had a very close relationship with her lesbian daughter and was involved in a close intersectional friendship with Manuel, a forty-two-year-old gay white man. Having gay male friends and a lesbian daughter "helps me," Barbara said. "I experience their lives and their frustrations, and it helps me to understand what gay people go through." Manuel also connected Barbara's sensitivity to her relationship with her daughter: "I can look to Barbara to be nurturing in a way my mother never would have [been], not to say that I want to set her up as my mother. But there is the fact that she is a mother and she understands what rejecting a child would mean; there's an empathy there. And I do believe that there is an empathy between us, with me being a gay man from an unsupportive family and her being a mother of a lesbian and very supportive. It would be impossible for me to say that that doesn't affect the relationship." In becoming wise in her relationship with her daughter, Barbara developed a connection to and understanding of gay male and lesbian life that she brought into her friendship with Manuel.

Barbara's position as someone who was wise in the lesbian and gay male community transcended beyond her friendship with her daughter and Manuel. She and her sixty-four-year-old white and straight husband, Bob, were both actively involved in Parents, Families, and Friends of Lesbians and Gay Men (PFLAG) and met Manuel through the organization, which was set up specifically to advocate for straight people to become "wise" and provide support and empathy for LGBT individuals. Barbara and Bob joined PFLAG more than a decade ago when Barbara's daughter came out to them as lesbian. Bob described how his relationships with gay men and lesbians in general, and with his thirty-year-old lesbian friend Sarah in particular, affected his awareness about LGBT issues: "My self-description is I am a recovering homophobe and find it very hard for any straight person to say, 'Oh, I'm completely over all of that.' I like to think that I'm on the road to becoming completely over all of that, but I'm going to have to admit that I'm a recovering homophobe trying to become over it. . . . But in that way, it does good for me to talk to Sarah. It helps me as much as I hope it helps her." Bob's comment reflected his awareness that, although he was in a wise position with respect to LGBT communities, he understood that homophobia is a deeply rooted belief system that needed to be actively resisted. Thus, his statements suggested that for straight people who have access to and benefit from heterosexual privilege, complacency is incompatible with being wise.

Sarah, who maintained meaningful friendships with both Bob and Barbara, explained their unique approach to serving as wise: "The reason they know I'm gay is that they came out as parents of a queer kid before I ever [came out to them as a lesbian], so it was like they opened up before I even had to say anything, and that's not something I get very often, definitely [not] from grown-up straight people. It's like, wow—they actually know how to come out [laughs]."

Sarah further reflected on Bob and Barbara's support for the lesbian and gay male communities. For example, "[Barbara] went to San Francisco Pride," she recalled. "I think [Barbara and Bob] have been parade monitors for the last two years, and this year she saw the dykes on bikes contingent, and she knows I have a motorcycle. She came to me and was like, 'I want to ride on the back of your motorcycle next year.' My mother would never—I mean, I couldn't even tell my mother I had a motorcycle, and to have somebody like that, who's sixty or something like that, want to be on the back of my motorcycle with a sign that says, like, 'I love this person'—it's huge." Barbara's desire to declare her love and support of Sarah publicly by participating in the pride parade alongside representatives of the larger LGBT community was a powerful moment of activism. Such involvement with the gay male and lesbian communities extended beyond casual interaction and achieved an integration of social worlds.

## Expressions of Activism

Having gained an awareness of the marginalized social location that gay men and lesbians occupy through their intersectional friendship, many straight interviewees reported significant changes in their consciousness; some described themselves as willing to actively fight inequality. In such instances, straight participants recognized their intersectional friendship as a source of new insight into how heterosexism affects the lives of lesbians and gay men. Some straight members of intersectional dyads became acutely aware of how heterosexism affects lesbians and gay men when they either were mistaken for homosexual or were present when harassment occurred. Paul recalled a situation that arose when he borrowed Jill's car:

> I borrowed [Jill's] car and didn't realize it had the rainbow sticker thing on it.[5] I had no idea it was on the car; nor would I have known what the hell it meant. But anyway, I came out, and somebody had—They didn't write on the car, they had stuck [stuff] just all over it, and then [Jill] goes, "Oh, no. Not the sticker." "What sticker?" But then I'm thinking, OK, well, even if they saw the sticker, how would they know—how the hell would they know? Then I'm thinking, well, shit, somebody actually sees me get out of the car, that sort of thing, then just—[They must have] actually sped back [to vandalize the car]. So then I guess that brought it home. I was pretty pissed. That was the first time—a small piece of experience that I'm sure she's had to deal with.

Paul situated his anger in realizing not only that he had been the target of vandalism, but also that this intolerance was something Jill encountered or feared regularly. This insight gave Paul a greater degree of awareness and sensitivity toward lesbians and gay men. Paul explained that had he not experienced this, he probably would still be fairly intolerant, "just like all my other jock friends."

Straight women in the study described themselves as more likely than straight men did to be motivated to take action on behalf of their gay male friends. Their own experiences with sexism may in part account for this, because it allows them to identify more easily with heterosexism (Rubin 1985). Many straight women described feeling compelled to act when they understood their friend to be the perceived target of attacks. In other instances, straight women took on struggles because they considered how their gay male friend would be affected by the intolerance of some actions. Karyn, a thirty-one-year-old straight white woman, explained how her friendship with Pete, a thirty-two-year-old Asian American gay man, shaped her reaction to a situation that arose when she was working as a teacher at the same high school she and Pete had attended as students:

> I went back to the same school that [Pete and I] went to, and there was this whole big issue that the drama teacher had chosen a play that was gay-themed, and it got censored by the administration, and . . . it started this whole ball of wax where I turned into a gay rights spokesperson. It was very much because of Pete, you know, because any time anybody said anything, I just took it very personally. I was like, there are other students in this school just like Pete who are listening to these kinds of things. . . . I just [took] it very specifically as though they were saying it specifically about him.

In personalizing expressions of heterosexism to imagine the effects on a close friend, many straight participants were motivated to attack expressions of prejudice. Monique, a thirty-one-year-old straight white woman, discussed how having Jesse, a thirty-one-year-old gay Latino, as her best friend has caused her to speak out against intolerance, not only on his behalf, but on behalf of all gay men: "To me, it's the anger and the violence and the hatred that [gay men] are subjected to just makes no sense, and that's what drives me absolutely crazy. It makes no sense—I mean, having a gay best friend has definitely increased my sensitivity. . . . I really hate injustice, know what I mean? And unfortunately there's not a lot I can do about [stopping genocide in] Rwanda, but I can definitely do something when fifty-year-old conservative assholes make gay jokes in a derogatory way." She continued:

> I've tried to explain it to [people]. I'm like, look, even if you're not standing outside of the Westboro Baptist Church holding up signs that say "God Hates Fags" or something, your little jokes and all that stuff, you're just as responsible for Matthew Shepard's death because you create an atmosphere in which . . . gay people are less than human or they have to make some kind of fucking apology to you for who they are. And, you know, [they say], "Oh, it's OK as long as you keep it in the closet. Why do you have to be so up front about it?" So I would definitely say that my relationship with Jesse has brought that home to me in a very concrete way, not just a theoretical but a

concrete way, you know? The people who have the nerve to say to me that he's going to go to hell or that God hates him or that he should hide some part of himself or that he should apologize in any way for the way God has made him or whatever, fuck that.[6]

Whether in struggles to change school practices or by challenging those who make ignorant comments, these women used interactions to resist heterosexism. Monique's comments, for example, demonstrate that she understands that heterosexism on the individual, interactional level is related to systemic heterosexism. Thus, she showed critical insight in connecting heterosexist attitudes to larger social inequalities; however, merely challenging interpersonal discrimination—either in attitudes or in actions—does not necessarily prompt widespread institutional change. According to Seidman et al. (1991: 27):

> There has been a considerable relaxing of social repression at the personal and interpersonal levels. Many individuals have fashioned affirmative gay identities; the symbolic and social boundaries between gays and straights has lessened considerably . . . It is equally clear, however, that the U.S. remains a nation organized by the institution of heterosexuality. If it operates less through repression, and if it is less directed at regulating individuals at the interpersonal level, it remains embedded at the institutional level as manifested in law, social policy, civic disenfranchisement, institutional practices, and public culture.

Hence, as previously discussed, movement toward equality at the interpersonal level intervenes with prejudicial attitudes and helps to foster a greater acceptance of sexual difference. In addition, these interpersonal gains promoted a greater degree of freedom in living as an openly gay man or lesbian. Despite such advances, many effects of heterosexism remain at the institutional level. More formal efforts aimed at policy and systemic social reforms have emerged to address the persisting social inequality based on heterosexism.

The mission of PFLAG is to fight heterosexism on the individual and systemic levels. As noted, two straight members of the intersectional dyads in the sample, Barbara and Bob, were active PFLAG members. Barbara explained that she became an activist through her participation in PFLAG:

> It's helped me to be a better advocate for equal rights for gay people. We learned they have to have protection in employment—they can be fired for being gay or perceived as gay. When [the conservative right] tried to get the end

of the Employment Nondiscrimination Act, we went to Washington to lobby for that bill to pass. It still hasn't passed yet [at the federal level]. So through their frustration, [I have become] a better advocate. I might not have paid any attention [to] things like domestic partnership, [but] we worked with PFLAG to get people signed up for domestic partnerships. It was quite a joy.

The political actions that occur through groups such as PFLAG are part of a growing contemporary movement of alliance across sexual orientation.[7] Many of the other articulations of such alliances are based in schools, with thousands of chapters of the Gay–Straight Alliance (GSA) forming throughout the country over the past decade (Russell, Muraco, Subramaniam, and Laub 2009; Sweat 2005). The organizations based in high schools (Herdt, Russell, Sweat, and Marzullo 2004) explicitly promote tolerance and diversity and seek to counter heterosexism, sexual prejudice, and gay bashing in school settings. GSAs encompass a range of activities, from social events to political organizing, and reflect a grassroots movement to promote sexual justice that relies on alliance across sexual orientations (Herdt et al. 2004). Within the context of the GSAs, it is common for teenaged women to become straight allies for their gay male friends (Herdt et al. 2004), a finding that is also consistent with the intersectional friendship data.

Beyond the high-school context, straight women have been active advocates on behalf of gay men. As discussed, this may be due to their own experiences with oppression based on sex and gender. One manifestation of this alliance was the organization Straight Women in Support of Homos (SWISH),[8] founded in 2003 by a small group of straight women who wanted to participate in New York City's Gay Pride Parade to support their gay male friends. According to the organization's website, SWISH is "a gay–straight alliance [that] provides opportunities for straight women and men to contribute their time, energy, and talents to furthering the gay rights movement." The stated mission of SWISH involved creating strategic partnerships with other organizations that promote education, advocacy, and antidiscrimination activities for LGBT communities. SWISH described its membership as made primarily up of "straight, savvy, cosmopolitan women and our dearest gay male friends. We have the pink, feminine aesthetic and the martini glasses and the kitschy chatter. But our pride for our gay friends, both men and women, runs deep. Politically and socially we are gay, through and through." While SWISH may have relied on conventional images of gay men and straight women to promote the group, its goals were political and intersectional alliance. It should be noted that none of the interviewees discussed any affiliation with, or awareness of, SWISH, yet the organization's existence reflected a larger trend of straight women's interest in the political well-being of their gay male friends. The process of straight women's social bonding to gay men has been characterized by other scholars as a form of political resistance (Maddison 2000; Thompson 2004).

In the context of organizations such as Gay–Straight Alliances and SWISH, straight women (as well as some straight men) engage in acts of resistance to heterosexism. Some expressions of activism are limited to conversations, while others assume a long-term commitment to political and social change. All of these expressions are significant, however, in that they originate from or are shaped to some degree by intersectional relationships.

The most common way for straight people to become politicized in activist ways is by participating in mostly straight-defined organizations such as these. Yet many of the straight participants have been involved in events that were focused primarily on gay men or lesbians. As mentioned earlier, Barbara and Bob served as parade monitors for the San Francisco Freedom Day Parade, an LGBT pride event. In earlier years, Ruth, a 46-year-old straight white woman, rode on a float in the same parade with the members of her punk band, who were mostly queer. Leyla also led the way in helping Ethan feel more comfortable in the gay male community by introducing him to gay dance clubs and bookstores when he was newly out. At a gay pride event to which she says she "dragged" Ethan, Leyla had a run-in with protesters:

> I created a scene with picketers, which I guess is weird, because the only heterosexual person who was there was the one who was getting mad and yelling at them. . . . I started prancing around [the picketers]. I kind of acted like I was a lunatic. And I basically said—You know, 'cause they were saying derogatory things about "places you would go to if you lived that lifestyle," you know, "h-e-double hockey sticks"—So I told them, "I'd rather go to h-e-double hockey sticks than be on earth with you [the picketers]." And they left. Then the comment of the lady in front of us in line was, "That was intense." And, you know, Ethan's just sitting there laughing, covering his eyes, 'cause he was so embarrassed. But I knew he was kind of happy that I did it. He's my best friend. Like I said, if anybody ever did anything to him, I don't believe in violence, but if pushed or provoked, if somebody does something to him, I'm coming to his defense. That's it. Period.

What prompts Leyla and other straight individuals in intersectional friendships to engage in gay-themed events while others remain involved in more straight-centered organizations is unclear. Many of the straight participants voiced similar devotion to their gay or lesbian friends but did not take part in any form of activism. Yet clearly, when faced with overt heterosexist actions, Leyla felt compelled to fight on Ethan's behalf. In recognizing that she, as the only (perceived) straight person present, was the person who confronted the picketers, Leyla hinted at the possibility that her status as a heterosexual and its accompanying privilege—even at a gay-themed event—gave her a greater sense of entitlement and then outrage when she realized that her friend was one of the targets of the protest. Since Leyla was not the target of gay oppression, she was given the *choice* to act (hooks 1984), which subsequently may have made her the most likely person to speak out.

## ENLIGHTENMENT INTERRUPTED

Overwhelmingly, the interviewees reported that through their intersectional friendship they had gained greater awareness of and sensitivity to the inequalities experienced by their lesbian and gay male friends. Many of the straight interviewees said that their friendships reduced their prejudice, provided them with a greater understanding of inequality, and motivated them to take political action on the behalf of gay men and lesbians. Even with these important benefits, however, involvement in an intersectional friendship does not necessarily promote the idea of liberation for all people. Nor does membership in an oppressed group always promote a greater understanding of inequality rooted in systems other than sexuality, such as class and gender (Ward 2000). Some comments reflected a class bias. For example, Mark, a twenty-year-old mixed-race gay man, commented that his relationship with Cristina, a thirty-year-old straight Latina who had many contacts in the beauty industry, gave him greater access to a social network to which he aspired. He described the network as "very much older, more sophisticated, non-trash. No spam-eating trailer-park trash, not that I hang around with those people. Very business-oriented. Different types of people. We went to a party the other night and it was, you know, good people." Here Mark distinguished "good people" from "spam-eating trailer-park trash," both of which clearly indicate social class. In addition, he clarified that he did not associate with people in the latter category and thus distanced himself from poor or working-class people. As a gay man, Mark is subject to heterosexist oppression; however, his comments suggested that he did not have tolerance for those who suffer from class-based inequalities.

Class bias was conflated with gender bias in comments Antonio made about his lesbian friend, Justine. "My brother Milton saw [Justine] and, like, obviously she was dressed in rags," he said, "so he knew [she was a lesbian]." This comment reflects a conflation of class and gender with lesbianism. To be clear, Antonio's comment expressed his perception of his brother's impression of Justine's appearance. Yet Antonio was complicit in the assumption that dressing in "rags" equated with lesbianism. Antonio felt that Justine did not meet straight society's expectations of gender, as such manifestations are class-conscious; thus, in Antonio's eyes, his brother instantly could identify Justine as a lesbian.

More commonly encountered than class bias were straight participants' comments that reflected either some degree of heterosexism or a method of distancing oneself from homosexuality. While some straight interviewees were very supportive of their intersectional friend, their words suggested they were not entirely comfortable with gay male or lesbian same-sex individuals. Throughout the interviews, comments by several participants indicated that their tolerance for people from traditionally disadvantaged communities has limitations.

Some straight interviewees expressed support of an other-sex gay or lesbian friend but were less comfortable with same-sex gay men or lesbians, a finding consistent with previous studies of attitudes about friendships that cross sexual orientation (Herek 2000, 2002). For example, although they supported their friends' same-sex attractions and relationships, many straight participants admitted that they are uncomfortable thinking of themselves engaging in same-sex behavior. Paul, who is straight, said that although he is "pretty open-minded," he is uneasy at the prospect of "two guys together." Yet Paul's lesbian friend, Jill, explained that when they went to gay clubs, Paul played around and flirted with other men. "He just eats it up," she said. "He'll dance with the guy. It's very, very cool. And he's very comfortable, until they touch him. You know, he doesn't like to be touched by some guy or whatever, but he's very comfortable with the whole gay thing." Here, Jill presents Paul as free of bias. Given Paul's own comments that he is uneasy at the thought of "two guys together," along with Jill's explanation that Paul is comfortable with gay men until they touch him (even though he reportedly has danced with them), this depiction does not seem entirely accurate. Paul took a clear line with regard to how comfortable he felt with attention from gay men: he participated in interactions that were marked as gay until they included a physical dimension perceived as sexual. Feeling discomfort with unwanted physical attention is not necessarily an expression of heterosexism, yet it is difficult to ascertain what the implications or motivations for Paul's behavior were, given the limited information on this topic provided by the interview.

Intersectional friendships' potential to challenge social norms may be limited in the way that some dyads criticize other out-group members and thus reinforce certain stereotypes and inequalities. This was present in the way Mark, who is gay, and Cristina, who is straight, talked about lesbianism. "I joke around with her: 'Cristina, you're a lesbian,'" he said, "and she's like, 'Ew, no.' She's so not. . . . We've joked about her [sexual orientation], like, 'Cristina, you want her,' and Cristina's like, 'Ew.'" While Cristina seemed genuinely comfortable having a very close friendship with Mark and identified herself as having close lesbian friends during the interview, she was not comfortable with images of herself sexually involved with another woman. Because she is straight, this is consistent with her orientation. In responding to Mark's teasing that she's a lesbian by saying "Ew," however, Cristina effectively distances herself from same-sex sexual behavior.

Perhaps the gay man–straight woman dyad acted as a unit that reinforced expectations of gender and sexuality more generally, so that women who acted in gender-nonconforming ways were viewed negatively and perceived as an out-group. In a previous chapter, I addressed how intersectional friendships in some instances served to police gender norms (although they also encouraged gender outlaw behavior). Particularly relevant was the case of gay men's praising their straight female friends for successful accomplishments of conventional femininity (West and Zimmerman 1987). Lesbians are often perceived as gender-nonconforming because their choice of sexual object is another woman (Ponse 1978). Hence, in the case of Mark and Cristina, a dyadic influence may have been at work so that these friendship members colluded to deride lesbian culture because it does not abide by traditional gender norms. The data are not sufficient to support or refute this possibility. I did not ask specific questions about homosexuality in general; nor did I ask straight women questions about lesbians or straight men questions about gay men. Yet future research that qualitatively examines processes of reproducing inequality as the dyadic level would benefit this discussion.

Discriminatory attitudes sometimes persisted in intersectional friendships in this study, although the more common result of such mixed contacts was growing awareness of inequality. According to many participants, having a deep intersectional friendship promoted a wider sense of open-mindedness overall simply through understanding how inequality affected a friend. Many gay men who felt limited by heterosexism in their lives described how they came to recognize gender inequality, as well. For instance, Pete discussed how his friendship with Karyn made him more politically astute with regard to sexism: "I do find myself standing up to other people is when it's more related to women's issues in general. I don't think I'm capable of being a feminist, but I can certainly understand women's issues and women's studies. I don't want to say I was very aware of things, but I wouldn't have been at the level where I am now without what Karyn has brought in."

In another such instance, Frank, a thirty-two-year-old white gay man, identified his lifelong friendship with Rebecca, a thirty-two-year-old mixed-race straight woman, as inspiring him to challenge sexism:

> My relationship with Rebecca . . . has made me a very staunch feminist. One example I'm thinking of particularly [was] in grade school and junior high school, when she was really involved with the . . . whole beauty pageant scene, which I had no interest in. Unlike the typical fag who's totally into that, I had no interest whatsoever. The only reason I was involved at all was because she was, and I knew it was important to her, and so I, you know, I got to sort of see the inside of that sometimes and frankly found it really disturbing. But, you know, I knew it was important to her, so it was something I kind of paid attention to as a result. . . . I think I had fairly feminist attitudes before that, but kind of being involved and seeing what it did to her as far as reinforcing her attitudes about self-image and beauty and what's actually important to her life, you know, my reaction was to put those even farther away, to actively seek other ways of verifying myself.

Frank's friendship with Rebecca provided him with a greater awareness of the effects of sexism vis-à-vis her childhood participation in beauty pageants. Thus, Frank developed a feminist awareness of how women's worth is tied to appearance and has consciously decided not to perpetuate that bias in his own life.

Frank's friendship with Rebecca also affected his understanding of racial oppression. "[Rebecca] was always the minority," he said. "She is half-Japanese and was the only non-white child in our grade school—certainly in our grade level, and sometimes in the entire school—which is certainly not true [of the town] anymore. The town has changed a lot since then. But that for her was always a challenge, and I think that being with her as she's experienced a lot of the difficulties that [prejudice and discrimination] involved has given me a much deeper appreciation for any kind of otherness or differentness and helped me to understand what it meant to be gay and to be a minority." Through his secondhand experience of Rebecca's status as the only mixed-race person in her town, Frank developed greater sensitivity about living as an "other" in a social context. This understanding has helped Frank shape his understanding of his own gayness in the heteronormative social context. While this recognition did not necessarily motivate Frank to engage in political activism, the awareness brought about by his connection to Rebecca was a politicized one with respect to creating a sense of alliance across categories of difference.

Many gay men in the sample addressed how exposure to sexism through close friendships with straight women has made them resist gender norms more actively. Such revelations, however, were largely absent in the straight men's comments. None of the straight men reported having become a feminist because of a close friendship with a lesbian, although two of the straight men in the sample stated that they had long histories with radical politics more generally. Several straight men identified their lesbian friend as having sensitized them to issues of lesbianism; however, none discussed the sex and gender oppression the friend faced as a woman. Because the straight men did not address gender as an issue in the friendship, it is difficult to ascertain whether they did not see lesbians as suffering from gender oppression or whether straight male privilege allowed them to ignore sexism altogether.

## THE POLITICS OF INTERSECTIONAL FRIENDSHIP

As shown throughout this chapter, the potential for intersectional friendships to be political was realized along a continuum. Interactions with straight people gave gay men and lesbians a greater sense of security in participating in the larger straight society. In addition, the shared history and affinity present in intersectional friendship, and bred through contact, led to the lessening of prejudicial attitudes for straight individuals. In more significant cases, straight individuals served the role of the wise in gay male and lesbian communities, which resulted in a blending of social worlds across sexual orientation. In many cases, the wise became activists, either momentarily in response to heterosexist comments or in longer-term organizational commitments to institutional change through participation in PFLAG or Gay–Straight Alliances.

Although intersectional friendships often broadened consciousness of hetero-sexist discrimination, many individuals remained unaware of other forms of oppression and may have reinforced social inequality through their comments and actions. Hence, many intersectional friendships advanced political outcomes, but despite the gains made within and because of these bonds, these relationships were not utopian.

By participating in intersectional friendships, the interviewees engaged in bonds that can be characterized as political. By challenging the social order through the creation of unlikely alliances, friendship bonds to some degree are political. For example, friendship among and between gay men and lesbians takes on a political dimension when situated in a contemporary social landscape that threatens their access to equal political, legal, and social rights and privileges. According to Nardi (1992: 116), "Gay friendship can be seen as a political statement, since at the core of the concept of friendship is the idea of being oneself in a cultural context that may not approve of that self. For some, the need to belong with others in dissent and out of the mainstream is central to the maintenance of self and identity (Rubin). The friendships formed by a shared marginal identity thus take on powerful political dimensions as they organize around a stigmatized status to confront the dominant culture in solidarity."

While Nardi's findings suggest the strongest of friendship bonds are likely to occur between those with a common marginal identity, friendships between those without a shared marginalized identity do also form. In this study, participants maintained strong bonds without a shared marginalized position. Participants demonstrated how strong bonds emerge in friendships that cross categories of oppression. Thus, while the individuals in intersectional friendships did not share the same marginal identities and thus did not organize around that stigmatized status, the bonds of friendship in which they engaged do confront aspects of the dominant culture and create a sense of solidarity.

In building a strong connection across sex and sexual-orientation categories, these intersectional friendships challenge the idea that gay men and lesbians are fundamentally and universally different from straight people. Such a move debunks any possible explanation for differential treatment, both socially and politically. Furthermore, through their close connection to gay men and lesbians, straight members of social networks may develop understandings of heterosexism, which may motivate them to become activists for LGBT rights. Perhaps, then, one of the most radical aspects of intersectional friendships is simply that they bring groups from different places in the social hierarchy together. Such an act complicates one of the primary expectations of friendship: that it is essential that people who enter into this voluntary bond be social equals (Jerrome 1984; Wiseman 1986). Defying this expectation suggests that friendship is a context in which it is possible to contest social inequality on the interpersonal level, a finding consistent with the tenets of contact theory and Goffman's discussion of stigma.

Thus, intersectional friendships have both progressive and repressive tendencies. On the one hand, through close and mixed contacts, the intersectional friendships that I studied promoted awareness and tolerance on the interpersonal level. On the other hand, the friendships showed a limited ability to create social change at the societal level, despite the actions of many straight individuals motivated by gay male and lesbian friends. In addition, while these intersectional friendships reportedly provided both a greater appreciation for difference and a context in which heterosexism was challenged, discriminatory attitudes coexisted with movement toward social progress.

Analyzing the inner working of the intersectional friendship, particularly with regard to moments of activism and unrealized political potential, is an important avenue for understanding how and why inequality persists at the level of interaction. While blending the social worlds of gay men, lesbians, and straight people is one means to fight oppressive conditions, the full potential of these bonds remains unrealized. Yet the knowledge that friendship sensitizes some individuals enough to fight discrimination at both the interactional and the institutional level provides hope for wider social change.

# 7

# THE FUTURE OF
# INTERSECTIONAL
# FRIENDSHIPS

*I think maybe, we all have different cultural experiences and perspectives and . . . the role of*
*women in society is not a central part of the power structure and the role of gay people in*
*general are not central in the power structure, might increase the ability to dialog around*
*differences and similarities because you come from something that is not automatically*
*rewarded.*

—Ken, *a thirty-five-year-old mixed-race gay man*

THE INTERSECTIONAL FRIENDSHIPS that I have highlighted here exist in
the shadow of both the social progress made toward acceptance of homosexuality and the legal battles to deny the civil rights of gay men and lesbians. As
I completed this manuscript, the culture wars over same-sex marriage were
being played out and rehashed in state referenda and political debates. For
much of the 1990s and 2000s, propositions limiting the rights of lesbian, gay,
and bisexual individuals have been placed on ballots, have passed, and have
been followed in many states. New Hampshire, Iowa, and New York legalized
same-sex marriage, while voters in California, Arizona, and Florida passed
state propositions that serve as the most recent incarnations of Defense of
Marriage Act prohibiting same-sex marriage. The proposition in California
came about as a result of the California Supreme Court's decision in May 2008
that judged the prohibition of same-sex marriage unconstitutional; as of this
writing, the court battles are continuing. This issue likely will play out in the
judicial courts and in the courts of public opinion for years to come.

Hence, despite Seidman's (2002) observation that interpersonal relations
and feelings of mainstream society toward LGBT individuals are more favorable
and accepting than in past decades, those who oppose the civil rights of gay
men, lesbians, and bisexuals insist on trying to regulate family life by limiting
access to it. This is the social context in which the intersectional friendships

presented here have thrived. On the one hand, the friendships are an extreme example of Seidman's claim that interpersonal relationships have shaped cultural norms so that overt acts of homophobia are less tolerated than they were in previous eras. In fact, we could characterize intersectional friendships as being the model for how affinity across social categories leads to greater understanding and alliance. On the other hand, despite these overall positive feelings, gay men and lesbians face real legal obstacles to civil rights and protections as a result of those who believe same-sex-oriented individuals should not be allowed to marry, parent, and have equal employment protections under the law.[1]

The existence of intersectional friendships within our contemporary social context raises two questions. What implications does this context have for the future of intersectional friendships? And what implications do intersectional friendships have for the future? In this final section, I address how we can look to intersectional friendships as a model for postmodern relationships and political alliance and discuss the potential for shifting social contexts to influence the future of intersectional friendships.

## INTERSECTIONAL FRIENDSHIPS AS A MODEL
## FOR POSTMODERN RELATIONSHIPS

It is almost a cliché to say that the world is globalizing at increasing rates. Yet the reality is that, as a result of global mobility, most of us interact with people very unlike ourselves at some point during the day, be it at the grocery store or at the post office, in the classroom, on the Internet, at the airport, or on the subway. In many cases, we form acquaintanceships, if not friendships, with some of these individuals. While demographic similarity is one of the most agreed-on components of friendship formation and maintenance (Brehm 1985; Weinstock 2000), friendships that bridge sexual orientation, sex, race, class, and religion provide close connection, as well as meaningful insight into the lives of others. Friendships across categories of difference can create strong social and political bonds that facilitate alliance and understanding (de Souza Briggs 2007; Miller 2002). Thus, intersectional friendships can provide insight not only into friendships between gay men and straight women and between lesbians and straight men, but also into social relationships between and among people from different social locations.

The data from the present study are consistent with these prior findings but also add a layer of complexity because stereotypes and conventional beliefs about gender, sexuality, and family are also reinforced within the intersectional friendships. The tensions between convention and social progress are not unique to intersectional friendships. Prior research about friendships between gay and straight men show that there are limits to the straight men's acceptance of different dimensions of gay men's lives and identities (Fee 1996; Price 1999). These limitations—in particular, straight men's avoidance of conversations about gay men's romantic relationships (Price 1999)—are consistent with Seidman's (2002) assertion that favorable feelings of acceptance on the interpersonal level have been stunted. Yet we do not know whether such limitations exist regardless of whether a friendship crosses categories of sex, sexual orientation, religion, or race. In other words, some dimensions of friendship itself, or of relationships more generally, may allow individuals to accept a person's individual identity while ignoring, or even rejecting, aspects that are viewed as distasteful or that cause discomfort. In the intersectional friendships I studied, for example, Antonio did not discuss Justine's devotion to a pagan religion with her because that caused conflict between them, given his Catholicism. In future research, a useful topic for study would be to focus on the positive and negative dimensions of various friendship types to see how people negotiate the distinctions. In particular, it would be helpful to know whether the tensions are related to differences in social locations, different individual expectations for behavior, or lack of tolerance for these differences more generally.

2In referring to relationships as "postmodern," I mean that they are various pand fluid (e.g., Stacey 1996); one size does not fit all in terms of norms and expectations of the contemporary social context, which also is continually shifting. Friendship may be the most postmodern of relationships; typically, people maintain a multiplicity of friendships, none operating just like any others. Thus, all friendships are remarkable. Ultimately, the intersectional friendships examined here are remarkable particularly because the individuals in the relationships view crossing identity categories as unremarkable, which is similar to findings about interracial marriages (Rosenblatt, Karis, and Powell 1995). When asked to characterize how identity affects their intersectional friendship, most of my study participants indicated an awareness of how their own social locations differed from that of their intersectional friends. Gay male and lesbian interviewees were the most likely to identify the intersectional nature of their friendships as presenting challenges, which ranged from straight friends' expecting them to embody stereotypes to having different access to normative family life. In general, most of the participants admitted during the interviews that they rarely thought about the friendship as crossing sex or sexuality categories and that they had thought about the implications of this difference more during our conversation than they ever had before—and then only because I prompted them with questions. When considering their relationships, the interviewees clearly saw their intersectional friends first and foremost as friends, and secondarily as a bond that crossed categories of sex and sexual identity. Yet we cannot overlook that sex and sexual-identity categories affect how these friendships operate. It is precisely because of their intersectional nature that the friendships uniquely navigate the strong social norms of compulsory heterosexuality and social scripts that dictate male–female interactions be romantic. In other words, identity matters.

The intersectional friendships in the study also are instructive in showing how people have assembled postmodern families. In these friendships, people unrelated by origin or by law formed family ties. While this is not a new concept, particularly for immigrant communities and for economically oppressed and LGBT communities (Chatters, Robert, and Jayakody 1994; Ebaugh and Curry 2000; Stack 1974; Weston 1991), choosing to integrate gay and straight people into one family structure reinforces Stacey's (1996, 1998a) definition of the postmodern family as varied and fluid. More significant is the inclusion of straight people in chosen family structures. Many straight interviewees had access to normative family structures and yet also chose to add their lesbian or gay male friend to their families. Likewise, the lesbians and gay men in the study saw fit to incorporate their straight friend into their chosen families. Contrary to conservatives' contemporary attempts to limit definitions of family, individuals involved in intersectional friendships define family according to the durability and significance of relationships.

Shifts in the contemporary social context have made alternative or postmodern family structures all the more significant. Marriage is not compulsory, even for childbearing. Those who marry wait longer to do so. In the past decade, we have seen the rise of the "urban tribe" (Watters 2003) and the "quirkyalones" (Cagen 2004), labels applied primarily to urban young adults of all sexual orientations, sexes, and races, who construct family relationships from friends as a way to foster community without formal commitments. These informal family structures rub shoulders with single-parent families, same-sex-parented families, multigenerational families, immigrant families, grandparent-headed families, military families who experience deployment of a loved one, and other variations of family life. The constellation of these various structures represents postmodern relationships; intersectional friendships are one point in the web of social connection that can help us understand how to navigate intimate connections across categories of difference.

## OTHER AVENUES FOR INTERSECTIONAL RESEARCH

The work presented here does not address the constellation of possible friendship combinations across sex and sexual orientation. When I started this project, my goal was to develop a greater understanding of friendships between gay men and straight women, and between lesbians and straight men, to see how men and women interact in the presumed absence of sexual tension and expectations. Thus, I limited the sample to the intersectional friendships included in the book: friendship pairs between gay men and straight women and between lesbian women and straight men. This limitation, while necessary for the scope of this project, excluded other pairings, such as the same-sex friendships of lesbians and straight women; the same-sex friendships of gay men and straight men; same-sex and other-sex bisexual friendships; and so on. To develop the fullest possible understanding of how sex and sexual orientation affect close friendships and social relationships more generally, and to improve the current state of knowledge, future research should be expanded to include these dimensions and provide a direct comparison of friendship types.

Expanding studies of intersectional friendship to include a multitude of sex and sexual-orientation pairings is complicated, however, by the fluidity of sexual orientation—and, sometimes, sex (Butler 1990). In some ways, sexual orientation has a temporal quality in that someone who identifies as a lesbian today may begin to identify as bisexual, which means that her relationships may also be affected by shifting identities. Likewise, sample participants who identified as heterosexual at the time of the interview could become involved in same-sex relationships or engage in same-sex sexual behavior or begin to identify as gay men or lesbians, or, alternatively, a gay man or lesbian in the sample might decide that he or she is bisexual or straight. Each of these shifts would affect whether friendships and relationships are defined as intersectional and might require a different strategy or degree of navigation of attraction and expectations within the friendship.

Gender identity is another dimension in these friendships that deserves further exploration. Much of the discussion in this study relied on easily understood stereotypical or conventional expectations of gender to illustrate how gender operates in intersectional friendships. We know, however, that gender identity and expression, like sexual orientation, is a fluid construct (Butler

1990). A future study that included an examination of the influence of gender identity and expression on friendship interactions would provide a new layer of understanding. A more nuanced examination of the distinctions between gender expression by gay men, straight men, lesbians, and straight women would also be informative, because it would provide greater knowledge of how sex and gender are and are not connected to close social relationships. Specifically, in a study of friendship between lesbians and straight men, gender expression for both individuals may affect how they interact together and are perceived by others. A femme gender expression in a lesbian may increase outsiders' perception that the friends are a heterosexual couple, whereas a butch gender expression would likely signal other interpretations of the relationship. Similarly, a gender-nonconforming straight man might be a more interesting candidate for friendship with a lesbian because he might seem less concerned about preserving his masculinity through thoughts and actions. The differences between and among gender variations for gay men, lesbians, straight men, and straight women would provide an even deeper understanding of how gender, as a fluid category that does not necessarily co-occur with sex (Ponse 1978), influences social interactions and relationships.

A related issue is the lack of research about transgender friendships and relationships more generally. We know virtually nothing about transgender men's and women's relationships beyond the dramatized stories of how they and their loved ones have dealt with transitioning or being transgender in a gender-normative society (see Witten 2004). Very little research exists about transgender individuals' relationships beyond their romantic partnerships. An exploration of friendships amongst transgender individuals and between transgender men and women and those of other gender identities is needed to provide evidence for how gender, shifting and non-normative, shapes and affects friendship ties and relationships more generally.

The present research provides a glimpse of how these intersectional friendships operated at one point in time. We do not know, therefore, whether the gay men's fears that their family ties with straight women would sever when the women married came to fruition. We do not know whether the pairs continue to grow old together. And we do not know how these friendships navigated time and distance. Because they are like other friendships, intersectional friendships must also break up or experience conflict over time (Duck and Wright 1993; Rose and Serafica 1986). I wonder, for example, whether these friendships are still intact today. If not, what caused the rift? Was it the "darker side" of friendships that I discussed in chapter 2 that severed ties? Was it parenthood and the long-term commitment of one (or both) of the friendship members that made her or him less present in the friendship? Another possibility is that the friendships are still intact but over time have become less intense or intimate. If this is the case, I wonder: do the friends still consider the relationships family? Do straight women still regard themselves as gay men in straight women's bodies? Are the straight friends still acting as allies to gay men and lesbians? These lingering questions can, to some degree, be attributed to the nature of cross-sectional research: if we conduct interviews at one point in time, we only can address the information provided by the individuals in that specific context. Conducting longitudinal research that follows the intersectional friends over several decades would be a useful strategy to address many of the questions that remain about intersectional friendships, including the shifting of identities and evolution of the relationships.

## SHIFTING SOCIAL CONTEXTS AND THE FUTURE
## OF INTERSECTIONAL FRIENDSHIPS

As I have mentioned, one of the most hotly contested contemporary issues is same-sex marriage. While other nations (e.g., Argentina, Canada, the Netherlands, Spain) have granted equal rights of marriage to same-sex couples, same-sex marriage remains an issue controlled at the state level in the United States.[2] Despite the ongoing battles, it seems inevitable, given that state courts consistently have upheld the denial of same-sex marriage as unconstitutional, that same-sex marriage eventually will be legally sanctioned in the United States. The provision of equal access to marriage would be a positive civil-rights decision for gay men and lesbians that likely will have ramifications for intersectional friendships.

As I discussed in chapter 3, intersectional friendships often are familial connections. Gay male participants perceived their familial ties with straight women to be more transient or in jeopardy as a result of her entrance into heterosexual marriage and family life. What, then, will happen when same-sex marriage becomes more commonplace? If gay men and lesbians gain access to formalized family life through marriage and parenthood, will intersectional friendships still play significant roles in family building? While we cannot predict the future, if we take straight people's family lives as a basis for comparison, intersectional friendships may be difficult to maintain if they are competing for attention and commitment with marriage and children (Pogrebin 1987; Werking 1997).

Perhaps, gay men and lesbians will be better than their straight counterparts have been at maintaining intersectional friendships by balancing the demands of marriage and parenthood. The history of gay men's and lesbians' creation of family formations and social networks that exist outside social norms—in other words, the building of queer family networks—suggests creativity in and commitment to managing and blending family and friendship ties (Weston 1991). Yet as is true for straight men and women, not all gay men and lesbians wish to marry and parent and thus will continue to build and maintain chosen-family structures. Still, as gay men and lesbians gain the rights of equal marriage and parenthood, their chosen-family bonds with intersectional friends may not be as significant because of commitments to formal, nuclear family life. In other words, just as Ben and Connor voiced concerns about how their friendships with Ming and Nadia, respectively, would weather the women's entrance into straight marriage and parenthood, many more intersectional friendships may feel, and be, tenuous.

Norms of sexual behavior are another dimension of the social context that appear to be ever evolving. Here, again, a culture war exists in the tension between "abstinence only" as the federally mandated and funded form of sex education in public schools and the sensationalized public panic over teenagers' "hooking up" and entering into casual, rather than committed, sexual relationships (Curtis and Hunt 2007; Irvine 2006; Manning, Giordano, and Longmore 2006). These public tensions affect how people conduct their personal relationships in myriad ways. Currently, the norms dictate that sex and friendship are mutually exclusive, as I discussed in chapter 5. Yet the terms "friends with benefits," "hooking up," and "fuck buddies" are commonplace descriptors of friendships that are close and that include sex but not commitment and interactions whose purpose is sex that are perhaps friendly, but fleeting.

One issue to emerge from the regulation of sexual and relational life is a social norm that dictates the mutual exclusivity of sex and friendship. This friendship norm certainly reflects a social order that gives primacy to monogamous, married families headed by straight men. The social norm of friendship's and sexual behavior's being mutually exclusive also shapes intersectional friendships, not necessarily in the dynamic between the friends, but through its influence on the greater social context. In particular, there is a pressure for individuals to be *either* friends *or* romantic partners. Also, these friends must not be seen as a barrier or threat to an existing or future romantic relationship, which is socially valued as the most important kind of relationship. These unwritten rules are expected to translate into consistent behavior between friends; clearly, such expectations are difficult to navigate. Because these dynamics are not expected to be relevant in intersectional friendships, such friendships seem ideal to their members despite the challenges that the friends themselves voiced throughout my study.

All categories of the friends who were interviewed also discussed lack of competition between themselves and their intersectional friends as a great benefit of the relationships. Most straight men and women in the study turned to lesbians and gay men, respectively, to provide intimate bonds that did not come with pressure to conform to compulsory heterosexuality and normative gender behavior. Gay men identified unconditional love free from sexual pressure and interpersonal competition as a benefit of their friendships with straight women. Lesbians valued, among many other attributes, straight men's company in public situations to deflect unwanted sexual attention from men. Thus, several of the listed benefits of intersectional friendships were related to freedom from managing sexual tension or expectations of a romantic relationship that might be present in other friendships or interactions.

To a certain extent, intersectional friendships may have emerged as way to cope with repressive social norms that regulate sex, sexual orientation, and gender. Without question, the interviewees involved in these friendships have forged meaningful and intimate bonds in myriad ways, and these friendships might have emerged in any social context. Yet the friendships emerged and were maintained in a contemporary social context in which one of the highest-rated television shows was the sitcom *Will and Grace*, about the friendship between a gay man and a straight woman, and one of the most popular daytime talk shows was hosted by Ellen DeGeneres, who openly identifies as a lesbian and has been involved in highly publicized same-sex relationships. These friendships also emerged as same-sex marriage was beginning to be hotly contested across the United States. Much like the tensions within the intersectional friendships, a tension exists in the surrounding social context. On the one hand, gay men and lesbians are part of our cultural consciousness and, for some of us who are heterosexual, fully integrated into our everyday lives in the roles of best friend, brother, aunt, co-worker, mother, or neighbor. On the other hand, gay men and lesbians continue to be subjected to repressive social regulation and viewed as "other" by many heterosexuals. In righting some of the injustices experienced by gay men and lesbians, both historically and in the present, we have come far, but we still have a long way to go.

# PROFILES OF INTERVIEW

# RESPONDENTS BY DYAD

### GAY MEN AND STRAIGHT WOMEN

1. Gary: thirty, white, no partner
   Zoë: thirty, white, graduate student, no partner
2. Connor: thirty-seven, white, web Internet design, partner
   Nadia: thirty, white (Iranian American), customer service, married
3. Ben: twenty-eight, Asian (Chinese), high-technology industry, partner
   Ming: twenty-eight, Asian (Chinese), high-technology industry, married
4. Pete: thirty-two, Asian American, partner
   Karyn: thirty-one, white, academic, no partner
5. Frank: thirty-two, white, research science, no partner
   Rebecca: thirty-two, mixed race (Asian and white), business executive, married
6. Derek: thirty-two, white, legal secretary, no partner
   Crystal: thirty, Latina, legal secretary, no partner
7. Scott: forty-six, white, engineer, partner
   Ruth: forty-six, white, graduate student, no partner
8. Mark: twenty-one, Asian (Filipino American), beauty industry, partner
   Cristina: thirty, Latina, student and beauty industry, no partner
9. Manuel: forty-two, white, partner (married)
   Barbara: fifty-nine, white, student, married
10. Ken: thirty-five, mixed race (white/ and Latino), social services, partner
    Carrie: thirty, white, educator, no partner
11. Jesse: thirty-one, Latino, student, partner
    Monique: thirty-one, white, medical industry, married
12. Mitch: forty-two, Latino, customer service, no partner
    Danae: thirty-one, Latina, customer service, no partner
13. Ethan: twenty-three, Latino, student and customer service, no partner
    Leyla: twenty-four, white (Iranian American), student, no partner
14. Seth: twenty-seven, white, student, no partner
    Shayna: twenty-five, white, full-time mother, married

15. Justine: thirty-six, mixed race (black and white), partner
    Antonio: twenty-eight, Latino, customer service, no partner
16. Margaret: thirty-seven, white, partner
    Wallis: thirty, white, partner
    Guy: twenty-nine, white, customer service, no partner
17. Debbi: thirty-nine, white, graduate student, partner
    Carl: forty-three, white, no partner
18. Charlene: twenty-eight, white, partner
    (Alec did not complete interview)
19. Brenda: thirty-seven, white, no partner
    Dan: forty-one, white, academic, married
20. Vanessa: twenty-eight, black, graduate student, no partner
    Bruce: thirty-four, Asian, graduate student, partner
21. Janet: thirty-five, white, partner
    Jon: thirty-eight, white, married
22. Jill: thirty-one, mixed race (white and Latino), social services, partner
    Paul: thirty-seven, white, high-technology industry, no partner
23. Sarah: thirty, white, student, partner
    Bob: sixty-four, white, married
24. Melissa: thirty-five, Latina, higher education administration, partner
    James: thirty-five, white, educator, married
25. Emily: forty-one, white, environmental management, partner (married)
    Patrick: forty-one, white, environmental management, married
26. Cassandra: twenty-nine, white, student, partner
    Stuart: thirty-five, white, customer service, no partner

# RESEARCH METHODOLOGY

Here I provide details about the composition of the participants and about the research methodology to give readers a full picture of how I conducted the study. Some of this material is presented in the introduction, but I repeat details, such as the demographic information and the process of collecting data, to give the clearest account of my methodological choices.

## THE PARTICIPANTS

Data were collected in face-to-face interviews I conducted with fifty-three people who were engaged in twenty-six close intersectional friendship dyads and one triad at the time of the interviews, which occurred between October 2002 and August 2003. The participants were primarily residents of the San Francisco Bay Area and surrounding counties, although six of the interviewees lived in Southern California.[1] The interviewees self-identified their gender as male or female and their sexual orientation as straight, gay, or lesbian (although one identified as "queer").[2] The total sample included twenty-eight women (thirteen lesbian, fourteen straight, one queer) and twenty-five men (thirteen gay, twelve straight). There are more women than men in the study because I was unable to interview the male halves of the dyads in two cases; also, the triad included in the study was composed of two women and one man. The participants ranged in age from twenty-one to sixty-four, with a median age of thirty-two; the racial composition was 59 percent white, 17 percent Latino, 19 percent Asian, and 4 percent black. Appendix 1 contains a list of participants with corresponding demographic information and identifies her or his intersectional friend.

The participants were recruited using a convenience and purposive snowball sampling method, in which one participant refers the researcher to another, beginning with my contacts in the San Francisco Bay Area lesbian, gay, bisexual, and transgender (LGBT) communities and expanding through the participants' social networks. These methods were ideal for sampling intersectional friends because the targeted population is not easily located using other methods of data collection. For example, building a random and representative population sample would have been exceptionally difficult, because the actual population size of intersectional friends is unknown. Some participants were contacted through LGBT community organizations in the Bay Area and recruited when they received a flyer I had distributed, participated in meetings where I had made requests, or saw advertisements on community bulletin boards. In my efforts to find such friends, I distributed recruitment letters saying that, in order to learn more about friendship, I sought to interview adults who were part of a close friendship that included a gay man and a straight woman or a lesbian and a straight man and listed my contact information for those who might be interested in participating. The advertisements I placed on the community bulletin boards had two different taglines: "Any lesbian/straight male friends out there?" and "Will and Grace?" (in reference to the television show). The text of the advertisements was similar to that of the recruitment letters sent to the community organizations.

## THE INTERVIEWS

I conducted each interview according to the same schedule (see appendix 3), although I did not strictly abide by the order of the prompts and added questions when relevant. The interview schedule asked questions about five primary areas: friendship formation and maintenance, the significance of these friendships, the role of the friendship within the participant's larger social network, the role of gender and sexuality in the friendship, and the individual's contributions to and experiences of the friendship. The questions were designed to prompt discussion about these friendships according to the listed themes, but other topics also emerged throughout each interview. Overall, the interviews flowed like structured conversations between participants and me. I attempted to create rapport with the participants from our first contact, whether it was by phone or by email. I first explained that my interest in studying intersectional friendships stemmed from academic concern, as well as personal significance, given my own significant intersectional friendship. The interviews lasted forty-five minutes to two hours and were tape recorded (with permission). All interviews were conducted in a convenient setting chosen by the participant. For example, some were in public settings, such as cafés and libraries, while others took place at the residence of the participant. I interviewed members of twenty-four friendships individually and maintained confidentiality about what one friend said about the other. In other words, I would not share what one friend had said about the other, even when asked directly. In one case, I interviewed both members of the friendship dyad together, at their request. In another instance, both members of a lesbian couple were present in the interview to discuss their straight male friend. Thus, I interviewed members of a total of twenty-six friendship units.

While I had easy rapport with most of the interviewees, a couple of interviews were awkward. The awkwardness seemed to stem from the interviewees' uncertainty about my sexual orientation. Despite my attempts to be clear that my own intersectional friendship was with a gay man and, under the parameters of the study, it would follow that I identify as a straight woman, two interviewees perceived me as lesbian. In these cases, I clarified my identity so as not to mislead them into thinking they were disclosing information to someone from their identity in-group. I did not disclose my identity from the outset of the interactions as a general practice because I feared that doing so would be viewed as a heterosexist distancing mechanism. When asked, I was always very clear about my identification.

In a few cases, the interviewees were either my acquaintances or were referred to me by a member of my social network, so such confusion was minimized. Creating rapport was easier with these interviewees, because we could start by talking about the person (or people) we knew in common. Occasionally, however, having a shared acquaintance seemed to make the participant more guarded about the information she or he shared with me. For example, one interviewee hesitated to tell me much about her intersectional friend's reaction to a recent breakup, because she perceived me to be a member of her friend's larger social network. Another interviewee asked me whether his frank discussion of the frustration he feels with his intersectional friend (a mutual acquaintance) made me uncomfortable. In addition, some individuals assumed that because I had been referred by an acquaintance, I knew more about their lives than I actually did, so I often needed to ask clarifying questions in the interviews.

In general, my identity and presentation seemed beneficial to the interview process. Although heterosexual, I am comfortable maneuvering in and out of gay male, lesbian, and straight communities, because I have an extensive social network of close relationships that includes individuals from all of these groups. Also, I am relatively young and female, and I lived in an urban neighborhood in the San Francisco Bay Area while I was conducting the interviews. These characteristics, combined with my experiences in an intersectional friendship, which I shared with participants during the interview process, gave me a fair amount of access to the intimate details of the participants' lives.

## PRESENTATION AND ANALYSIS OF THE INTERVIEW DATA

To preserve the confidentiality of the participants, I use pseudonyms as identifiers. Also, throughout the book I identify the ages and occupations of the individuals or industries in which they worked only when that is relevant to the details of the analysis. In such cases, I slightly alter the age and occupation so they coincide with the individual's general age range and area of employment. In doing so, I make every attempt to make it difficult to identify which participant said what, particularly because detailed descriptions of situations or incidents could make the statements easily identifiable, especially to a close friend. It goes without saying that as someone who studies friendships, I feel that it is important to protect participants and avoid potentially damaging those relationships.

Data were coded into the most prevalent themes and then qualitatively analyzed under the principles of grounded theory, which uses a systematic set of procedures to develop and inductively derive theory about a phenomenon (Glaser and Strauss 1967; Strauss and Corbin 1990). Initially, I noted the themes that emerged from participant responses to interview questions and then reviewed each interview transcript line by line with these themes in mind (Muraco 2006). As I coded, I electronically cut and pasted the pieces of the interview data into thematic files (see, e.g., Lofland and Lofland 1995), which eventually became the chapters of this volume.

Throughout the coding process, participants generally were treated as individual cases rather than as dyads. To gain the fullest possible understanding of individuals' perceptions and meanings of similar experiences; however, particular responses from both members of the dyad were paired during the analysis process. For example, in the examination of the kinship functions fulfilled by friends, I compared the responses of both dyad members to see whether there were differences by sex and sexual orientation in the types of assistance provided.

## METHODOLOGICAL IMPLICATIONS

In addition to improving our understanding of intersectional friendships, this study presents a model for examining social relationships more generally. Rather than simply asking participants about their social network and identifying when they had friends of different sexualities and gender from themselves, I sought to examine one significant social pairing to investigate the inner workings of this relationship with a degree of depth. To this end, I interviewed both members of the friendship to understand both sides of the relationship from the perspective of each member, but I interviewed them separately in an attempt to remove the dyadic effect that interviewing the individuals together might have had.

In the one case where I interviewed the friends together—a situation that was presented to me when I arrived to conduct an interview with what I had understood to be only one of the friends—the interview process was much different from the others. Watching that particular dyad interact gave me greater insight into the dynamics of the friendship and allowed each of the friendship members to build on recollections, correct inaccurate memories, and tell each other how much they valued the relationship. While examining interactions between all participant dyads would have further illuminated the dynamics of these bonds, such a methodological approach would also have produced a study that focused more on the processes than the individual meanings of interaction.

Conducting the research with friends interviewed separately, however, provided information that likely would not have been disclosed in contexts in which both friends were present. Many individuals, for example, expressed frustration about the friend to me as way to explain the challenges these friendships face. Some frustrations emerged in reaction to "bad" decisions the friend had made, while others surfaced as one friend described past struggles or some negative patterns of behavior in the relationship. For example, I probably would not have learned about the sexual tension present in some of the intersectional friendship bonds if I had interviewed the participants in each other's company, because while describing those tensions interviewees referred to the fact that they and their friends did not discuss it. Moreover, I suspect that most of the individuals in the study would not have discussed a friend's compromised mental health and past suicidal feelings in their presence, as many of these conversations were preceded by, "He won't hear this, will he?" I have also chosen not to include some of these confidences in my analyses, because they were said "off the record" and could be hurtful to participants' friendship. It is my greatest goal to avoid damaging the friendships I study by carefully monitoring the ethical ramifications of sharing particular material.

Interviewing the friends separately also allowed me to get at some of the challenging issues operating in intersectional friendships. It is common for researchers of friendship to talk about friendships in idealized ways since friends often describe their own relationships in ways that reflect a wish for such a relationship more than their actual experiences of such bonds (Rubin 1985). Although I did not set out to focus on the negative aspects of these relationships, I did want to portray friendships with all the complexities they hold, particularly when they cross social locations. Differences in social power and privilege influence significant and intimate relationships, and it is valuable to understand how these elements affect intersectional friendships.

Throughout the interviews, most of the intersectional friendships were described in primarily positive ways, despite the disclosure of sometimes painful and difficult periods of time the friends had experienced together. Conducting the interviews, with very few exceptions, was a wholly positive experience for me. Most people I approached about participating in the study were enthusiastic about being interviewed about their friendship. The intersectional friendship is a relationship that lacks social recognition except in stereotypical depictions of gay men and straight women; making these friendships the focus of study implies that they are important and worthy of time and attention. In turn, the study participants opened up their lives to me in unexpected ways. In several instances, people I had never previously met prepared food for me so we could talk more casually over a meal. Others, recognizing that my status as a graduate student likely meant that I was struggling economically (which was true), insisted on buying me coffee and snacks when we met in cafés. Not one of my interviewees canceled or failed to show up—a rarity in interview research. Instead, participants repeatedly worked their schedules around mine, even though I made it clear to them that they were doing me the great favor of opening their lives to me. Overwhelmingly, participants' actions indicated that they shared my belief that intersectional friendships are an important topic of study.

# INTERVIEW SCHEDULE

1. So, tell me how you and "x" came to be friends . . .
2. So this means you've been friends for x years?
3. Have you always been so close, or have you lost touch for periods of time?
4. Can you recall a specific case of losing touch? Do you remember what made you reconnect?
5. How frequently would you say you talk to "x"? How often do you see "x"?
6. Did you know that "x" was straight/gay/lesbian when you first met him/her?
7. Did you ever have a "coming-out" conversation with "x"?
8. How did that conversation go? Do you remember details from that interaction?
9. Did your friend know about your sexual orientation?
10. Was either of you surprised? Was it an issue for either of you?
11. Most relationships have ups and downs. Can you tell me about some especially good and especially difficult times in this relationship?
12. How important would you say your friendship with "x" is to you?
13. Do you consult with "x" when making big life decisions, for example? Can you recall a specific example where this happened?
14. In general, how would you define a close or significant friend? Is this how you would characterize your friendship with "x"?
15. What kinds of things do you and "x" talk about? For example, do you talk about relationships? Feelings?
16. Are there any particular common interests that you and "x" discuss?
17. Are there topics you avoid discussing? Which in particular? Why do you think this is the case?
18. What kinds of activities do you do together?
19. Has your friendship with "x" given you experiences that you would not have had otherwise?
20. Has your friendship with "x" given you contact with groups or information that was not part of your everyday life? Can you give me an example of something in particular?

21. Would you characterize "x" as a "family" type of friend who is present for special occasions?
22. How do your other friends get along with "x"? Your family? Have you discussed your friend's sexual orientation with them?
23. Do any of the people in your life have problems with your friendship with "x"?
24. How does "x" get along with the people you date/your partner(s)? How do your partner(s) get along with your friend?
25. How important is it to you that your partner accept your friendship with "x"?
26. How important is it to you that "x" approves/gets along with your partner?
27. Have you ever sensed jealousy between "x" and a partner? Can you give a specific example? If problems arise, how are they negotiated?
28. Have you ever used "x" as a means of comparison for people you date? What kinds of comparisons do you make?
29. Do you have children? How do they feel about "x"? What is their relationship? Have you explained your relationship with "x" to them? Have you disclosed her/his sexual orientation to them? Why or why not?
30. Have you ever discussed the possibility of you and "x" co-parenting?
31. Is anything keeping you from doing so?
32. Is this friendship similar to other friendships with men? Other friendships with women? How? Do you have any specific examples?
33. Do you have friends in common? Share social circles?
34. Do you sometimes find yourself in an entirely gay/straight environment when you are with your friend? How does that feel to you? Can you think of particular examples?
35. In general, would you say that this friendship provides something that others do not? Can you give me a specific instance in which you have found this to be true?
36. What is the greatest benefit you get out of this friendship?
37. In general, what would you say are the benefits of friendships like the one you have with "x"? I am referring to friendships between gay men and straight women, lesbians and straight men. What are the pros and cons of these types of friendships?
38. Do you think "x"'s being a gay man/lesbian/straight man/straight woman affects your friendship in any particular way? How? Can you give me an example?
39. Do you think that "x"'s being gay/lesbian/straight has ever had a negative impact on your friendship? How about your being gay/lesbian/straight? Can you give me a specific example?
40. Has your friendship with "x" ever made you wonder about your own sexual orientation? Have you encouraged "x" to question hers/his?
41. Have you ever taken "x" somewhere as your date? Describe that situation for me. If not, then would you consider that a possibility? Can you explain why or why not? In these cases, do you inform others that "x" is "just a friend"?
42. Do you feel like people expect you two to get together romantically? Do they assume you might? How do you respond to these suggestions?

43. How detailed are your discussions with your friend about romantic relationships? How about the sexual details? Do you feel comfortable with that level of disclosure? Do you discuss your behavior with "x"? Does "x" discuss romantic relationships/sexual details with you? Is this similar to your discussions with other friends? Why do you think this might be different with "x"?

44. Have you or "x" ever tried to play matchmaker for each other? Why or why not?

45. Have you ever been sexually involved with "x"?

46. Do any television or movie characters remind you of you and "x"? Which ones?

47. Would you say that there is something unique about you that makes you open to having a close friendship with a gay man/lesbian/straight man/straight woman? How would you characterize this "something?"

48. Do you think there is something unique about "x" that makes him/her different from other heterosexuals/homosexuals? Can you give me specifics?

49. Have you encountered situations in which people make negative remarks about homosexuals/heterosexuals? How do you respond? Can you give me an example of a specific instance? Has your friendship with "x" changed how you feel about these kinds of comments/actions? How?

50. How do you think you would be different if you had never met "x"?

51. What do you wish were different about your relationship with "x"?

52. Do you feel that your friendship with "x" is fairly equal? Do you call each other/plan events pretty equally?

53. Is there anything else you would like to add? Any important aspects of the relationship that I failed to ask about?

# NOTES

## INTRODUCTION

1. The term "intersectional" was introduced by Crenshaw (1989), who discussed how black women's experience is more than the sum of their race and sex. Collins (1990) uses similar concepts in discussing the matrix of oppression.
2. Other friendship forms, particularly those between bisexual and heterosexual individuals and across the spectrum of sexual-orientation categories, could also be analyzed for the ways they reflect and perhaps shape contemporary social life, but they are not the focus of this book.
3. Warner's (1991: 3–17) definition of heteronormativity continues that its coherence is always provisional, and its privilege can take several (sometimes contradictory) forms: unmarked as the basic idiom of the personal and the social, marked as a natural state, or projected as an ideal or moral accomplishment. It consists less of norms that can be summarized as a body of doctrine than of a sense of rightness produced in contradictory manifestations—often unconscious, immanent to practice or to institutions. Contexts that have little visible relation to sex practice, such as life narrative and generational identity, can be heteronormative in this sense, while in other contexts, forms of sex between men and women might not be heteronormative. Heteronormativity is thus a concept distinct from heterosexuality. One of the most conspicuous differences is that it has no parallel, unlike heterosexuality, which organizes homosexuality as its opposite. Because homosexuality can never have the invisible, tacit, society-founding rightness that heterosexuality has, it would not be possible to speak of "homonormativity" in the same sense.
4. Throughout the book, I use the terms "straight" and "heterosexual" interchangeably, but in most cases I use "gay" or "lesbian" instead of "homosexual" because of the history of mental-health and medical professions' pathologizing same-sex desire and identities.

## 1 YOU'VE GOT TO HAVE FRIENDS

1. As I discuss in the introduction, these assumptions are based on compulsory heterosexuality, or the dominant cultural expectation that women will be innately sexually

attracted to men and men will be attracted to women. This cultural norm is reinforced by socialization practices (Myers and Raymond 2010; Thorne 1986).

2. Fine's (1986) description of occupation choice is largely based on middle-class (professional) career possibilities.

3. Heterocentrism is implicit in most discussions of same- and cross-sex friendship; discussions of women's or men's friendships in prior research generally assume that the friends in the dyad are heterosexual unless they are specifically identified as crossing categories of sexual orientation. The discussion of same-sex friendship here thus engages with prior studies.

4. There is a tendency within gay male and lesbian communities also to expect consistency with respect to the sex of sexual partners (e.g., bisexuality is marginalized). However, the effects are not the same as the process that Ponse (1978) and Tripp (1975) suggest, because in general at least two elements identified in the principle in consistency (gender identity and roles) are afforded a greater level of nonconformity in gay male and lesbian cultures.

## 2 SNAPSHOTS

1. San Francisco, along with New York City and Los Angeles, was one of the areas hardest hit by the AIDS epidemic in the 1980s. As chronicled by Shilts (1987) and others, AIDS disproportionately affected the gay male communities living in urban areas.

2. Research about AIDS and mental health has addressed the phenomenon that many gay men who lived in areas most affected by the AIDS epidemic experienced multiple losses of friends, partners, lovers, and community members (Neugebauer, Rabkin, Williams, Remien, Goetz, and Gorman 1992; Remien and Rabkin 1995).

3. One study of multiple losses related to HIV and AIDS found that in a sample ($N = 141$) of gay and bisexual men in Vancouver, British Columbia, the mean number of people lost in a nearly eight-year period was 19.62, with 53 percent of individuals reporting between one and six losses, 27 percent reporting seven to twenty-four losses, and 20 percent reporting twenty-five to two hundred losses (Oram, Bartholomew, and Landolt 2003). Given that this study took place in a city that was less affected by the AIDS epidemic than San Francisco, where Scott and Ruth were living, we would expect the average losses to have been even greater than the staggering number reported by Oram and colleagues.

4. In this comment, Bruce seems to be using "social capital" as it is defined by Bourdieu (1986: 51): "Social capital is the aggregate of the actual or potential resources which are linked to possession of a durable network of more or less institutionalized relationships of mutual acquaintance and recognition . . . which provides each of its members with the backing of the collectively owned capital, a 'credential' which entitles them to credit in the various senses of the word."

5. These instances are consistent with whiteness being an unmarked social position that endows its member with privilege vis-à-vis people from racial-minority back-

grounds. This dynamic has been the subject of many theorists who discuss race and white privilege, such as Frankenberg (1994) and Collins (1990).

6. The mission of PFLAG is to "[promote] the health and well-being of gay, lesbian, bisexual and transgender persons, their families and friends through: support, to cope with an adverse society; education, to enlighten an ill-informed public; and advocacy, to end discrimination and to secure equal civil rights. Parents, Families and Friends of Lesbians and Gays provides opportunity for dialogue about sexual orientation and gender identity, and acts to create a society that is healthy and respectful of human diversity" (Parents, Families, and Friends of Lesbians and Gays [PFLAG] 2009).

## 3 WE ARE FAMILY

1. One such example is the federal Defense of Marriage Act (DOMA) of 1996, which allowed states to decide whether or not they would legally sanction same-sex marriages and recognize same-sex marriages that have been legally sanctioned in other states. The DOMA also redefined "spouse" as a husband or wife of the opposite sex. The text of the bill clarifies that the purpose of the DOMA is "to define and protect the institution of marriage." Many states have passed their own versions of the DOMA since 1996. In addition, in the past decade the parental rights of gay men and lesbians have been fiercely contested politically and legislatively. Currently, many states have laws and pending propositions that limit the parental rights of gay male, lesbian, bisexual, and transgender individuals.

2. Many same-sex identified individuals resist using the term "family" because they view it as reflecting a wholly heterosexist and historically oppressive dimension of relational life that negates homosexuality as a viable identity (Weeks, Heaphy, and Donovan 2001). Yet at the risk of further reifying family as the paragon for all social relationships and thus further reinforcing a heterosexist ideology of relationships, I use the existing terminology regarding family to address the kinship connections within intersectional relationships because this is the only vocabulary available to discuss the connections I describe. Thus, the following discussion draws from Weeks (1991), who acknowledges that the continued use of the term "family" to characterize a multiplicity of relationships underscores the lack of available language to adequately describe significant bonds.

3. It is likely that the easy usage of these terms is related to location effects from sampling in the San Francisco Bay Area. This region is known for its support of gay male and lesbian liberation; the most recent example was the highly publicized 4,100-plus marriage licenses given to same-sex couples in San Francisco in February 2004. Thus, the attitudes and experiences voiced by a population drawn from this region are expected to reflect this unique context.

4. As I noted in the introduction, Warner (1991: 3–17) explains heteronormativity as "the institutions, structures of understanding, and practical orientations that make heterosexuality seem not only coherent—that is, organized as a sexuality—but also privileged."

5. In 2004, Massachusetts became the first U.S. state to allow same-sex civil marriages.

California and Connecticut followed in 2008, but the right to marry was overturned by California voters by a narrow margin in the 2008 election and is still being contested in court. Currently, Massachusetts, Vermont, New Hampshire, Connecticut, Iowa, New York, and the District of Columbia allow same-sex marriage, while a few others permit civil unions and domestic partnerships. Civil unions and domestic partnerships do not provide same-sex couples with access to federal programs such as Social Security and citizenship. Those same-sex couples who enter legal civil unions are eligible for the same state rights as married couples, but these rights likely are not portable across state lines. Domestic partnerships are valid in the cities and states that offer them and confer various local rights, such as health care for registered partners, but are not portable and do not offer any federal protection (National Gay and Lesbian Taskforce 2011).

6. According to the Human Rights Campaign, as of 2011, gay and lesbian individuals have been granted second-parent adoptions in 16 additional states (Alabama, Alaska, Delaware, Hawaii, Iowa, Louisiana, Maryland, Minnesota, Nevada, New Hampshire, New Mexico, North Carolina, Oregon, Rhode Island, Texas, and Washington) at the trial court level, which means they were approved only in particular counties of the states. In these states, there remains a lack of affirmative case law (Human Rights Campaign [HRC] 2011).

## 4 GENDER COPS AND ROBBERS

1. As I discuss in the introduction, "queer" is another term that the participants of this project and scholars use to describe identities, theories, and analytical frameworks.

2. The term "sex-positive" refers to a pro-sex form of feminism that arose as an alternative to the anti-pornography stance within feminism. Pro-sex feminism supports sex as a potentially positive force in individual lives and celebrates diversity, differing desires and relationships structures, and individual choices based on consent (Queen and Comella 2008).

3. Unfortunately, Alec could not be interviewed for this study. The material from Charlene's interview appears in the text only when it supports a theme that also was raised by other participants.

4. Cassandra is referring to her partner's transition from female to male. When transgender people go through a transition, there is a range of possible changes they may be seeking to experience. For some, the transition is a mental shift from one gender to another. Others physically alter their bodies to resemble the felt identity through sex reassignment, taking hormones, or other changes. For a more in-depth discussion of transgender issues, see Stryker and Whittle (2006).

## 5 WHAT'S SEX GOT TO DO WITH IT?

1. This is not to deny that bisexuality is a recognized social and sexual identity. However, bisexuality is not free from the socially imposed definitions of identity. Typically, bisexuals are characterized according to binary categories, as well, and their sexual

orientation is regulated depending on the sex of a current romantic interest or partner. In addition, there is a subcultural aspect of same-sex partnerships being compulsory within the context of gay male and lesbian communities so that bisexuality is marginalized (Garber 1996).

## 6 THE PERSONAL IS POLITICAL

1. The concept of social location can be inferred from Berger and Luckmann (1967), who theorize that all knowledge and understanding emerges from a perception of the social world that originates from a social position. This social position takes into account various elements of an individual's social identity, as well as the time and place in which she or he lives.

2. As I noted in earlier chapters, Rich (1980) defines compulsory heterosexuality as the dominant cultural expectation that women will be innately sexually attracted to men and men will be attracted to women. The norm of compulsory heterosexuality structures our social perceptions of all social relationships, including friendships.

3. As of 2011, six states and the District of Columbia (in 2010) have enacted marriage equality laws: Connecticut (in 2008), Iowa (in 2009), Massachusetts (in 2004), New Hampshire (in 2010), Vermont (in 2009), and New York (in 2011). In California, Colorado, Connecticut, the District of Columbia, Illinois, Indiana, Iowa, Maine, Massachusetts, New Jersey, New York, Oregon, Vermont, and Washington, same-sex couples can jointly petition to adopt statewide. A person can petition to adopt the child of her or his partner (called second-parent adoption) in California, Colorado, Connecticut, the District of Columbia, Illinois, Massachusetts, New Jersey, New York, Pennsylvania, and Vermont (HRC 2011). According to the HRC (2011), gay and lesbian individuals have been granted second-parent adoptions in sixteen additional states (Alabama, Alaska, Delaware, Hawaii, Iowa, Louisiana, Maryland, Minnesota, Nevada, New Hampshire, New Mexico, North Carolina, Oregon, Rhode Island, Texas, and Washington) at the trial court level, which means the adoptions were approved only in particular counties of the states.

4. Several aspects of the intersectional friendship context set it apart from intergroup relationships that cross racial categories. First is the issue that homosexuality is not as visually recognizable as race. Hence, some straight people can be mistaken for being gay men or lesbians, whereas most white individuals are not assumed to members of racial-minority groups. Second, and more important for this particular sample of intersectional friends, is that many of the friendships predated an individual's "coming out" as gay or lesbian. This is the case in nine of the twenty-six dyads included in the study. These cases suggest that an established relationship in some instances may provide a sufficient bond to withstand a shifting understanding of sexual orientation within friendship. In such instances, if the straight individual was truly homophobic, he or she likely would not have sustained a close friendship tie.

5. The sticker Paul referred to is a rainbow flag, a symbol of gay and lesbian pride and liberation.

6. Monique was referring to Matthew Shepard, a young gay man who was killed in a grisly incident of gay bashing in Laramie, Wyoming, in 1998. The events of his death and the resulting criminal trial were highly publicized and often controversial and were dramatized in filmic and theatrical performances of *The Laramie Project*. Monique also refers to the extreme and overt homophobia demonstrated by the Westboro Baptist Church, established by Fred Phelps. Members of the church regularly demonstrate at funerals at which the deceased are gay men. Members of the Westboro Baptist Church picketed the funeral of Matthew Shepard, carrying signs that read "God Hates Fags," as well as other profane statements: see the website at http://www.godhatesfags.com/wbcinfo/aboutwbc.html.
7. These interviews took place before the national focus turned to the struggle for same-sex marriage rights in the United States. Thus, it was not part of the now rampant public discourse, and none of the participants spoke about what would become the major civil-rights push for same-sex marriage that began shortly after the interviews ended.
8. SWISH defines itself as "the most fabulous gay-straight alliance (for adults) on the planet!" The organization began as a resource for straight women who support gay men but has since expanded to include heterosexual male members. The organization is active in thirty-two states and four countries, and has over three hundred and fifty followers on the Facebook social networking site: see the website at http://www.swishpride.org.

## 7 FUTURE OF INTERSECTIONAL FRIENDSHIPS

1. Eight states have enacted nondiscrimination in employment acts that specifically protect sexual orientation, and twelve states and the District of Columbia have enacted nondiscrimination in employment acts that specifically protect sexual orientation and gender identity (HRC 2011). In these states, there remains a lack of affirmative case law. No federal nondiscrimination act has passed to date.
2. Same-sex marriage was made legal in the Netherlands in 2000; in Belgium in 2003; in Spain and Canada in 2005; in South Africa in 2006; and in Norway and Sweden in 2009 (Pew Forum on Religious and Public Life 2009).

## APPENDIX 2

1. Two of the interviewees in Los Angeles were members of a friendship dyad with a San Francisco Bay Area resident. In addition, in my travels to Los Angeles, I located two additional dyads that fit the criteria of the study and arranged to interview their members. In two more cases, the participants had relocated to other parts of the country, and I was fortunate enough to be able to travel to their new places of residence to meet with them.
2. As noted, "queer" is a more political and inclusive term for sexual minorities. Of those interviewees who identified as queer, one was a woman in a romantic relationship with a transsexual man, and three considered more bisexual than lesbian.

# REFERENCES

Acker, J. 1988. Class, gender, and the relations of distribution. *Signs*, 13, 473–97.

Adams, R. G., and G. Allen. 1998. Contextualising friendship. In R. G. Adams and G. Allen (Eds.), *Placing friendship in context* (pp. 1–17). Cambridge: Cambridge University Press.

Adams, R. G., R. Blieszner, and B. de Vries. 2000. Definitions of friendship in the third age: Age, gender, and study location effects. *Journal of Aging Studies*, 14, 117–33.

Allan, G. 1989. *Friendship: Developing a sociological perspective*. Boulder: Westview.

Allport, G. W. 1954. *The nature of prejudice*. Reading, Mass.: Addison-Wesley.

American Psychological Association. 2008. *Answers to your questions: For a better understanding of sexual orientation and homosexuality*. Washington: American Psychological Association. Retrieved from www.apa.org/topics.sorientation.pdf.

Anderson, E. 1999. *Code of the street: Decency, violence, and the moral life of the inner city*. New York: W. W. Norton.

Anderson, L. A. 1998. Desiring to be together: A theological reflection on friendship between black lesbians and gay men. *Theology and Sexuality*, 9, 59–63.

Antonucci, T. C., and H. Akiyama. 1987. An examination of sex differences in social support among older men and women. *Sex Roles*, 17, 737–49.

Argyle, M. 1987. *The psychology of happiness*. London: Methuen.

Arnup, K. 1994. Finding fathers: Artificial insemination, lesbians, and the law. *Canadian Journal of Women and the Law*, 7, 97–115.

Barker, J. C, G. Herdt, and B. de Vries. 2006. Social support in the lives of lesbians and gay men at midlife and later. *Sexuality, Research and Social Policy*, 3, 1–23.

Bartlett, N. H., H. M. Patterson, D. P. VanderLaan, and P. L. Vasey. 2009. The relation between women's body esteem and friendships with gay men. *Body Image*, 6, 235–41.

Baumeister, R. F., and M. R. Leary. 1995. The need to belong: Desire for interpersonal attachments as a fundamental human motivation. *Psychological Bulletin*, 17, 497–529.

Berger, P. L., and T. Luckmann. 1967. *The social construction of reality: A treatise in the sociology of knowledge*. New York: Anchor Books.

Berscheid, E. Snyder, and A. M. Omoto. 1989. Issues in studying close relationships:

Conceptualizing and measuring closeness. In C. Hendrick (Ed.), *Close relationships* (pp. 63–91). Newbury Park, Calif.: Sage Publications.

Bornstein, K. 1994. *Gender outlaw: On men, women, and the rest of us.* New York: Vintage.

Bourdieu, P. 1986. The forms of capital. In J. Richardson (Ed.), *Handbook of theory and research for the sociology of education* (pp. 241–58). New York: Greenwood.

Brehm, S. S. 1985. *Intimate relationships.* New York: McGraw-Hill.

Butler, J. 1990. *Gender trouble: Feminism and the subversion of identity.* New York: Routledge.

———. 1991. Imitation and gender insubordination. In D. Fuss (Ed.), *Inside out: Lesbian theories, gay theories.* (pp. 13–31). New York: Routledge.

Cagen, S. 2004. *Quirkyalone: A manifesto for uncompromising romantics.* New York: Harper Collins.

Cahill, S., K. South, and J. Spade. 2000. *Outing age: Public policy issues affecting gay, lesbian, bisexual, transgender elders.* New York: Policy Institute of the National Gay and Lesbian Task Force Foundation.

Calasanti, T., and N. King. 2005. Firming the floppy penis: Age, class, and gender relations in the lives of old men. *Men and Masculinities,* 8, 3–23.

Cancian, F. M. 1987. *Love in America.* Cambridge: Cambridge University Press.

Carrington, C. 1999. *No place like home: Relationships and family life among lesbians and gay men.* Chicago: University of Chicago Press.

Castro-Convers, K., L. A. Gray, N. Ladany, and A. E. Metzler. 2005. Interpersonal contact experiences with gay men. *Journal of Homosexuality,* 49, 47–76.

Chatters, L. M., J. Robert, and R. Jayakody. 1994. Fictive kinship relations in black extended families. *Journal of Contemporary Family Studies,* 25, 297–313.

Chauncey, G. 1994. *Gay New York.* New York: Basic.

Cherlin, A. J. 2002. *Public and private families: An introduction.* New York: McGraw-Hill.

Clarke, V. 2002. Sameness and difference in research on lesbian parenting. *Journal of Community and Applied Social Psychology,* 12, 210–22.

Clarke, V., and C. Kitzinger. 2005. "We're not living on planet lesbian": Constructions of male role models in debates about lesbian families. *Sexualities,* 8, 137–52.

Cohen, T. F. 1992. Men's families, men's friends: A structural analysis of constraints on men's social ties. In P. M. Nardi (Ed.), *Men's friendships* (pp.115–31). Newbury Park, Calif.: Sage.

Collins, P. H. 1990. *Black feminist thought: Knowledge, consciousness, and the politics of empowerment.* Boston: Unwin Hyman.

———. 1991. Learning from the outsider-within: The sociological significance of black feminist thought. In M. M. Fonow and J. A. Cook (Eds.), *Beyond methodology: Feminist scholarship as lived research* (pp. 35–59). Bloomington: Indiana University Press.

———. 1998. Intersections of race, class, gender, and nation: Some implications for black family studies. *Journal of Contemporary Family Studies,* 29, 27–37.

Connell, R. W. 1992. A very straight gay: Masculinity, homosexual experience, and the dynamics of gender. *American Sociological Review,* 57, 735–51.

———. 1995. *Masculinities.* Berkeley: University of California Press.

Conner, K., and M. Cohan. 1996. Negotiating difference: The friendship of a lesbian-identified woman and a heterosexual man. In J. S. Weinstock and E. D. Rothblum (Eds.), *Lesbian friendships: For ourselves and each other* (pp. 205–24). New York: New York University Press.

Cooley, C. H. 1922. *Human nature and the social order.* New York: Scribner.

Coontz, S. 1992. *The way we never were: American families and the nostalgia trap.* New York: Basic.

Corbett, K. 1999. Homosexual boyhood: Notes on girlyboys. In M. Rottnek (Ed.), *Sissies and tomboys: Gender nonconformity and homosexual childhood* (pp. 107–39). New York: New York University Press.

Crenshaw, Kimberlé. 1989. Demarginalizing the intersection of race and sex: A black feminist critique of antidiscrimination doctrine, feminist theory and antiracist politics. *University of Chicago Legal Forum,* 1989, 139–67.

Crosby, F., S. Bromley, and L. Saxe. 1980. Recent unobtrusive studies of black and white discrimination and prejudice: A literature review. *Psychological Bulletin,* 87, 546–63.

Curtis, B., and A. Hunt. 2007. The fellatio "epidemic": Age relations and access to the erotic arts. *Sexualities,* 10, 5–28.

de la Cruz, M., and T. Dolby. 2007. *Girls who like boys who like boys.* New York: Penguin.

de Souza Briggs, X. 2007. "Some of my best friends are . . .": Interracial friendships, class, and segregation in America. *City and Community,* 6, 263–89.

De Vault, M. L. 1991. *Feeding the family: The social organization of caring as gendered work.* Chicago: University of Chicago Press.

De Vries, B., and D. Megathlin. 2009. The dimensions and processes of older GLBT friendships and family relationships: The meaning of friendship for gay men and lesbians in the second half of life. *Journal of GLBT Family Studies,* 5, 82–98.

Diamond, L. M. 2002. Having a girlfriend without knowing it: Intimate friendships among young sexual-minority women. *Journal of Lesbian Studies,* 6, 5–16.

Dillaway, H., and C. Broman. 2001. Race, class, and gender differences in marital satisfaction and divisions of household labor among dual-earner couples. *Journal of Family Issues,* 22, 309–27.

Dorfman, R., K. Walters, P. Burke, L. Hardin, T. Karanik, J. Raphael, and E. Silverstein. 1995. Old, sad and alone: The myth of the aging homosexual. *Journal of Gerontological Social Work,* 24, 29–44.

Dovidio, J. F., S. L. Gaertner, and K. Kawakami. 2003. Intergroup contact: The past, present, and the future. *Group Processes and Intergroup Relations,* 6, 5–20.

Duck, S. 1999. *Relating to others.* Philadelphia: Open University Press.

Duck, S., and J. Wood. 1995. *Confronting relationship challenges.* Thousand Oaks, Calif.: Sage.

Duck, S., and P. H. Wright. 1993. Reexamining gender differences in same-gender friendships: A close look at two kinds of data. *Sex Roles,* 28, 709–27.

Eagly, A. H., W. Wood, and A. B. Diekman. 2000. Social role theory of sex differences and similarities: A current appraisal. In T. Eckes and H. M. Trautner (Eds.), *The developmental social psychology of gender* (pp. 123–74). Mahwah, N.J.: Lawrence Erlbaum Associates.

Ebaugh, H. R., and M. Curry. 2000. Fictive kin as social capital in new immigrant communities. *Sociological Perspectives,* 43, 189–209.

Eder, D., C. Evans, and S. Parker. 1995. *School talk: Gender and adolescent culture.* New Brunswick: Rutgers University Press.

Egelman, W. 2004. *Understanding families: Critical thinking and analysis.* Boston: Pearson.

Fee, D. 1996. Coming over: Friendship between straight and gay men. Ph.D. diss., Department of Sociology. University of California, Santa Barbara.

——. 2000. "One of the guys": Instrumentality and intimacy in gay men's friendships with straight men. In P. Nardi (Ed.), *Gay masculinities* (pp. 44–66). Thousand Oaks, Calif.: Sage.

Fehr, B. 1996. *Friendship processes.* Thousand Oaks, Calif.: Sage.

——. 2000. The life cycle of friendship. In C. Hendrick and S. S. Hendrick (Eds.), *Close relationships: A sourcebook* (pp. 71–82). Thousand Oaks, Calif.: Sage.

Felmlee, D. H. 1999. Social norms in same- and cross-gender friendships. *Social Psychology Quarterly,* 62, 53–67.

Felmlee, D. H., and S. Sprecher. 2000. Close relationships and social psychology: Intersections and future paths. *Social Psychology Quarterly,* 63, 365–76.

Fine, G. A. 1986. Friendships in the workplace. In V. J. Derlega and B. Winstead (Eds.), *Friendship and social interaction* (pp. 185–206). New York: Springer-Verlag.

Frankenberg, R. 1994. *White women, race matters.* Minneapolis: University of Minnesota Press.

Frye, M. 1983. *Politics of reality: Readings in feminist theory.* Trumansburg, N.Y: Crossing Press.

Fujino, D. C. 1997. The rates, patterns, and reasons for forming heterosexual interracial dating relationships among Asian Americans. *Journal of Social and Personal Relationships,* 14, 809–28.

Gagnon, J. H., and W. Simon. 1973. *Sexual conduct: The social sciences of human sexuality.* Chicago: Aldine.

Galupo, M. P. 2007a. Friendship patterns of sexual minority individuals in adulthood. *Journal of Social and Personal Relationships,* 24, 139–51.

——. 2007b. Women's close friendships across sexual orientation: A comparative analysis of lesbian–heterosexual and bisexual–heterosexual women's friendships. *Sex Roles,* 56, 473–82.

Galupo, M. P. and S. St. John. 2001. Benefits of cross-sexual orientation friendships among adolescent females. *Journal of Adolescence,* 24, 83–93.

Gamson, J., and D. Moon. 2004. The sociology of sexualities: Queer and beyond. *Annual Review of Sociology,* 30, 47–64.

Garber, M. B. 1996. *Vice versa: Bisexuality and the eroticism of everyday life.* New York: Simon and Schuster.

Gentry, C. S. 1987. Social distance regarding male and female homosexuals. *Journal of Social Psychology,* 127, 199–208.

Glaser, B., and A. Strauss. 1967. *The discovery of grounded theory.* Chicago: Aldine.

Goffman, E. 1963. *Stigma: Notes on the management of spoiled identity*. New York: Simon and Schuster.

Goldberg, A.E., and K. R. Allen. 2007. Imagining men: Lesbian mothers' perceptions of male involvement during the transition to parenthood. *Journal of Marriage and Family*, 69, 352–65.

Green, R. 1987. *The sissy-boy syndrome and the development of homosexuality*. New Haven: Yale University Press.

Greif, G. L. 2009. *The buddy system: Understanding male friendships*. Oxford: Oxford University Press.

Grigoriou, T. 2004. Friendship between gay men and heterosexual women: An interpretative phenomenological analysis. *Families and Social Capital* ESCR Research Group, 1–39.

Gross, A. E., S. K. Green, J. T. Storck, and J. M. Vanyur. 1980. Disclosure of sexual orientation and impressions of male and female homosexuals. *Personality and Social Psychology Bulletin*, 6, 307–14.

Grossman, A. H., A. R. D'Augelli, and S. L. Hershberger. 2000. Social support networks of lesbian, gay, and bisexual adults 60 years of age and older. *Journal of Gerontology: Psychological Sciences*, 55B, 171–79.

Gubrium, J. F., and J. A. Holstein. 1990. *What is family?* Mountain View, Calif.: Mayfield.

Halberstam, J. 1998. *Female masculinity*. Durham: Duke University Press.

Hartmann, H. I. 1981. The family as the locus of gender, class, and political struggle: The example of housework. *Signs*, 6, 366–94.

Hendrick, S. S. 2003. *Understanding close relationships*. Boston: Allyn and Bacon.

Herdt, G., S. T. Russell, J. W. Sweat, and M. Marzullo. 2004. Sexual inequality, youth empowerment, and the GSA: A community study in California. In N. Teunis and G. Herdt (Eds.), *Sexual inequalities and social justice* (pp. 233–52). Berkeley: University of California Press.

Herek, G. M. 1986. On heterosexual masculinity: Some psychical consequences of the social construction of gender and sexuality. *American Behavioral Scientist*, 29, 563–77.

——. 1994. *Assessing heterosexuals' attitudes toward lesbians and gay men: A review of empirical research with the ATLG scale*. Thousand Oaks, Calif.: Sage.

——. 2000. Sexual prejudice and gender: Do heterosexuals' attitudes toward lesbians and gay men differ? *Journal of Social Issues*, 56, 251–66.

——. 2002. Gender gaps in public opinion about lesbians and gay men. *Public Opinion Quarterly*, 66, 40–66.

Herek, G. M., and J. P. Capitanio. 1996. "Some of my best friends": Intergroup contact, concealable stigma, and heterosexuals' attitudes toward gay men and lesbians. *Personality and Social Psychology Bulletin*, 22, 412–24.

Hochschild, A. R. 1983. *The managed heart: Commercialization of human feeling*. Berkeley: University of California Press.

Hochschild, A. R., and A. Machung. 1989. *The second shift: Working parents and the revolution at home*. New York: Viking.

Homans, G. C. 1961. *Social behavior: Its elementary forms.* New York: Harcourt, Brace and World.

hooks, b. 1984. *Feminist theory: From margin to center.* Boston: South End.

Hopke, R. H., and L. Rafaty. 1999. *A couple of friends: The remarkable friendship between straight women and gay men.* Berkeley, Calif.: Wildcat Canyon.

Human Rights Campaign (HRC). 2011. Website: http://www.hrc.org. Retrieved January 31, 2011.

Ibsen, C. A., and P. Klobus. 1972. Fictive kin term use and social relationships: Alternative interpretations. *Journal of Marriage and the Family,* 34, 615–20.

Ingraham, C. 1999. *White weddings: Romancing heterosexuality in popular culture.* New York: Routledge.

Inman, C. 1996. Friendships among men: Closeness in the doing. In J. T. Wood (Ed.), *Gendered relationships* (pp. 95–110). Mountain View, Calif.: Mayfield.

Institute for Women's Policy Research (IWPR). 2010. *The gender wage gap 2009.* IWPR no. C350: http://www.iwpr.org/ publications/pubs/the-gender-wage-gap-2009. Retrieved January 11, 2011.

Irvine, J. M. 2006. Emotional scripts of sex panics. *Sexuality Research and Social Policy,* 3, 82–94.

Jackman, M. R. 1994. *The velvet glove: Paternalism and conflict in gender, class, and race relations.* Berkeley: University of California Press.

Jackman, M. R., and M. Crane. 1986. "Some of my best friends are black . . .": Interracial friendships and whites' racial attitudes. *Public Opinion Quarterly,* 50, 459–86.

Jackson, R. M. 1977. Social structure and process in friendship choice. In C. S. Fischer, R. M. Jackson, C. A. Stueve, K. Gerson, L. M. Jones, and M. Baldassare (Eds.), *Networks and places: Social relations in the urban setting.* New York: Free Press.

Jagose, A. M. 1996. *Queer theory: An introduction.* New York: New York University Press.

Jerrome, D. 1984. Good company: The sociological implications of friendship. *Sociological Inquiry,* 32, 696–718.

Johnson, B. R., and C. K. Jacobson. 2005. Contact in context: An examination of social settings on whites' attitudes toward interracial marriage. *Social Psychology,* 68, 387–99.

Johnson, F. 1996. Friendships among women: Closeness in dialogue. In J. Wood (Ed.), *Gendered friendships* (pp. 79–94). Mountain View, Calif.: Mayfield.

Kao, G., and K. Joyner. 2004. Do race and ethnicity matter among friends?: Activities among interracial, interethnic, and intraethnic adolescent friends. *Sociological Quarterly,* 45, 557–73.

Kimmel, M. 1996. *Manhood in America: A cultural history.* New York: Free Press.

———. 2000. Masculinity as homophobia. In E. Disch (Ed.), *Reconstructing gender: A multicultural anthology* (pp. 132–139). Mountain View, Calif.: Mayfield.

Kinsey, A. C., W. P. Pomeroy, and C. E. Martin. 1948. *Sexual behavior in the human male.* Philadelphia: Saunders.

———. 1953. *Sexual behavior in the human female.* Philadelphia: Saunders.

Kocet, M. M. 2001. An examination of friendship between gay men and its impact on psychological well-being and identity disclosure: A case study. Ph.D. Diss. Department of Social Psychology. University of Arkansas, Little Rock.

Larson, R. W., and N. Bradney. 1988. Precious moments with family members and friends. In R. M. Milardo (Ed.), *Families and social networks* (pp. 107–26). Newbury Park, Calif.: Sage.

Levitt, H. M., and K. R. Hiestand. 2004. A quest for authenticity: Contemporary butch gender. *Sex Roles*, 50, 605–21.

——. 2005. Gender within lesbian sexuality: Butch and femme perspectives. *Journal of Constructivist Psychology*, 18, 39–51.

Lindsey, K. 1981. *Friends as family.* Boston: Beacon.

Lofland, J., and L. H. Lofland. 1995. *Analyzing social settings: A guide to qualitative observation and analysis.* Belmont, Calif.: Wadsworth.

Lorber, J. 1994. "Night to his day": The social construction of gender. In J. Lorber (Ed.), *Paradoxes of gender* (pp. 13–36). New Haven: Yale University Press.

MacRae, H. 1992. Fictive kin as a component of the social networks of older people. *Research on Aging*, 14, 226–47.

Maddison, S. 2000. *Fags, hags, and queer sisters: Gender dissent and heterosocial bonds in gay culture.* New York: St. Martin's Press.

Manning, W. D., P. C. Giordano, and M. A. Longmore. 2006. Hooking up: The relationship contexts of "nonrelationship." *Sex Journal of Adolescent Research*, 21, 459–83.

Martin, K. A. 2009. Normalizing heterosexuality: Mothers' assumptions, talk, and strategies with young children. *American Sociological Review*, 74, 190–207.

McKenna, K. Y. A., A. S. Green, and M. E. J. Gleason. 2002. Relationship formation on the Internet: What's the big attraction? *Journal of Social Issues*, 58, 9–31.

McPherson, M., M. E. Brashears, and L. Smith-Lovin. 2006. Social isolation in America: Changes in core discussion networks over two decades. *American Sociological Review*, 71, 353–75.

McPherson, M., L. Smith-Lovin, and J. M. Cook. 2001. Birds of a feather: Homophily in social networks. *Annual Review of Sociology*, 27, 415–44.

Mead, G. H. 1934. *Mind, self, and society.* Chicago: University of Chicago Press.

Mills, C. W. 1959. *The sociological imagination.* New York: Oxford University Press.

Miller, N. 2002. Personalization and the promise of contact theory. *Journal of Social Issues*, 58, 387–410.

Moon, D. 1995. Insult and inclusion: The term fag hag and gay male "community." *Social Forces*, 74, 487–510.

Morahan-Martin, J., and P. Schumacher. 2003. Loneliness and social uses of the Internet. *Computers and Human Behavior*, 19, 659–71.

Morell, C. M. 1994. *Unwomanly conduct: The challenges of unintentional childlessness.* New York: Routledge.

Muraco, A. 2006. Intentional families: Fictive kin ties between cross-gender, different sexual orientation friends. *Journal of Marriage and Family*, 68, 1313–25.

Musick, K. 2007. Cohabitation, non-marital caregiving, and the marriage process. *Demographic Research*, 16, 249–86.

Myers, D. G. 2000. The funds, friends, and faith of happy people. *American Psychologist*, 55, 56–67.

Myers, K., and L. Raymond. 2010. Elementary school girls and heteronormativity: The girl project. *Gender and Society*, 24, 167–88.

Nardi, P. M. 1992. That's what friends are for: Friends as family in the gay and lesbian community. In K. Plummer (Ed.), *Modern homosexualities: Fragments of lesbian and gay experience* (pp. 108–20). London: Routledge.

——. 1999. *Gay men's friendships: Invincible communities.* Chicago: University of Chicago Press.

——. 2000. "Anything for a sis, Mary": An introduction to gay masculinities. In P. M. Nardi (Ed.), *Gay masculinities* (pp. 1–11). Thousand Oaks, Calif.: Sage.

Nardi, P. M., and D. Sherrod. 1994. Friendships in the lives of gay men and lesbians. *Journal of Social and Personal Relationships*, 11, 185–99.

National Gay and Lesbian Taskforce. 2011. Relationship recognition for same-sex couples in the U.S.: http://www.thetaskforce.org/reports_and_research/relationship_recognition. Retrieved July 30, 2011.

Nestle, J., and J. Preston. 1995. *Sister and brother: Lesbians and gay men write about their lives together.* San Francisco: Harper Collins.

Neugebauer, R., J. G. Rabkin, J. B. W. Williams, R. H. Remien, R. Goetz, and J. M. Gorman. 1992. Bereavement reactions among homosexual men experiencing multiple losses in the AIDS epidemic. *American Journal of Psychiatry*, 149, 1374–79.

O'Boyle, C. G., and M. D. Thomas. 1996. Friendships between lesbian and heterosexual women. In J. S. Weinstock and E. D. Rothblum (Eds.), *Lesbian friendships: For ourselves and each other* (pp. 240–50). New York: New York University Press.

O'Connor, P. 1992. *Friendships between women: A critical review.* New York: Guilford Press.

O'Meara, J. D. 1989. Cross-sex friendship: Four basic challenges of an ignored relationship. *Sex Roles*, 21, 525–43.

Oram, D. Bartholomew, and M. A. Landolt. 2003. Coping with multiple AIDS-related loss among gay men. *Journal of Gay and Lesbian Social Services*, 16, 59–72.

Oswald, R. F. 2000. A member of the wedding?: Heterosexism and family ritual. *Journal of Social and Personal Relationships*, 17, 349–68.

——. 2002. Resilience within the family networks of lesbians and gay men: Intentionality and redefinition. *Journal of Marriage and Family*, 64, 374–83.

Page-Gould, E., R. Mendoza-Denton, and L. R. Tropp. 2008. With a little help from my cross-group friend: Reducing anxiety in intergroup contexts through cross-group friendship. *Journal of Personality and Social Psychology*, 95, 1080–94.

Parents, Families, and Friends of Lesbians and Gays. 2009. About PFLAG: http://community .pflag.org/page.aspx?pid=237. Retrieved June 29, 2011.

Parker, S., and B. de Vries. 1993. Patterns of friendship for women and men in same and cross-sex relationships. *Journal of Social and Personal Relationships*, 10, 617–26.

Pew Forum on Religious and Public Life. 2009. *Gay marriage around the world*: http://pewforum.org/Gay-Marriage-and-Homosexuality/Gay-Marriage-Around-the-World.aspx/ Retrieved January 31, 2011.

Pharr, S. 1988. *Homophobia: A weapon of sexism*. Little Rock: Chardon Press.

Pogrebin, L. C. 1987. *Among friends: Who we like, why we like them, and what we do with them*. New York: McGraw-Hill.

Ponse, B. 1978. *Identities in the lesbian world: The social construction of self*. Westport, Conn.: Greenwood.

Price, J. 1999. *Navigating differences: Friendships between gay and straight Men*. New York: Harrington Park Press.

Quam, J. K., and G. S. Whitford. 1992. Adaptation and age-related expectations of older gay and lesbian adults. *The Gerontologist*, 32, 367–77.

Queen, C., and L. Comella. 2008. The necessary revolution: Sex-positive feminism in the post-Barnard era. *Communication Review*, 11, 274–91.

Quimby, K. 2005. Will and Grace: Negotiating (gay) marriage on prime-time television. *Journal of Popular Culture*, 38, 713–31.

Rafaty, L., and R. H. Hopke. 2001. *Straight women, gay men: Absolutely fabulous friendships*. Berkeley, Calif.: Wildcat Canyon.

Rapp, R. 1987. Toward a nuclear freeze?: The gender politics of Euro-American kinship analysis. In J. Fishburne Collier and S. J. Yanagisako (Eds.), *Gender and kinship: Essays toward a unified analysis* (pp. 119–31). Stanford: Stanford University Press.

Rasulo, D., K. Christensen, and C. Tomassini. 2005. The influence of social relations on mortality in later life: A study on elderly Danish twins, *The Gerontologist*, 45, 601–8.

Reeder, H. 1996. What Harry and Sally didn't tell you: The subjective experience of heterosexual cross-sex friendship. Ph.D. diss., Department of Sociology. Arizona State University.

Remien, R. H., and J. G. Rabkin. 1995. Long-term survival with AIDS and the role of community. In G. M. Herek and B. Greene (Eds.), AIDS, *identity, and community: The* HIV *epidemic and lesbians and gay men* (vol. 2) (pp. 169–86). Thousand Oaks, Calif.: Sage.

Reskin, B. F. 1984. *Gender at work: Perspectives on occupational segregation and comparable worth*. Washington: Women's Research and Education Institute of the Congressional Caucus for Women's Issues.

Rich, A. 1980. Compulsory heterosexuality and lesbian existence. *Signs*, 5, 631–60.

Rose, S., and F. C. Serafica. 1986. Keeping and ending casual, close, and best friendships. *Journal of Social and Personal Relationships*, 3, 275–88.

Rose, S. M. 1985. Same- and cross-sex friendships and the roles of psychology and homosociality. *Sex Roles*, 2, 63–74.

Rosenblatt, P. C., T. A. Karis, and R. D. Powell. 1995. *Multiracial couples: Black and white voices*. Thousand Oaks, Calif.: Sage.

Rubin, L. B. 1985. *Just friends: The role of friendship in our lives*. New York: Harper and Row.

Rumens, N. 2008. Working at intimacy: Gay men's workplace friendships. *Gender, Work, and Organization*, 15, 9–30.

Russell, S. T, A. Muraco, A. Subramaniam, and C. Laub. 2009. Youth empowerment and high school gay–straight alliances. *Journal of Youth and Adolescence*, 38, 891–903.

Sabin, E. P. 1993. Social relationships and mortality among the elderly. *Journal of Applied Gerontology*, 12, 44–60.

Schilt, K., and L. Westbrook. 2009. Doing gender, doing heternormativity: "Gender normals," transgender people, and the social maintenance of heterosexuality. *Gender and Society*, 23, 440–64.

Schneider, B. E. 1992. Lesbian politics and AIDS work. In K. Plummer (Ed.), *Modern Homosexualities: Fragments of Gay and Lesbian Experience*. (pp. 160–74). London: Routledge.

Seidman, S. 2002. *Beyond the closet: The transformation of gay and lesbian life*. New York: Routledge.

Seidman, S., C. Meeks, and F. Traschen. 1999. Beyond the closet?: The changing social meaning of homosexuality in the United States. *Sexualities*, 2, 9–34.

Shea, L., L. Thompson, and R. Blieszner. 1988. Resources in older adults' old and new friendships. *Journal of Social and Personal Relationships*, 5, 83–96.

Shelton, J. N., T. E. Trail, T. V. West, and H. B. Bergsieker. 2010. From strangers to friends: The interpersonal process model of intimacy in developing interracial friendships. *Journal of Social and Personal Relationships*, 27, 71–90.

Shepperd, D., A. Coyle, and P. Hegarty. 2010. Discourses of friendship between heterosexual women and gay men: Mythical norms and an absence of desire. *Feminism and Psychology*, 20, 205–24.

Sherif, M., O. J. Harvey, B. J. White, W. R. Hood, and C. W. Sherif. 1961. *The robber's cave experiment: Intergroup conflict and cooperation*. Norman: University of Oklahoma Press.

Shilts, R. 1987. And the band played on: Politics, people and the AIDS epidemic. New York: St. Martin's Press.

Solano, C. H. 1986. People without friends: Loneliness and its alternatives. In V. J. Derlega and B. A. Winstead (Eds.), *Friendship and social interaction* (pp. 227–46). New York: Springer-Verlag.

Stacey, J. 1996. *In the name of the family: rethinking family values in the postmodern age*. Boston: Beacon.

——. 1998a. *Brave new families: Stories of domestic upheaval in late 20th century America*. Berkeley: University of California Press.

——. 1998b. Gay and lesbian families: Queer like us. In M. A. Mason, A. Skolnick, and S. D. Sugarman (Eds.), *All our families: New policies for a new century* (pp. 117–43). New York: Oxford University Press.

Stack, C. B. 1974. *All our kin: Strategies for survival in a black community*. New York: Harper and Row.

Stanley, J. L. 1996. The lesbian's experience of friendship. In J. S. Weinstock and E. D. Rothblum (Eds.), *Lesbian friendships: For ourselves and each other* (pp. 39–64). New York: New York University Press.

Stein, A. 1997. *Sex and sensibility: Stories of a lesbian generation*. Berkeley: University of California Press.

Stein, P. J. 1981. *Single life: Unmarried adults in social context.* New York: St. Martin's Press.

Stephan, W. G., and K. Finlay. 1999. The role of empathy in improving intergroup relations. *Journal of Social Issues,* 55, 729–43.

Strauss, A. L. 1959. *Mirrors and masks.* New York: Free Press.

Strauss, A. L., and J. M. Corbin. 1990. *Basics of qualitative research: Techniques and procedures for developing grounded theory.* Newbury Park, Calif.: Sage.

Strazdins, L., and D. H. Broom. 2004. Acts of love (and work): Gender imbalance in emotional work and women's psychological distress. *Journal of Family Issues,* 25, 356–78.

Stryker, S. 1980. *Symbolic interactionism: A social structural version.* Menlo Park, Calif.: Benjamin Cummings.

Stryker, S., and S. Whittle. 2006. *The transgender studies reader.* New York: Routledge.

Swain, S. O. 1992. Men's friendships with women: Intimacy, sexual boundaries, and the informant role. In P. M. Nardi (Ed.), *Men's friendships* (pp. 153–72). Newbury Park, Calif.: Sage.

Swann, W. B., and S. J. Read. 1981. Acquiring self-knowledge: The search for feedback that fits. *Journal of Personality and Social Psychology,* 41, 1119–28.

Sweat, J. W. 2005. Crossing boundaries: Identity and activism in gay–straight alliances. Ph.D. diss., Department of Sociology, University of California, Davis.

Szymanski, D. M. 2004. Relations among dimensions of feminism and internalized heterosexism in lesbians and bisexual women. *Sex Roles,* 51, 145–59.

Taylor, M. C. 1999. The significance of racial context. In D. O. Sears, J. Sidanius, and L. Bobo (Eds.), *Racialized politics: Values, ideology, and prejudice in American public opinion.* Chicago: University of Chicago Press.

Thomas, W. I. 1967. The definition of the situation. In J. G. Manus and B. N. Meltzer (Eds.), *Symbolic interaction: A Reader in social psychology* (pp. 331–36). Boston: Allyn and Bacon.

Thompson, D. 2004. Calling all fag hags: From identity politics to identification politics. *Social Semiotics,* 14, 37–48.

Thorne, B. 1986. Girls and boys together . . . but mostly apart: Gender arrangements in elementary schools. In W. Hartup and Z. Rubin (Eds.), *Relationships and development* (pp. 167–84). Hillsdale, N.J.: Erlbaum.

Tillmann-Healy, L. M. 2001. *Between gay and straight: Understanding friendship across sexual orientation.* Walnut Creek, Calif: AltaMira.

Townsend, P. 1957. *The family life of old people: An inquiry in East London.* London: Routledge and K. Paul.

Trail, T. E., J. N. Shelton, and T. V. West. 2009. Daily interracial interactions and interpersonal behaviors. *Personality and Social Psychology Bulletin,* 35, 671–84.

Tripp, C. A. 1975. *The homosexual matrix.* New York: McGraw-Hill.

Ueno, K. 2005. Sexual orientation and psychological distress in adolescence: Examining interpersonal stressors and social support processes. *Social Psychology Quarterly,* 68, 258–77.

Vaquera, E., and G. Kao. 2008. Do you like me as much as I like you?: Friendship reciprocity and its effects on school outcomes among adolescents. *Journal of Social Science Research*, 37, 55–72.

Verbrugge, L. M. 1977. The structure of adult friendship choices. *Social Forces*, 56, 576–97.

Vidal-Ortiz, S. 2002. Queering sexuality and doing gender: Transgender men's identification with gender and sexuality. *Gender Sexualities*, 6, 181–233.

Walker, K. 1994. Men, women, and friendship: What they say, what they do. *Gender and Society*, 8, 246–65.

Ward, J. 2000. Queer sexism: Rethinking gay men and masculinity. In P. M. Nardi (Ed.), *Gay masculinities* (pp. 152–75). Thousand Oaks, Calif.: Sage.

Warner, M. 1991. *Fear of a queer planet: Queer politics and social theory*. Minneapolis: University of Minnesota.

Watters, E. 2003. *Urban tribes: A generation redefines friendship, family, and commitment*. New York: Bloomsbury.

Weeks, J. 1991. *Against nature: Essays on history, sexuality, and identity*. London: Rivers Oram Press.

Weeks, J., B. Heaphy, and C. Donovan. 2001. *Same sex intimacies: Families of choice and other life experiments*. London: Routledge.

Weinstock, J. S. 1998. Lesbian, gay, bisexual, and transgender friendships in adulthood. In C. J. Patterson and A. R. D'Augelli (Eds.), *Lesbian, gay, and bisexual identities in families* (pp. 122–53). New York: Oxford University Press.

——. 2000. Lesbian friendships at midlife: Patterns and possibilities for the 21st century. *Journal of Gay and Lesbian Social Services*, 11, 1–32.

——. 2004. Lesbian ex-lover relationships: Under-estimated, under-theorized, and under-valued? In J. S. Weinstock and E. D. Rothblum (Eds.), *Lesbian ex-lovers: The really long-term relationships* (pp. 1–10). Binghamton, N.Y.: Harrington Park.

Weinstock, J. S., and L. A. Bond. 2002. Building bridges: Examining lesbians' and heterosexual women's close friendships with each other. *Journal of Lesbian Studies*, 6, 149–61.

Weisz, C., and L. F. Wood. 2005. Social identity support and friendship outcomes: A longitudinal study predicting who will be friends and best friends four years later. *Journal of Social and Personal Relationships*, 22, 416–32.

Werking, K. 1997. *We're just good friends: Women and men in nonromantic relationships*. New York: Guilford.

West, C., and S. Fenstermaker. 1995. Doing difference. *Gender and Society*, 9, 8–37.

West, C., and D. H. Zimmerman. 1987. Doing gender. *Gender and Society*, 1, 125–51.

West, L., J. Anderson, and S. Duck. 1996. Crossing the barriers to friendships between men and women. In J. Wood (Ed.), *Gendered relationships* (pp. 111–27). Mountain View, Calif.: Mayfield.

Weston, K. 1991. *Families we choose: Lesbians, gays, kinship*. New York: Columbia University Press.

Wilmot, W. W., and W. N. Shellen. 1990. Language in friendships. In H. Giles and W. P.

Robinson (Eds.), *Handbook of language and social psychology* (pp. 413–31). Oxford: John Wiley and Sons.

Wiseman, J. P. 1986. Friendship bonds and binds in a voluntary relationship. *Journal of Social and Personal Relationships,* 3, 191–211.

Witten, T. M. 2004. Life course analysis: The courage to search for something more. *Journal of Human Behavior in the Social Environment,* 8, 189–224.

Wolff, J. L., and J. D. Kasper. 2006. Caregivers of frail elders: Updating a national profile. *Gerontologist,* 46, 344–56.

Woolwine, D. 2000. Community in gay male experience and moral discourse. *Journal of Homosexuality,* 38, 5–37.

Wright, D. 1999. *Personal relationships: An interdisciplinary approach.* Mountain View, Calif.: Mayfield.

Wright, P. H. 1982. Men's friendships, women's friendships, and the alleged inferiority of the latter. *Sex Roles,* 8, 1–20.

——. 1985. The acquaintance description form. In S. Duck and D. Perlman (Eds.), *Understanding personal relationships: An interdisciplinary approach* (pp. 39–62). Thousand Oaks, Calif.: Sage.

Zinn, M. B., and B. T. Dill. 2000. Theorizing difference from multiracial feminism. In M. B. Zinn, P. Hondagneu-Sotelo, and M. A. Messner (Eds.), *Gender through the prism of difference* (pp. 23–29). Boston: Allyn and Bacon.

## INDEX

Cross-sex heterosexual friendships, 26–27
Crystal (straight woman), 70, 84, 95

Dark side of friendships, 33
Debbie and Carl (lesbian woman/straight man), 63; Debbie's sense of personal safety with Carl, 90; gender norms and, 88
DeGeneres, Ellen, 153
Derek and Crystal (gay man/straight woman), 70, 84, 95
Discrimination, 141; in employment, 121; without hostility, 128. See also Inequality; Same-sex marriage and relationships

Emily and Patrick (lesbian woman/straight man), 37–41, 126; on chosen vs. biological family, 61
Emotional support, 64–66; as challenge to gender roles, 94; as reinforcement of gender roles, 5, 87–88
Ethan and Leyla (gay man/straight woman), 63, 97, 107, 118–19, 137–38; on getting old together, 66

"Fag hag," 21, 95–96
Family and family norms, 58–62, 74, 145–46, 148; conceptualizations of, 75; conservatives' view of, 77, 148; evolving of, 5; financial support and, 64–65; functions of, 58–59; heterosexism of term and, 57; historical transformation of, 75–77; non-normative structures of, 57–58; parental characteristics of, 62–63; parenting and, 69–72; postmodern families and, 148; primacy of, over friendships, 5; reinforcement of, 146; siblings and, 63; substitution principle in, 5, 9, 19–20, 62; tenuousness in, 60. See also Heterosexual marriage and weddings; Intersectional friendships as chosen family

Femininity, 32, 80–81, 86, 93; heterosexual, 86; policing of, 88–89; praising of conventional, 84–85, 140–41
Feminist theory and social inequality, 31
Financial support, 64–65
Frank and Rebecca (gay man/straight woman), 13–14, 53, 109–10, 141–42; complications from sexual tension between, 110
Friendships, intersectional. See entries for Intersectional friendships
Friendships (general), 14–15, 19–20, 34; adolescent, 17–18; belongingness hypothesis and, 15; contact theory and, 33; cross-sex heterosexual, 26–27, 102–3; dark side of, 33; formation of, 16–17; health benefits of, 16; heteronormativity and, 4, 19; identity development, social interaction, and, 28–29; interracial, 17–18, 21, 60–61; lack of research on importance of, in adult life, 5; between lesbian women and gay men, 24; in mid-life, 19; romantic relationships vs., 58, 102–3; same-sex, same-orientation, between gay men and lesbians, 19–20; same-sex heterosexual, 27–28; scripting theory and, 30–31; across sex and sexuality, 24–26; sexuality in, 116; similarity in, 51; straight women and, 35; as substitution for family, 19–20; substitution principle outside family norms, 5, 9; technology and, 16; in workplace, 16–17, 22

Gagnon, J. H., 30, 104–5, 112
Gary and Zoë (gay man/straight woman), 53, 84, 95–96, 98; sexual tension and, 111–12
Gay male friendships: sexual tension in, 19–20, 107–8, 143; acceptance of sexuality in, vs. other friendships, 116–17; as challenge to heteronormativity, 4; importance of, 19

Inequality (*cont.*)
124, 131; discrimination without hostility and, 128; feminist theory on, 31; in heterosexual relationships, 5; informing of, in lesbian/straight friendships, 123–24; intersectional friendships and, 119–20; oppressed peoples' inherent understanding of, 123; reproduction of, in intergroup contact, 128; sharing knowledge of, through social location, 123; straight awareness of, through intersectional contact, 124–26. *See also* Prejudice; Social change and transformation

Ingraham, C., 67

"Institutional difficulty," 5

Internalized heterosexism, 82

Interracial friendships, 17–18, 21, 60–61; white and black intergroup contact and, 125, 128

Intersectional friendships as chosen family, 11, 56–62, 119, 121; anxiety over possible dissolution of, 73–74; biological family vs., 61–62, 76; emotional support in, 64–66; financial support and, 64–65; growing old together and, 65–67; as historical transformation of family norms, 75–77; as metaphorical or real bond, 74–75; parental characteristics of, 62–63; parenting and, 69–72; postmodern families and, 148; role of gay/lesbian friends in straight weddings and, 68–69; as siblings, 63; tenuousness of, 58, 60. *See also* Heterosexual marriage and weddings

Intersectional friendships as political bonds, 12, 22, 119, 143–44; as challenge to normative bonds, 120; class bias and, 138–39; gay and lesbians as informants on oppression, 122–23; gay men/straight women and, 124, 133–35; Gay-Straight Alliance and, 136; heterosexual privilege and, 123–

24, 128, 131–33, 139–41; lesbian women/straight men and, 123–24; PFLAG and, 135–36; politicization of straight people and, 120, 124–29; sexism and, 141–42; stigmatized identities and, 129, 131–32; straight acceptance and tolerance and, 119–20, 124–26; straight people in position of wise and, 129–33. *See also* Activism; Prejudice; Social change and transformation

Intersectional friendships (gay men/straight women), 1–2, 35–36, 41–47, 52, 62–65, 118–19, 155; acceptance of gays/lesbians and, 127; activism and, 133–37; anxiety over chosen family status and, 73–74; of author, 8–9; benefit of lack of sexual tension in, 107–8, 109–10; "fag hags" and, 95–96; gender norms and, 13–14, 22, 81–84, 97–98, 140–41; list of friendships by couple, 156; male and heterosexual privilege awareness in, 124; media depiction of, 78–79; motivations in forming, 22–23; parenting and heterosexual family life of, 69–72; sexuality in, 86–87, 97–98; straight world access and, 121–22; as substitute for heterosexual relationship, 95; surrogacy and attitudes toward parenting, 70–72; trust and closeness in, 22; in workplace, 22–23. *See also by type of friendship*

Intersectional friendships (general), 1; age differences and, 51–52; as alternative model for male–female interaction, 15; areas of future research and, 147, 149–51; author's, 8; challenges of, for gays and lesbians, 147–48; as components of social structure and interaction, 7; conflict in, 53–55; effect of, on straight people, 13; existing scholarship on, 21; focus on close bonds in study of, 8; heteronormativity and, 4; homophobia and, 25–26; homosexual ghettoization and, 15; inequalities and, 6–7; interviews as research method and, 9–10; jealously in, 54–55; lack of scripts for intersectional friendship, 111–12; long-distance friendships and, 52–53; media depiction of, 1, 21; motivation of straight people in, 21–22; need for longitudinal research on, 151; primacy of family over, 5; similarity in, 51; social expectations of, based on gender and sexual norms, 2–4; social scripts and, 54–55, 105–6, 110–12; socioeconomics and, 52; stories of, 36–37; terminology of, 6–8; theoretical foundations of, 11

Intersectional friendships (lesbian women/straight men), 2–3, 37–41, 47–52, 74; acceptance of lesbians/gays and, 125–26; connection to family life and, 56–57, 70; emotional support in, 87–88, 90–91; gender norms and expectations in, 79, 88–94, 99, 117; lack of awareness of sexism in, 142; lack of study on, 23; list of friendships by couple, 156; male and heterosexual privilege awareness in, 123; male-coded activities in, 92–94, 99; positive attitudes toward lesbians and, 126; sexual relationships in, 113–14; sexual tension in, 101–2, 108–10

Jackman, M. R., 128
Janet and John (lesbian woman/straight man), sexual relationships of, 113–14
Janet (interviewee), 101–2
Jealously in friendships, 54–55, 108–9, 114
Jesse and Monique (gay man/straight woman), 53, 60–61, 83–84, 86, 95–96, 134–35; heterosexual weddings and, 69
Jesse (interviewee), 56
Jill and Paul (lesbian woman/straight

man), 61, 89, 94, 133, 139–40; increased tolerance through contact and, 125–26; resemblance of friendship to heterosexual relationship, 106
Justine and Antonio (lesbian woman/straight man), 89–90, 101–2, 126, 147; sexual tension in, 112

Karyn (interviewee), 95
Ken and Carrie (gay man/straight woman), 52, 111, 129–30
Kinship studies, 59–60

Language and identity, 86
Lesbian women: challenges of intersectional friendships and, 147; friendships with straight women and, 25; gender identity and, 32; gender nonconformity and, 81, 140; obstacles to parenting for, 69–70; positive attitudes toward, 126; positives of intergroup contact for, 129; same-sex same orientation friendships and, 19–20; sexual tension in friendships between, 20–21. *See also* Intersectional friendships (lesbian women/straight men)
Long-distance friendships, 52–53

Maddison, Stephen, 4–5; on gender dissent, 95
Manuel and Barbara (gay man/straight woman), 86–87, 130–31, 135–36
Margaret and Guy (lesbian woman/straight man), 110–11
Marginalized groups, 17, 122–23
Mark and Christina (gay man/straight woman), 78–79, 87, 138–39
Marriage and weddings. *See* Heterosexual marriage and weddings
Masculinity, 32, 80; challenge to hegemonic, in gay man/straight man friendships, 25–26; gay masculine norms and, 95, 98; male-coded

Self-concept, friendships and, 28–29
Seth and Shayna (gay man/straight woman), 70, 98
Sex and sexuality norms, 152; defined, 7; discussion of, in lesbian/straight man friendships, 88–89; effect of, gay male on straight women's, 97–98; intersectional friendships' reinforcement of, 117; lack of cultural interrogation of, 116–17; of monogamy, 116; principle of consistency and, 32, 82; reinforcement of, 146; sexuality of gay men and, 83–84. See also Scripts, scripting theory
Sexism, 82; gay men's awareness of, 141–42
Sexual orientation, 94, 125; alliances across, 7, 136–37; complexity of, 117, 149; continuum of, 110–11, 115; definition of, 7; friendships and, 18–19; gender identity and, 32–33; intersectional friendship and, 115; sexual behavior as not equivalent to, 7; social inequalities and, 6–7, 31. See also Discrimination; Inequality; Prejudice
Sexual tension, 6, 12, 101–2, 103; complications of, in intersectional friendships, 110–13; consummated, 113–14; as disruptive, 117; between Gary and Zoë (gay man/straight woman), 111–12; in gay male friendships vs. other friendships, 20–21, 107–8, 116–17; lack of, as positive quality, 86–88, 107–10, 115–18; in lesbian woman/straight man friendships, 90; navigation of, 116–17; in same sex/sexual orientation lesbian friendships, 20–21; unrequited, 113–15
Similarity in friendship formation, 16–17, 51, 146
Simon, J., 30, 112
Smith, L., 104–5
Social change and transformation, 119–20, 128–29, 135, 138; of families, 75–77
Social context: of friendships, 30–31; of intersectional friendships, 115–16, 145–46, 151–54
Social location differences, 12, 100, 123, 133, 146–47
Socioeconomics and friendship, 18, 52
Sports, 92
Stacey, J., 148
Stereotypes, 83–85; reinforcement of, 146; of women, 27
Stigmatized identities, 31, 129, 131–32, 143
Straight life and communities, 13; chosen family and, 59–60; discomfort with same-sex different sexual orientation, 125; gay and lesbian access to, 120–22, 142; motivations of forming intersectional friendships for, 21–22; politicization of, through intersectional friendships, 120, 124–29, 142; in position of the wise, 129–33
Straight men: emotions and, 94; friendships with gay men and, 24–25; lack of awareness of, of sexism of lesbian friends, 142; perception of gay men and, 33; positive attitudes toward lesbians and, 126; pressure of hegemonic masculinity on, 87–88; same-sex heterosexual friendships of, 27–28
Straight women: activism of, for gay friends, 133–37; enacting of oppression and privilege of, 124; friendships with lesbian women and, 25; motivations of, for forming intersectional friendships, 22; same-sex heterosexual friendships of, 27–28; weddings and surrogacy and, 72
Straight women in Support of Homos (SWISH), 136–37
Strauss, A. L., 86
Substitution principle, 5, 62
Surrogacy, 70–72

**ANNA MURACO** is an assistant professor of sociology at
Loyola Marymount University in Los Angeles.

Library of Congress Cataloging-in-Publication Data
Muraco, Anna
Odd couples : friendships at the intersection of gender
and sexual orientation / Anna Muraco.
p. cm.
Includes bibliographical references and index.
ISBN 978-0-8223-5177-1 (cloth : alk. paper)
ISBN 978-0-8223-5192-4 (pbk. : alk. paper)
1. Friendship. 2. Sexual orientation.
3. Man-woman relationships. I. Title.
HM1161.M87 2012
302.34086'6—dc23
2011030870